WITHDRAWN

D0906673

THE SEARCH FOR PEACE IN **AFGHANISTAN**

THE SEARCH FOR PEACE IN
AFGHANISTAN

From Buffer State to Failed State

BARNETT R. RUBIN

Yale University Press
New Haven and London

Designed by Sally Harris/Summer Hill Books
Set in Times Roman type by
Keystone Typesetting, Inc., Orwigsburg, Pennsylvania.
Printed by BookCrafters, Inc., Chelsea, Michigan.

Library of Congress Cataloging-in-Publication Data

Rubin, Barnett R.
    The search for peace in Afghanistan: from buffer state
to failed state / Barnett R. Rubin.
        p.   cm.
    Includes bibliographical references and index.
    ISBN 0-300-06376-8
        1. Afghanistan — Politics and government — 1973–1989.
    2. Afghanistan — Politics and government — 1989–   . I. Title.
    DS371.2.R86   1995
    958.104′5 — dc20   95-15694
                                                        CIP

A catalogue record for this book is available
from the British Library.

The paper in this book meets the guidelines for permanence
and durability of the Committee on Production Guidelines for
Book Longevity of the Council on Library Resources.

10   9   8   7   6   5   4   3   2

To the companions and friends of the way.
It is not our duty to finish the work,
but neither are we free to desist from it.

"I shall go far and far into the North, playing the Great Game."

Rudyard Kipling, *Kim*

"Turkistan, Afghanistan, Transcaspia, Persia . . . are the pieces on a chessboård upon which is being played out a game for the dominance of the world."

Lord Curzon, *Russia in Central Asia*

"The Great Game is over; the Russians have won."

State Department source, January 1980 (apocryphal)

"But helpless Pieces of the Game He plays
Upon this Chequer-board of Nights and Days;
Hither and thither moves, and checks, and slays,
And one by one back in the Closet lays."

Omar Khayyam

Contents

Preface

This is the second and final volume of my study of the origins, structure, and outcome of the war in Afghanistan. In the first volume, *The Fragmentation of Afghanistan: State Formation and Collapse in the International System,* I explored how Afghanistan's integration into the state system affected its society and politics. In this volume I focus on the international system itself. I analyze how shifting patterns of strategic conflict and cooperation altered the flow of money and weapons into the region, as the Great Powers in turn consolidated Afghanistan as a weak buffer state, helped tear it apart in a regional conflict, and then abandoned it as a failed state. Either work can be read separately, the first as a contribution to the understanding of comparative politics and the second as a contribution to the understanding of international relations. Read together, they are meant to advance the integration of these subfields into a common study of politics and to provide an integrated view of the interaction among different levels of political organization, from village elders to the U.N. Secretariat, in one of the century's most violent conflicts.

But this subject is of more than academic interest as we scan the horizon of the post–Cold War world. Where a nuclear holocaust once loomed, we now look on a panorama of seemingly chaotic conflicts, ethnic clashes, and failed states. While policymakers work to prevent the spread of nuclear and conventional weapons of mass destruction, a proliferation of small arms, massively applied, produces even more lethal results. Taken in isolation, each such conflict may seem to pose little threat to the comfortable West; taken together, the multiplicity of humanitarian disasters razes economies, sends millions of refugees on the routes of exile, and blocks political development that would improve security for all. Continued warfare in Afghanistan has halted plans to link the newly independent republics of Central Asia to the sea, has promoted the drug trade, and has spread conflict into surrounding areas. Reconstruction of the country that sacrificed more than any other in the endgame of the Cold War would not only repay an overdue debt but invest in a common future.

In the previous volume, I thanked many of those who helped me during the decade-long itinerary that led to these works. I will not repeat all of their names here, but they have all contributed to this work as well. Some organizations and individuals, however, deserve special mention for their role in this part of the project.

The fellowship I received from the Jennings Randolph Program of the U.S. Institute of Peace in 1989–90 provided vital support that enabled me to spend a year in Washington during the U.S.-Soviet negotiations regarding a transitional government in Afghanistan. A further grant from USIP for a different purpose enabled me to travel in May–June 1993 to Central Asia, where I was able to gather still more information.

Lawrence Lifschultz was the first to insist that I take seriously attempts to resolve the conflict diplomatically. Without his help and pressure, this work would not have come into being. Selig Harrison later joined this effort. Thanks to their introductions, I gained access to the U.N. Secretary General's Office, and in particular to Diego Cordovez, whose role in the research and conception of this book cannot be overstated. Through Diego, I met the other members of his team. Some, like Raymond Sommereyns, Charles Santos, and Benon Sevan, remain at the United Nations, where they are still valued interlocutors. Giandomenico Picco, though professionally playing a different role, has become a valued adviser and critic. Huseyin Avni Botsali, whom I finally caught up with in Tehran after he had left the United Nations, deserves thanks for preparing to receive me in Kabul in August 1992, though the rockets of Gulbuddin Hikmatyar prevented me from arriving. I particularly benefited from comments on the manuscript by Cordovez and Santos.

My colleagues at Human Rights Watch enabled me to travel to Afghanistan in 1989 and to Tajikistan in 1993. Each of these trips uncovered information that appears here. Patricia Gossman, who carried out Human Rights Watch/Asia's research on Afghanistan, provided more assistance and encouragement than can easily be acknowledged.

I must pay tribute to the professional foreign service officers of the United States, who bore my criticisms with goodwill and sometimes told me more than they should have, perhaps in the hope that I would see their point of view. Among those whose frankness I appreciated were Edmund McWilliams, the late Robert Peck, Robert Oakley, Peter Tomsen, Charles Dunbar, Teresita Schaffer, Steve Grummond, David Katz, and Richard Hoagland. My colleagues Peter Hauslohner and Richard Herrmann also provided indispensable help while they were serving in the Policy Planning Staff of the State Department. Steve Coll of the *Washington Post* generously shared with me CIA documents that he obtained under the Freedom of Information Act.

In Congress I thank former Rep. Steve Solarz for several opportunities to testify before him. I owe particular gratitude to Eric Schwartz for arranging these events and keeping me abreast of legislative developments.

I learned much from my colleagues from Moscow, most of all from Yuri Gankovsky, Nodari Simoniya, Vladimir Plastun, and Alexander Umnov. Mikhail Konarovsky and Alexander Titov of the Soviet, then Russian, Ministry of Foreign Affairs were generous with their time and insight.

Pakistan's professional diplomats, too, were unfailingly courteous and sometimes informative. Tariq Fatemi, Arif Ayub, the late Shahnawaz Khan, Riaz Mohammad Khan, Sahibzada Yaqub Khan, Jamshed Marker, Gen. Nur Hussain, and others over the years chatted over endless cups of tea and long lunches in New York, Washington, and Islamabad.

As for the Afghans, many shared with me over the years their frustrations at being excluded from the diplomatic discussions of their fate. Wakil Akbarzai and Mohammad Es'haq deserve particular mention for repeated assistance over the years. Hamed Karzai, Hamid Akbarzai, Rawan Farhadi, Abdul Rahim, Fatima Gailani, Muhammad Gailani, Qadir Amiryar, Zaid Siddig, Nangialai Tarzi, and so many others enriched me with their information and analysis. Amin Tarzi provided an insider's perspective on the U.N. mission of 1994–95. I owe special thanks to Gen. Abdul Wali and His Highness Zahir Shah for graciously welcoming me to their homes in Italy and to Sultan Mahmud Ghazi for facilitating that visit and for other aid. Eventually I also managed to contact officials of the Kabul regime; I would like to thank Miagol, Sarwar Yurish, Sulaiman Laiq, Sayyid Ikram Paigir, Muhammad Nabi Azimi, and Daud Kawian.

Most recently, Charles Norchi, the executive director of the International League for Human Rights, enabled me to visit Afghanistan again in 1994, together with an old friend, Edward Girardet, and a new one, Tracy Higgins.

Jack Snyder's comments on an early draft gave indispensable guidance to this work. The comments of an anonymous reviewer for Yale University Press helped me integrate the various parts of the argument. And I owe Ester Fuchs special thanks for first suggesting that my unwieldy project actually contained two books.

The Afghan conflict is not over yet. The hope that inspired this venture — for a peaceful and stable Afghanistan, a hope that in recent years has alternately grown and receded — seems again out of reach. As always, the hopes of the activist and the conclusions of the analyst sit uneasily together. It has been my intent neither to abandon the effort for peace when the analysis gave little hope of success nor to distort the analysis where hope sought a different conclusion. Readers will decide whether I have succeeded.

I have issued some harsh judgments in this work, but I hope they are based on sound information and analysis. Some of those who helped me will not approve of the conclusions that I drew from their confidences. No doubt I have made mistakes of fact, analysis, and judgment for which I alone bear responsibility. But the disaster I have tried to understand is our common responsibility. In this work I have tried to discharge my share.

New York, June 1995

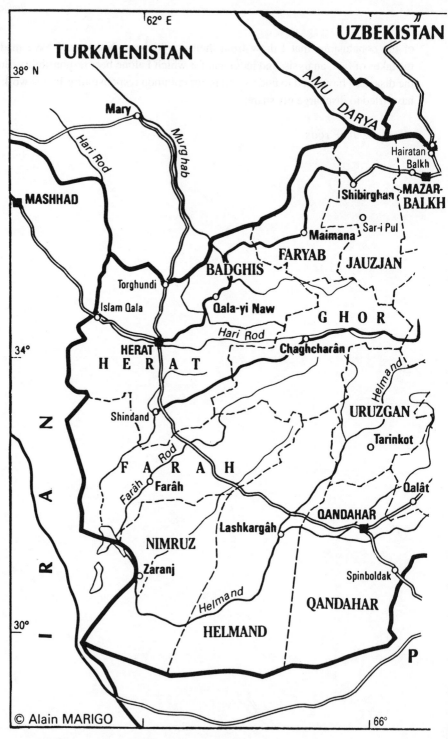

Political Map of Afghanistan and Surrounding Countries, January 1992

Note: Before 1992 the republics north of Afghanistan were part of the USSR.

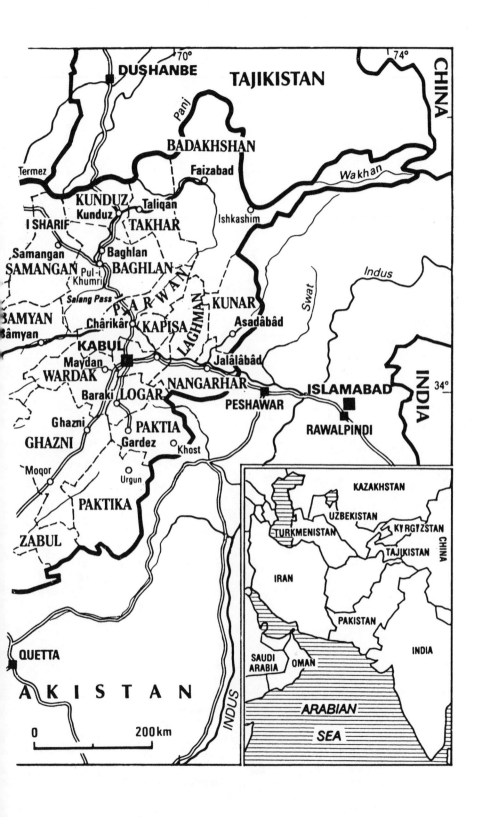

PART ONE

From Buffer State to Regional Conflict

As the British and Russian empires marched across the Indo-Gangetic plain and the Central Asian steppes in the nineteenth century, each confronted two threats to its borders: the advance of the opposing power and the depredations of what Prince Alexander Gorchakov called "lawless tribes." Continual resistance of the border peoples pushed each empire to expand further to protect its security, and the expansion of each in turn threatened the other.

Agreement on the independence of Afghanistan solved this dilemma, in theory, at least. The ruler of the buffer state, strengthened by foreign arms and cash, would both separate the empires and subdue the tribes. The international and domestic functions of the state were inextricably linked, and both developed out of international cooperation between the great powers of the day.

Cooperation between the region's imperial successors, the United States and the Soviet Union, continued through the 1970s. Resources from both Cold War alliance systems strengthened the central state in Afghanistan. At the same time, the decolonization of Asia forced Afghanistan into a race for "development," a development that created new political actors and destabilized relations between society and the state. The conflicts of new political actors drew in the superpowers as surely as had the raids of the tribes.

After the 1978 Communist coup and the 1979 Soviet intervention, cooperation between the great powers collapsed. External conflict penetrated and devastated the society of Afghanistan as it never had in the previous century: the United States and the Soviet Union poured fifty times more resources into the enterprise of destruction than they had into development. Successive attempts to restore cooperation failed. When one superpower collapsed and the other withdrew, Afghanistan was left once again an ungoverned land disturbing the borders of neighboring states whose manipulations of factional conflict aggravated the insecurity they sought to quell.

I *The Failure of International Conflict Resolution*

Along the road from Peshawar to the Afghan city of Jalalabad, the memorials to the British regiments set into the stony face of the mountains must now compete for the traveler's attention with the gaudy palaces of the heroin traders, new lords of the Khyber. The road enters Afghanistan at the top of the pass, in the shadow of yet higher mountains to the north and south, then meanders east, pitted and shredded by artillery explosions and tank treads that evince a previous historical epoch — the Cold War. Officials at the Afghan border post seem unsure what to do with the four of us, there on a mission for the International League for Human Rights. One of us enters our passport and visa numbers in the log book.

The burnt-out tanks and armored vehicles that littered the road when I saw it five years earlier, in January 1989, are long gone, cut up and sold for scrap in the bazaars of Peshawar. Here and there strings and white flags mark off a field — mines, keep out.

We traverse an irrigated plateau, green with the olive and orange trees of the Soviet-built Ghaziabad State Farm. In 1989, a few weeks before the last Soviet troops left Afghanistan, the farm had been captured by the Islamic resistance, the mujahidin. Though blood still stained the doorways, and much of the furniture had been chopped up for firewood, Save the Children (U.S.A.) sent Afghan agronomists to revive the farm. Five years later more and more stumps interrupt the rows of trees in the abandoned groves, cut down by the women and children who daily fan across the land in search of fuel.

A checkpoint: teenagers with Kalashnikov rifles and rocket-propelled grenades smile and wave us through. Looking at their scraggly beards, I doubt whether they can remember an Afghanistan before Soviet troops intervened at the end of December 1979. We emerge onto a rolling desert of sand and stone. A year before, two European United Nations employees and their Afghan guide and driver had been murdered here, apparently by Arab extremists training for *jihad* in this unpoliced, overarmed land.

We reach Samarkhel, the former military post whose capture signaled the start of the mujahidin's disastrous assault on the city of Jalalabad in March 1989. In a barren depression to the north, slightly hidden from the road, tents spread across the unwatered scrubland. Their inhabitants, six hundred families of the Safi tribe, fled their home region of Taghab in November, when a dispute within the ruling *shura* (council) of Jalalabad ignited a battle between the two main forces warring for the capital of the country.

Across the road, a chalkline grid marks the ground. Men in olive fatigues move methodically along the rectangles with metal detectors, searching for mines and unexploded munitions (they have already found two thousand pieces) before expanding the refugee camp. Something disturbed by the wind that sweeps down from the mountains explodes in the middle distance, raising a pillar of white smoke beyond the deminers.

On a plot of barren ground by the camp, men unload a truck that has just arrived from Kabul. Brightly dressed women with children in rags squat in the sun with small bundles of belongings. They swarm around us recounting their stories. I record these fragments:

> Twenty-five families from Kabul here came by private car. It cost Af 10,000 per person. We left the houses with all our property still in them. Families left the bodies of their family members killed in the fighting. The bodies are still there. If you can help us, then give us help. Otherwise, don't write anything. We spent last night in the cold with no shelter. For one week the children have had no food. We left the bodies and locked the doors. There is no protection for our property. What are we doing here? What should we do here? We have no way to get food. They were attacking on the ground and from the air. There were many kinds of ammunition. Everyone who had a Kalashnikov took what he wanted. Last Saturday, the first day of fighting, the fighting was inside the houses. They fired on and bombarded the houses. People were asleep when the fighting started. They were just taking property, and they had no other purpose. All the big stores and markets were looted. Shahzada market, the big money bazaar, was first looted and then burned.

> The parties attacked the houses and even took the food from the houses by force. One family was kicked out of their house and the house was occupied. You see all we have taken with us. We have nothing with us but the children. No medicine. No shelter. We never had to leave our houses while the communists and Soviets were there, but now we do. When the Soviets were there, there was no fighting.

> The aircraft were bombing. I hid underground. My niece here was injured. Her whole body was injured, because she was buried when the bombs fell. Four members of my family were martyred. Please pay attention to our lives here. . . .

A young man, evidently educated, approaches. He offers this analysis: "This is the result of the U.N. plan ordered for the Afghan people. And what happened to the people of Afghanistan? Even two brothers are killing each other."

Nowhere have hopes for peace and order at the end of the Cold War been mocked more cruelly than in Afghanistan. Here the superpowers had waged the deadliest regional conflict of the Cold War endgame, and here the United States and the USSR first reached an agreement on one of these conflicts. The Geneva Accords were intended not only to promote a political solution in Afghanistan but to launch a new era of international cooperation. "When the Afghan knot is untied," Soviet President Mikhail Gorbachev predicted at the beginning of 1988, "it will have the most profound impact on other regional conflicts." Likening such conflicts to "bleeding wounds which can result in gangrenous growth on the body of mankind," Gorbachev claimed that an Afghan settlement would improve the chances for peace "in the Middle East, in connection with the Iran-Iraq war, in Southern Africa, in Kampuchea, or in Central America."[1]

In the years following the Geneva Accords, the superpowers indeed went on to elaborate an international "regime" — a set of "principles, norms, rules, and decision-making procedures around which actor expectations converge in a given issue-area" — for the peaceful resolution of such regional conflicts.[2] Foreign troops would leave, outside arms aid would end, and internationally sponsored negotiations would lead to an internationally sponsored transition to a new government, chosen in free and fair elections. Variations of this model were tried in many of the cases Gorbachev mentioned. By the end of 1991, the United States and the dissolving USSR finally agreed to authorize the United Nations to implement such a plan in Afghanistan.

But if the Geneva agreement had furnished one of the first symbols of hope for peace and world order after the Cold War, Afghanistan's post-Soviet descent into further bloodshed and anarchy despite (or because of) the U.N.-sponsored peace plan exemplified the dazzling frustration of those hopes. Like Somalia, Croatia, Bosnia and Herzegovina, Moldova, Georgia, Azerbaijan, Armenia, Tajikistan, Liberia, Zaire, Rwanda, and Haiti, Afghanistan typified "the failed nation-state, utterly incapable of sustaining itself as a member of the international community." Such states "descend into violence and anarchy — imperiling their own citizens and threatening their neighbors through refugee flows, political instability, and random warfare."[3] Rather than devote to the peace the resources they had committed to the war, the United States disengaged, the USSR disintegrated, and the international community turned its attention elsewhere. Gorbachev's words are forgotten in most places, but not in Afghanistan. In September 1993, a village elder named Haji Mahmud Zamin told an American reporter: "We were a tool they used and threw away. They got their victory, so now their policy is, 'Who is Afghanistan? We don't know them. They are strangers.' Do you remember what Gorbachev said when he proclaimed Soviet troops were going to leave Afghanistan? He called Afghanistan a bleeding wound. What happens when you don't treat a wound? It becomes infected."[4]

Paradigms of Peacemaking

On February 8, 1988, Gorbachev had interrupted normal television programming with the dramatic speech that Haji Mahmud Zamin remembered. Gorbachev made public a hitherto secret decision: Soviet troops, he announced, would withdraw from Afghanistan within ten months from the effective date of a U.N.-sponsored agreement. The war in which those troops had intervened had already killed nearly a million of Afghanistan's 15–17 million people, had driven more than 5 million Afghan refugees to neighboring countries, and had displaced 2–3 million more within the country's borders.[5]

Less than ten weeks later, on April 14 in Geneva, representatives of the governments of the Soviet Union, the United States, Afghanistan, and Pakistan signed an agreement under which Soviet troops left Afghanistan by February 15, 1989. Yet by the end of 1994, nearly all of the conflicts mentioned by Gorbachev had advanced further toward settlement than the still-raging war in Afghanistan.

The United Nations began its mediation effort in Afghanistan under the rules of diplomacy that had developed since the Peace of Westphalia in 1648 and were codified in the Charter of the United Nations. Diplomacy, according to those rules, consisted of negotiation among the accredited representatives of recognized states. The agenda of diplomacy included disputes between states as articulated by their governments, but it excluded questions within the domestic jurisdiction of each state, particularly about the composition of governments and the nature of the regimes through which they ruled their citizens. In the Cold War the superpowers had evolved certain tacit rules of the game about what types of regimes and regime changes were acceptable in different regions. But conflict between the superpowers over precisely this issue — in the Third World in general, and even more acutely in Afghanistan — had been a principal cause of the breakdown of détente in the 1970s.[6]

The prohibition of explicit negotiation over domestic issues placed obstacles in the way of resolving conflicts like that in Afghanistan. The Afghan sides were fighting over what kind of regime should rule their country and how the state itself should be constituted. The Soviet Union had intervened on the side of the group that controlled the Afghan state, while the United States, Pakistan, Saudi Arabia, Iran, China, and other Western, Islamic, and anti-Soviet powers supported a disparate opposition. Moscow had flagrantly violated the international norm against interference in domestic affairs by invading Afghanistan to install a client regime, but that regime continued to hold Afghanistan's seat in the United Nations and to enjoy *de facto* recognition from the international community — including Pakistan and the United States, both of which retained diplomatic missions in Kabul — and the Soviets and their clients refused to bargain over the nature of the regime. The U.N. officials to whom fell the task of elaborating a mutually acceptable agenda for negotiation argued that the warring parties should first resolve the international disputes over the presence of Soviet troops, external aid to the antigovernment forces, and the flight of Afghan refugees to neighboring countries. A discreet "second track" of negotiations could begin discussions on a future Afghan government. "Second-track" negotiation had long been available to address issues that could not figure on an official agenda. Through unofficial exchanges or intermediaries, parties to a conflict could pursue an agreement without committing to paper anything that would compromise sovereignty. Concurrence on these international issues, together with informal agreements that could evolve on the second track, would create conditions for a domestic settlement. Afghan national traditions of conflict resolution and compromise would reemerge in the less polarized environment.

As Gorbachev's New Thinking developed, the Soviet leadership became less interested in the ideological stamp of the Afghan regime. The main goal of Soviet foreign policy was to reduce tensions with the United States, thereby freeing Moscow to pursue domestic reforms. New Thinking also recognized that the sort of militarized vanguard-party regime that ruled in Afghanistan was viable only with a level of military support that Moscow no longer wanted to give — and perhaps not even then. Gorbachev's search for a way to transform these regimes without simply abandoning Soviet clients led him to relax objections to negotiating over domestic issues in regional conflicts.

On November 13, 1986, the Soviet Politburo had secretly decided to withdraw the USSR's troops from Afghanistan by the end of 1988 and to encourage the replacement of the communist regime with a broader coalition, a regime of "national reconciliation."[7] As a result of the Soviet decision the role of the United Nations began to change, though still within the bounds of traditional diplomacy. The Soviet government now encouraged the U.N. Secretary General's Office to take a more active role in developing a second track. By 1987, however, when the United Nations began actively to promote the second track, the American and Pakistani governments suspected that negotiating over a new government in Kabul was simply a ploy to delay a Soviet withdrawal.

The second track failed to produce a transitional government before the expiration of the Soviets' self-imposed deadline, and the parties to the Geneva negotiations returned to the official agenda. Even then, the Accords that the negotiators had drafted differed from the agreement that actually took effect. The text of the Accords provided that aid to the resistance would cease on the day the

Soviets started their nine-month troop withdrawal. Mujahidin supporters in the United States (including President Ronald Reagan and Secretary of State George Shultz) resisted this provision, and the Soviets were more determined to disentangle themselves from Afghanistan than to insist on full compliance with the Accords. When the Soviets rejected an American proposal for "negative symmetry" — ending military aid to clients of both sides — the United States announced that if Moscow reserved the right to aid Kabul, Washington reserved the right to aid the resistance ("positive symmetry"). The two sides left the Accords unaltered, but the United States included its claim to positive symmetry in letters to Soviet Foreign Minister Eduard Shevardnadze. Gorbachev and Shevardnadze considered this a betrayal of an agreement that had been laboriously worked out, but they recognized that withdrawal from Afghanistan, on whatever terms, was necessary for success in reducing tensions with the United States.[8]

First the United Nations and then Soviet diplomats explored the possibility of a negotiated transition after the troop withdrawal. A major obstacle was the patent illegitimacy of the Afghan regime, which even the most moderate resistance groups refused to recognize as a partner in negotiation. The Soviets might not have agreed at that time to any acceptable political solution, but the mujahidin and their supporters never seriously tested their intentions. The Reagan administration and the regime of Gen. Mohammad Zia ul-Haq in Pakistan misread both the Soviet reasons for withdrawal and the political situation in Afghanistan, analyzing both in line with Cold War logic according to bipolar models of relative strength. They discounted both the domestic changes in the Soviet Union and the complexity of Afghan society and politics. The Soviets had withdrawn, the mujahidin's backers believed, because generous aid to the valiant resistance had raised the costs too high. With the Soviets gone, the puppet regime would fall before the onslaught of the resistance. Hence Washington and Islamabad saw no reason to support a negotiated or mediated political solution and instead pressed for a military victory. Massive military aid continued to flow, especially to the most extremist groups, which were deemed most effective on the battlefield.

In fact, when the Soviets withdrew, the bipolar conflict declined in intensity, and the alliances sustained by that conflict showed increasing strains. The United States, its regional partners, and the various mujahidin groups had different objectives and found it harder to cooperate. The mujahidin resisted Pakistani attempts to place favored Islamist radical groups in power. The fragmentation of power as much as the regime's illegitimacy was becoming the real obstacle to a political settlement in Afghanistan.[9]

By the end of 1989, however, the Berlin Wall had fallen, and a series of reforms and revolutions had transformed and then carried off the Soviet-sponsored regimes of Eastern Europe, seemingly signaling an end to Europe's legacy of war and division, which had aggravated "bleeding wounds" around the globe.

Washington now accepted that the changes in Moscow were genuine and sought a more cooperative relationship in Afghanistan as elsewhere. In late 1989 the two sides began a dialogue on the structure of a transition in Afghanistan. Progress was blocked both by the steadfast refusal of the mujahidin to negotiate openly with the "puppet" regime (though most had back channels to Kabul) and, in 1991, by the growing power of hard-liners in Moscow. The latter's defeat in the coup of August 1991 led quickly to a U.S.-Soviet agreement on Afghanistan. Not long after, on December 25, Gorbachev appeared once again on worldwide television, this time to announce his resignation and the dissolution of the Union of Soviet Socialist Republics. Among all the other changes then convulsing the world, an agreement took effect the week after Gorbachev's speech between the United States and the USSR (or the latter's successors) to complete the work begun at Geneva in 1988. Washington and Moscow would end both deliveries of weapons and aid for the purchase of weapons to all parties in Afghanistan and would work toward a U.N.-sponsored political solution of the civil war.

Without the Soviet Union, however, the United States lacked not only an enemy but a partner. Afghanistan became one of the first conflicts to show that the end of strategic bipolarity could replace cold war with hot peace. Eleven weeks after President Gorbachev's last speech, on March 18, 1992, President Najibullah of Afghanistan appeared on television to announce his own resignation. In a speech written for him by U.N. envoy Benon Sevan, Najibullah said that his resignation would take effect once the United Nations had established an "interim government," to which he would transfer all "powers and executive authority."[10] The loss of both Soviet aid and the Soviet model, however, soon deprived him of any "powers and executive authority" to transfer. Less than a month later, as Najibullah tried to leave the country on the night of April 15, his mutinous armed forces blocked him from the airport, and he sought refuge in the U.N. offices in Kabul.

Even before the establishment on April 28 of an interim government by a shaky coalition of mujahidin, an iconic post–Cold War scene began to play itself out on the streets of the Afghan capital. As had happened in Mogadishu and was soon to happen in Sarajevo, ethnic and factional battles killed thousands, devastated the city, blocked food and medical supplies, and increasingly threatened to split the country. Unending civil war engulfed the capital.[11]

Transition to Democracy as Conflict Resolution

Under the evolving, informal international regime for conflict resolution, the United States and USSR were to actively promote international involvement to bring some form of democracy to countries torn by conflict. The Reagan and Bush administrations had long advocated elections in many countries, not only to resolve conflict but to legitimate right-wing regimes fighting leftist insurgencies, as in El Salvador. After flirting briefly with the idea of abandoning human rights in foreign policy altogether in favor of the fight against terrorism and communism, the Reagan administration had found a different alternative to the Carter administration's human rights policy. The rights policy of the Carter administration had focused on the security of the person — freedom from torture and arbitrary killing, for example — a category in which many right-wing governments engaged in counterinsurgency had exceedingly poor records. The Reagan administration, however, argued that "democracy," largely identified with the holding of competitive elections, constituted the best protection of human rights.[12] Communist regimes, of course, had exceedingly poor records in this area.

Some human rights advocates argued that while democracy might indeed offer an antidote to the pursuit of politics through armed conflict, elections alone could not establish democracy.[13] Democracy, in this view, requires a civil society, in which public association and freedom of expression are effectively protected by law. Such protections have meaning only if the use of force by the state itself is regulated by law. A protected civil society is essential to democracy's function as a form of conflict resolution. Assurance that the loser in an election can survive, participate, and compete again is key to convincing armed political groups to enter the political arena. Law-bound, civilian control of the police and armed forces, which removes the threat of force against opposition, is particularly necessary to genuine democracy. In El Salvador in the mid-1980s, to pick an egregious example, opposition to the government was legal but often fatal.

A generation of social scientists, meanwhile, had studied the determinants of democracy and the conditions necessary for its emergence. Some analysts emphasized social and economic development, while others argued that culture played the fundamental role. Because economic development seemed more feasible than cultural transformation, the different approaches led to divergent predictions. But proponents of both positions agreed that the prospects for democracy were slim in the large number of poor countries with "authoritarian" or "non-Western" cultures.[14]

In the 1970s an emergent school of thought focused instead on the contingency and the dependence upon political strategy of both the breakdown of democratic regimes and the (re-) democratization of authoritarian regimes. While acknowledging that social and economic conditions affected the prospect for democratization, these studies emphasized that political actors had multiple choices, especially during periods of high uncertainty accompanying transitions, and that they could learn from experience. Their choices were limited, though, by unpredictable and external factors, including, very importantly, influences from the international system.[15] Social scientists also came to see "culture" not as a given but as a social and even political construct. They began to refute the concept of "bounded" cultures coterminous with political units.

At the same time, like the human rights advocates, these analysts increasingly emphasized the importance for democratization of the development of elements of a civil society under the old regime. Authoritarian regimes under which society had not developed a range of legally protected associations, whether because of repression, poverty, or a low level of integration of the population into a national society, had less chance for democratization.

Shain and Linz focused particularly on the problem of the interim government. They developed a typology of transitional governments: a provisional revolutionary regime of the opposition, an incumbent-controlled transition, a coalition of incumbents and opposition, and an international transitional regime. Their studies emphasized the importance of the "legality" of the state for any interim government charged with organizing democratic elections.[16] By definition, an interim government is one whose role is to prepare a process by which a more legitimate government can be chosen; it therefore at least implicitly admits that its own legitimacy is questionable. State legality assures that the military, police, administration, and courts will continue to carry out legally issued orders despite the weak legitimacy of the interim political authorities. Conversely, where state legality has broken down or has never existed, interim governments are unlikely to establish stability or democracy. Without a legal order, legitimacy is meaningless. Even when all sides sincerely agree to hold elections, if the voters are not registered, if no one in the country has the skills or means to print, distribute and count ballots, if there is no reasonably neutral security force to guard the polling places, then free and fair elections cannot be held.

The new international regime for conflict resolution through the holding of "free and fair elections" seemed consistent with the new social science paradigm of regime change in its accent on voluntarism and its deemphasis of "objective" determinants in favor of international factors. It ignored, however, the insistence of the paradigm on the importance of the development of civil society and its prerequisite, a law-bound state. Indeed, ignored in the general norms of the regime were those questions most closely linked to the integrity of basic state institutions. Although the regime specified the goal of the process (free and fair elections), it included few guidelines on how to organize the interim government. It also was unclear and inconsistent about how, when, and whether to disarm combatants, and about the degree of accountability for those guilty of crimes and violations of human rights during the conflict. The regime also failed to specify what agent of the international community should engage in mediation and oversee the transition. The U.N. Secretary General's Office took responsibility in some cases, states or regional organizations acted as mediators in others. In still other cases, the Security Council compensated for the weakness of state institutions by sending armed forces or officials to oversee the disarming of hostile forces, administration of the transition, and the conduct of elections.

Shain and Berat considered Namibia and particularly the U.N. Transitional Authority in Cambodia (UNTAC) models for what they called "international interim governments." Both of these, of course, operated under Security Council resolutions pursuant to agreements reached with the active involvement of at least some of the permanent members. This mandate allowed these operations to exercise some state-like powers. UNTAC, for instance, presided over a coalition of the four major parties to the conflict, controlled five ministries, and in general was authorized to exercise many of the prerogatives of a state.[17]

Such interim governments, Shain and Berat argued, are likely to be imperative when: "deep-seated historical rivalries are so profound and so violent and so seemingly irresolvable that the construction of an interim regime with the potential for creating real long-term stability is minimal"; the conflict is "exacerbated by the strong influence and sometimes actual physical presence of foreign powers"; "the political and socioeconomic rivalries among aspirants for power . . . may be so intense that they preclude the possibility of the acceptance of an incumbent leading the transition as a caretaker, a complete victory of an opposition group that installs a provisional government, or the creation of power-sharing interim rule among the rivals for power"; and "this impasse may be reinforced by the very high level of accumulation of weapons which are dispersed widely without any faction having a clear-cut ability to exert monopoly over them."[18]

Berat and Shain originally mentioned eight components of the international interim government model, including the disarming of all factions, the participation by all factions in free elections, certification of the election as free and fair by international monitors, and the stationing of U.N. security forces in the country as a stabilizing influence even for some time after the election of a permanent government. Such an interim government would be administered by the United Nations under a Security Council resolution required for dispatching armed forces.[19] Under this model, the international community establishes precisely the key precondition for democratization, a law-bound state. The international community both provides the forces to bind the state to obey the law and determines in large part what are the relevant laws, according to the terms of the agreement and human rights standards. The internationally dispatched armed forces gain a monopoly over the means of violence by disarming the contending factions. The international community establishes an administration run by objective and law-respecting bureaucrats from outside the country. These bureaucrats organize and administer a free and fair election, while the U.N. armed force authorized by the Security Council remains in the country for some time to back up the law-bound administration and enforce the results of the election.

In fact, an international authority that assumes responsibility for political legitimacy and enjoys an effective monopoly of force within a territory is not an interim government at all but rather an interim state. Helman and Ratner correctly recognize that such an arrangement is a response to "failed states," not just to a problem of transition to democracy.[20] The essential difficulty with this international interim government model is that the very factors that make it desirable decrease the likelihood that the international community will establish — or even attempt to establish — such an authority. When conflicts are so severe that the state breaks down — or, more accurately in many cases, when intense conflict exacerbated by wide availability of weapons results from competitive mobilization in response to state breakdown — an interim government leading to a change in regime must take upon itself the additional burden of rebuilding the state.[21] Rebuilding the state demands the acquisition of a near-monopoly on at least the most drastic forms of violence in an environment where automatic weapons may be easier to obtain than shovels.[22] Building state power in an environment characterized by widespread military organization among the population requires a level of force (and other resources) that the international community has been unwilling and perhaps unable to mobilize in more than a few cases.

In Afghanistan, the forces required to implement such a model exceeded anything the international community was willing to consider. Rather than invoke the powers of the Security Council, the United States and the USSR, supported by a General Assembly resolution, merely asked the secretary general to use his good offices to promote a negotiated solution. Until 1994 no plan put forward by the United Nations ever addressed the key but apparently insuperable problem of the multiplicity of well-equipped, poorly disciplined, competitive armed forces. Furthermore, the intelligence agencies of key international sponsors of various antagonists never fully abandoned the goal of victory or predominance through military means — or at least they never believed that their rivals had, which produced the same effect.

The widespread belief after the end of the USSR that the decline of communism and the overthrow of bureaucratic authoritarian regimes "has left democracy almost unchallenged as the supreme principle of political legitimacy," remains true, but, in omitting state power from the equation, it implies more than it can deliver.[23] That Islam rather than democracy has provided the main ideological and symbolic focus of mobilization in Afghanistan is not the main problem. No ideology alone constitutes the obstacle to conflict resolution, and no ideology alone can resolve the conflict. Indeed, as the postcommunist civil war has dragged on, ideological claims and appeals have been notable for their impotence and irrelevance. Cast adrift by the collapse of empires and states, people who seek refuge in religious and ethnic mobilization are not living in some past century, driven by ancient hatred. The main obstacle to civic order is not the culture they have created but the weapons the superpowers have provided. The security of some and the insecurity of others forge a simultaneous, integrated, but fragmented world. The agony of the citizens of Kabul, and the fury of those who have subjected them to agony, represent this century's experience at least as much as the security that we, the Soviets, and our imperial predecessors tried to guarantee by constructing a system of states, a system that great powers imposed on a rugged and unruly territory called Afghanistan.

2 The International System, State Formation, and Political Conflict

The state of Afghanistan took shape within its current borders as imperial powers sought to transform a turbulent dynasty into a buffer state. This externally promoted transformation inevitably entailed interactions between international and domestic politics. These arenas became more closely entwined than can easily be accounted for even by theories of interaction between separable domains. States do not arise through domestic processes and then interact through international ones; until a state demarcates its boundaries this distinction cannot exist. Because modern states are partly defined by their boundaries with other states, the formation of a state system logically precedes the formation of individual states. The creation of boundaries, furthermore, changes the interactions within as well as across the boundaries.[1]

The state system evolved over centuries, and different states developed in different ways. Depending on their natural resources, political and social structures, and geographical locations, various territories became different kinds of states, with different structures of administration, military forces, and political authority. The mode and chronology of incorporation into the international system left a lasting imprint on the patterns of politics in these states.[2]

In the process of anarchic war under which the European core of the state system developed, only those states with the military capability of defending their existence survived. This process created strong states with the capacity to tax and mobilize their citizens.[3] The system of unregulated anarchy gradually gave way to a more cooperative one in which mutually recognized sovereignty regulated state interaction. Colonization spread the system of territorial nation-states across the globe, and decolonization left it in place. European imperialism, like European state formation, started as an unregulated scramble for power but turned into an organized international regime dominated by the major Western European states. During the early period of colonialism, economic exploitation of the colonies was the primary motivation of the imperial powers. As the system developed, however, the dominant states sought strategic positions to protect their routes of communications and to insulate their empires from competitors. Early colonial states, in short, developed commercial and extractive mechanisms, but later ones concentrated on military and security concerns.[4]

During the latter period in particular, the imperial powers tried to regulate their competition and prevent conflict in the borderlands by convening congresses and conventions through which each recognized the boundaries of the others' colonies and of buffer states.[5] The identities of such states thus reflected the relations of force and strategic needs of the imperial powers rather than the political or social structures within their borders. Some buffer or colonial states (including Afghanistan) built on preexisting political institutions that could be useful to the colonial powers in legitimating indirect rule. Nonetheless, Uganda was not the same as the kingdom of Buganda, and Afghanistan was not the same as the Durrani empire of the Afghans.

Because these states, both before and after independence, fulfilled strategic functions for imperial or hegemonic powers, those powers sustained their existence even when their rulers (whether juridically subordinate or sovereign) had few if any of the capacities that characterized those states that survived the wars of Europe. With the elaboration of an international regime of universal sovereignty after World War II, codified by a provision in the Charter of the United Nations for the right of self-determination for all peoples, major states committed themselves to uphold the independence and integrity of states regardless of the capacity of state institutions to defend themselves. Hence, as Jackson and Rosberg argued primarily from African cases, juridical sovereignty, which derived from international recognition, no longer demanded the ability to defend oneself from predatory foreign powers or to control the state's territory and population.[6]

Such states did not always disintegrate. The Cold War in particular provided important resources to rulers who could exploit the new form of global strategic conflict. The end of the Cold War, in turn, stripped some regions of their strategic value, depriving precariously situated political elites of their margin for maneuvering. Change in the structure of the international system can thus promote either order or anarchy *within* the recognized boundaries of states. It is an oversimplification to attribute anarchy to the international system and authority to domestic politics.[7]

States elaborated the regime of universal juridical sovereignty to solve security dilemmas: by promising not to take over other territories, they could avoid escalating reactions by rivals. States often intervened more or less covertly to establish preferred orders in strategic areas, but they could no longer legitimately conquer them. The regime for regional conflict resolution at the end of the Cold War, in turn, provided a framework for international cooperation to end domestic anarchy in disintegrating states while preserving their juridical sovereignty.

Afghanistan exemplified the dilemmas of sovereignty of the postcolonial state. The great powers drew its borders to create a buffer state between the British and Russian empires. They supported the state of Afghanistan by providing the ruling elites with ideologies, organizational models, and financial and coercive resources. A breakdown of the decades-long pattern of great-power cooperation in the 1970s led to war. Negotiations to end the war in the 1980s attempted to reinstate cooperation governing the flows of those power resources that both built and undermined the Afghan state.

Great-Power Cooperation and Modern Afghanistan

Afghanistan formally entered the modern state system after the second Anglo-Afghan war (1878–80) as a buffer between the British and Russian empires.[8] As the British Indian empire expanded to the northwest from its base in Calcutta and the Russians moved south from Orenburg, the two imperialist powers engaged in a contest for influence and advantage that became known as the Great Game.[9]

As each power consolidated its control, it confronted the dilemma described by Prince Alexander Gorchakov, the foreign minister of Tsar Alexander II, in a memorandum of December 1864 that he circulated to all European powers. "In the interest of the security of its frontiers and its commercial relations," wrote Gorchakov, all "civilised states" are eventually forced to conquer those "half-savage nomad populations" and "lawless tribes" beyond their borders. Russia and Britain alike had been "irresistibly forced, less by ambition than by imperious necessity, into this onward march." The greatest difficulty was in knowing where to stop.[10] This process created a security dilemma between Russia and Britain. Gorchakov circulated his memorandum to assure the rulers of Europe that Russia's continuing expansion across Asia was defensive in character. Yet Gorchakov's memorandum described the classic situation in which security dilemmas arise. If borders could be defended only by conquering the "lawless tribes," defensive and offensive action were practically indistinguishable. Each empire's attempt to secure its borders caused it to expand in a seemingly aggressive fashion toward the other. In accordance with the hypotheses of attribution theory, many on each side interpreted their rival's actions as evidence of inherent aggressiveness and their own actions as an unavoidable reaction. Fearing the other's aggression, each empire undertook "forward policies" that convinced the other of its aggressive intentions.[11]

A simple game theory model illustrates this dynamic and accents its resemblance to events of a century later. Each side had a defensive or cooperative strategy (*C*, consolidate the empire in place) and an aggressive or defecting strategy (*D*, advance toward or onto the opponent's territory). The possible combinations of these strategies yield four outcomes: *DC,* in which the first actor exploits the other; *CD,* in which the second actor exploits the first; *CC,* where the actors agree on a static defense to avoid clashes; and *DD,* where both advance, leading to conflict.[12] All actors prefer the *DC* outcome and want to avoid the *CD* outcome. Aggressive actors (identical to the enemy images each side has of the other) prefer *DD* to *CC,* as in the game of deadlock; defensive actors prefer *CC* to *DD,* as in the game of prisoners' dilemma. As long as each side perceives the other as aggressive, both aggressive and defensive factions on each side agree on a forward policy. But the defensive faction on each side would prefer a cooperative agreement that separated the two empires, if it could be monitored and enforced.

This security dilemma gave rise to the two Anglo-Afghan wars and numerous smaller skirmishes. Consolidation of Afghanistan as a buffer state resolved the dilemma. After the second Anglo-Afghan war, Britain forced Amir Abdul Rahman Khan of Afghanistan to conduct all foreign affairs through the British Government of India. The British, however, agreed to have only one representative in Afghanistan, an Indian Muslim, and the amir kept all foreigners out of his territory except for a handful of military technicians in his personal employ. Russia agreed that it had no interest in extending its influence into the territory of Afghanistan, which the two powers demarcated together, sometimes without consulting the amir. Most notably, they forced the amir to assume responsibility for the Wakhan corridor, a narrow strip of land in the Pamir Mountains, which today separates the Northern Territories of Pakistan from the Gorno-Badakhshan autonomous region of Tajikistan. This barren territory cost more to police than it produced in revenue, and the British paid the amir a subsidy to administer it, thereby assuring that the British and Russian empires would have no common border, and hence no border incidents.

Britain and Afghanistan also agreed not to extend their administration forward into what became the Pashtun tribal territories on the Afghan frontier; this boundary of the amir's administration became known as the Durand Line, after Sir Mortimer Durand, who demarcated it. Although Britain and later Pakistan claimed suzerainty — never recognized by an Afghan government — over the tribal territories, they have constituted a sort of unadministered buffer between Afghanistan and its eastern neighbor. All of these understandings were cemented in the Anglo-Russian Convention on Persia, Afghanistan, and Tibet in 1907. Cooperation between the rival empires was made easier by a common threat: Germany was not only amassing a huge army and navy in Europe but also making plans for a Berlin-to-Baghdad railroad.[13]

Making Afghanistan into a buffer state required more than drawing boundaries around it; a government had to be consolidated that could control the territories and boundaries. The Durrani confederation, one of three major groups of tribes from Afghanistan's preeminent ethnic group, the Pashtuns, had a long tradition of rule. Since 1747 various Durrani branches had built up a dynasty of varying strength, centered first in Qandahar, then in Kabul, with a powerful and often independent branch in Herat. After the first Anglo-Afghan war, all Afghan rulers came from the Muhammadzai clan of the Barakzai tribe of Durrani Pashtuns.

Although the Afghan government was formally a monarchy, the first British emissary to the court of Kabul, Montstuart Elphinstone, found in 1809 that it resembled a grouping of tribal republics. He predicted that the "anarchy and disorder which so often arise under the republican government of the tribes" would give rise to "alarms and confusion which will be forced on our attention." Elphinstone seems at first to have concluded that "the country would derive more advantage from the good order and tranquillity which an absolute monarchy, even on Asiatic principles, would secure." But discussions with Afghans changed Elphinstone's mind: "I once strongly urged to a very intelligent old man of the tribe of Meaunkhail [Miankhel], the superiority of a quiet and secure life, under a powerful monarch, to the discord, the alarms, and the blood which they owed to their present system. The old man replied with great warmth, and thus concluded an indignant harangue against arbitrary power: 'We are content with discord, we are content with alarms, we are content with blood, but we will never be content with a master.' "[14]

Afghanistan, Elphinstone came to believe, provided better raw material for good government under a republican constitution than the seemingly superior despotisms of China, India, and Persia. Like the United Nations nearly two centuries later, he argued that Afghanistan might be stabilized through a representative form of government based on Pashtun traditions. He sketched out a model that could have come straight from the work of Charles Tilly, wherein the king's need for taxes and conscription might lead him to craft national representative institutions from the existing tribal ones.

Nonetheless, Elphinstone remained pessimistic about the country's capacity to cohere:

> Such are the pleasing reveries to which we are led by a consideration of the materials of which the Afghaun government is composed, but a very little reflection must convince us, that these speculations are never likely to be realised. The example of neighbouring despotisms, and the notions already imbibed by the court of Caubul, preclude the hope of our ever seeing a King capable of forming the design; and there is reason to fear that the societies into which the nation is divided, possess within themselves a principle of repulsion and disunion, too strong to be overcome, except by such a force as, while it united the whole into one solid body, would crush and obliterate the features of every one of the parts.[15]

In the event, the British themselves sought to create such a force. The weapons and cash they supplied to Amir Abdul Rahman Khan (1880–1901) enabled the ruler to erect an absolutist state, capable of crushing more than forty revolts by local tribal-republican forces and of creating a brutal secret police force. Rudyard Kipling wrote of the Amir's use of professional soldiers, foreign aid, and heavy weapons to subdue the tribes:

> Abdhur Rahman, the Durani Chief, to the North and the South is sold.
> The North and the South shall open their mouth to a Ghilzai flag unrolled,
> When the big guns speak to the Khyber peak, and his dog-Heratis fly:
> Ye have heard the song — How long? How long? Wolves of the Abazai! . . .
>
> Abdhur Rahman, the Durani Chief, of him is the story told,
> He has opened his mouth to the North and the South, they have stuffed his
> mouth with gold.
> Ye know the truth of his tender ruth — and sweet his favours are:
> Ye have heard the song — How long? How long? — from Balkh to Kandahar.[16]

In alliance with the British, Abdul Rahman Khan began the project of turning Afghanistan into a pacified nation-state with a centralized government. The basic state structure he erected — a Pashtun ruler whose administration used a nominally centralized bureaucracy and army, as well as strategic foreign aid, to encapsulate a variety of local social structures — largely endured until 1992.

After 1919, the amir's grandson, King Amanullah Khan, declared independence and forfeited the British subsidy. His failure to find an alternative source of revenue and military aid left him defenseless when tribes and religious movements mobilized against his state-building efforts in 1928. After a nine-month interregnum, during which a Tajik social bandit ruled, the British supported the establishment of a new dynasty under one of Amanullah's former generals, Nadir Shah. Nadir Shah was assassinated in 1933 and succeeded by his nineteen-year-old son, Zahir Shah, who reigned until 1973.

Afghanistan in the Cold War

The Cold War provided new opportunities to the rulers of Afghanistan. During the 1950s, Prime Minister Daoud, a cousin of the king, played on the country's renewed status as a buffer — now between the USSR and the U.S.-sponsored Baghdad Pact (later CENTO) — to build an expanded state apparatus with foreign aid from both Cold War antagonists.

Under the Anglo-Russian Convention, both powers had abstained from directly intervening in Afghanistan. Afghanistan enjoyed a neutrality based on isolation, which it preserved by rebuffing German overtures during both World Wars. Stalin maintained this policy, never even establishing a Communist Party in Afghanistan, though he had done so in nearly every other country bordering on the Soviet Union by 1921.[17] Stalin's successors, however, decided to compete with the West in the postcolonial world, not only by supporting communist movements but by giving aid to governments whose nonalignment with the West served Soviet interests. Afghanistan was the first state to benefit from this policy. In response, the United States and others in the West also gave aid. Although the two blocs were competing for influence, they cooperated in giving aid to a common recipient, the state, which both sought to stabilize.[18]

The Soviet Union became the leading aid giver, in particular sponsoring the recruitment and equipping of a 100,000-man army. From 1956 to 1978 the Soviet Union provided Afghanistan with $1,265 million in economic aid and roughly $1,250 million in military aid, while the United States provided $533 million in economic aid. During the same period, 3,725 Afghan military officers — mostly from the elite air force and armored corps — were trained in the Soviet Union, sometimes for as long as six years, while Afghan officers took a total of 487 courses in the United States.[19] Small numbers were also trained in Egypt and India. The United States also engaged in teacher training, agriculture, and engineering. Islamic legal and educational officials were trained with the assistance of Egypt's al-Azhar University.

Nonaligned Afghanistan had turned to the Soviet Union for military aid only after being refused by the United States. The United States had recruited Afghanistan's new neighbor, Pakistan, into both CENTO and the Southeast Asia Treaty Organization (SEATO). Pakistan, an ally of the United States, opposed aid to Afghanistan, its rival in a bitter dispute over the areas of northwest Pakistan, including the tribal territories, that were inhabited by Pashtuns. The government of Afghanistan argued that the inhabitants of "Pashtunistan," as it called those areas, should enjoy the right to self-determination.

The rulers of Afghanistan exploited its location to make it into a borderline case of the rentier or "allocation" state, financing more than 40 percent of its state expenditures in every year from 1958 to 1968 and again from the mid-1970s from "revenue accruing directly from abroad"[20] (see Appendix A). These revenues included both foreign aid and, beginning in 1968, sales of natural gas to the USSR. Most of the rest of the state's revenue came from customs duties levied on a few agricultural exports. Such revenues, derived from links to the international state system and market, enabled the state leadership to expand the apparatus under its control without bargaining with or being accountable to its citizens, as it would have been in the model advocated by Elphinstone. The citizens were not called upon to finance the state's expansion with taxes derived from their own productive activity. Rather than try to penetrate the countryside and govern it, the Afghan state pursued a "cover-over" strategy of encapsulating local institutions with an administration laid over the existing society.[21]

The state elite did not rule the people of Afghanistan by representing them and managing the conflicts among them. Nor had it mobilized networks of clientelism into a national organization for a political struggle against colonialism (as in India, Tunisia, and elsewhere). Amir Abdul Rahman Khan had devoted his efforts to crushing, not institutionalizing, the tribal coalitions that had defeated the British during the Anglo-Afghan wars. And although subsequent rulers periodically convened an assembly called the Loya Jirga — Pashto for *great assembly* — that evoked the traditions of tribal republicanism described by Elphinstone, this congress was in nearly every case composed of appointed representatives who assented to the ruler's decrees. The institution on occasion demonstrated the potential to develop into a genuine representative body, but usually it illustrated the encapsulation, not the continuing power, of the tribes.

Rather than integrate various sectors of the population into a common, national political system, the state elite acted as an ethnically stratified hierarchy of intermediaries between the foreign powers who provided the resources and the groups who received the largesse of patronage. Most of the population considered the government only a source of kinship-linked patronage. Each local kinship-based group (*qawm*) remained isolated, tied to the nation-state only by personal ties to individuals in the state apparatus. Qawms formed no nationwide alliances to capture and exercise power. The consequent political fragmentation meant that the elite of the old regime had no political or organizational base from which to resist those who deposed them.

The structure of the old regime of Afghanistan imposed a pattern of ethnic stratification on the diverse and fragmented local societies. This stratification defined the relation of various groups to the state, although local systems of identity and ethnic relations differed from those defined by the state. The country was also divided into distinct regions with different ethnic compositions, as shown in Map 2.1.

The Muhammadzai-led state claimed to represent the national identity of Pashtuns (about 40–45 percent of the population).[22] Indeed, the word *Afghan* was originally the Persian term for Pashtuns, and Afghanistan denoted the territory of Pashtuns. In the 1920s King Amanullah's constitution, the country's first, defined an Afghan as any citizen of the state, but the term retains its ethnic meaning in popular usage, contributing to ambiguity about the ethnic character of state power and citizenship. The official religion of the state was from the beginning Sunni Islam, and the state's capital was the predominantly Persian-speaking city of Kabul.

The royal clan topped the ethnic hierarchy. Below them came the other Pashtuns, with some preference for Durranis. The Shia (about 15 percent of the

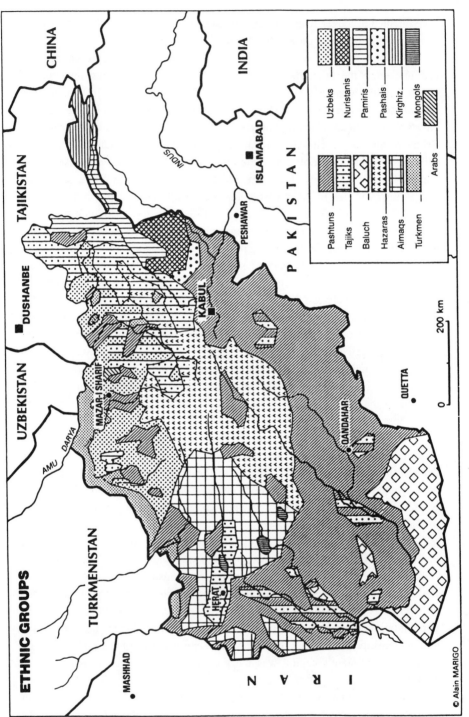

ETHNIC GROUPS

CHINA

TAJIKISTAN

UZBEKISTAN

TURKMENISTAN

IRAN

PAKISTAN

INDIA

ISLAMABAD

PESHAWAR

DUSHANBE

KABUL

MAZAR-I-SHARIF

HERAT

QUETTA

QANDAHAR

MASHHAD

AMU DARYA

INDUS

Pashtuns	Uzbeks
Tajiks	Nuristanis
Baluch	Pamiris
Hazaras	Pashais
Aimaqs	Kirghiz
Turkmen	Mongols
Arabs	

0   200 km

© Alain MARIGO

Map 2.1 *Approximate Geographical Distribution of Ethnic Groups in Afghanistan*

population), most of them belonging to the Hazara ethnic group, occupied the bottom of the social hierarchy. Between the Pashtuns and Hazaras were the other predominantly Sunni ethnic groups. Of these, the Tajiks, Sunni Persian-speakers of the northeast and west, served as junior partners of the Pashtuns in ruling the country.[23] Other groups of intermediate status included the Turki speakers of the north, mostly Uzbeks.

Breakdown of Cooperation

Foreign aid stimulated expansion of the state and produced new relations between state and society. In response to growing pressures from newly educated groups, Zahir Shah promulgated a new constitution with an elected, consultative parliament in 1964. For almost a decade Afghanistan enjoyed a form of constitutional rule known as "New Democracy," under which the government held two national elections. Although political parties were not permitted to compete in the parliamentary elections, various factions of the intelligentsia that had arisen from the state's expanded educational system began to organize politically, launching nationalist, communist, and Islamic movements with corresponding links to the international system.

The state increasingly relied on this group to run the expanding bureaucracy and to staff the growing army, but its members lacked political power or institutionalized channels of participation. Their education alienated them from the local power structures in the "small societies" of tribe, clan, or village, and those not from leading families or the royal clan had little hope of influencing the decisions of the state they served. Furthermore, because different parts of the educational system were aided by different foreign powers, the intelligentsia did not share a common metropolitan culture either but were inspired by different foreign ideologies and models.

Even as these competing political groups gained strength, the United States and USSR continued to compete for influence over a regime that both supported rather than backing political factions seeking to replace the regime. In 1973, however, Daoud overthrew his cousin Zahir Shah in a coup, abolished the monarchy, and proclaimed himself president. Both superpowers, as well as regional states, feared that the abolition of the monarchy without the institutionalization of an alternative political system could provoke a future succession crisis. Instability in the internal politics of a buffer state can easily generate security dilemmas among neighboring states, as each tries to assure that its rivals do not exploit the resulting opportunities. Such crises set off the Anglo-Afghan wars in the nineteenth century, and such a crisis set off the Soviet-Afghan war of the 1980s.

The crisis was harder yet to contain in the 1970s, when opposing ideological interests and perceptions of what constituted equitable agreements were under-mining superpower détente in several areas of the Third World. The Brezhnev leadership considered that the correlation of forces in the world was favorable to the expansion of Soviet influence through support for militarized vanguard-party regimes in Third World countries. The United States considered such expansion illegitimate. Under the Nixon doctrine the United States encouraged the develop-ment of regional hegemons to guard Western interests, a strategy that the Soviets perceived as encirclement. In Southwest Asia the Shah of Iran assumed this role. He tried to use his oil wealth to draw Afghanistan into a regional grouping under his leadership. Daoud eagerly seized this opportunity to increase his independence from Moscow, but the Kremlin under Brezhnev saw this shift as an attempt to reverse Afghanistan's policy of Soviet-friendly nonalignment.

The increasing tensions affected the foreign powers' attitudes toward do-mestic political forces in Afghanistan. Both the USSR and U.S.-supported Paki-stan increased aid to political groups challenging the Afghan regime, communists and Islamists respectively.[24] When the state collapsed, these strategies of defection became dominant.

The principal Soviet-oriented Communist organization in Afghanistan was the People's Democratic Party of Afghanistan (PDPA), founded in 1965. In 1967 the party split into two factions: Khalq, led by Nur Muhammad Taraki and Hafizullah Amin, and Parcham, led by Babrak Karmal.[25] The Soviets pressured them into reunion in 1977. Parcham and Khalq constituted distinct political and social groups. Parcham recruited from the middle and upper ranks of the urban elite. Many were Persian speakers, but the group also included many Pashtuns, mostly either urbanized or of relatively high (but not the highest) social status. Khalq recruited from the newly educated of rural background, mainly tribal Pashtuns from more humble backgrounds. Many of the leaders of both groups had studied or received military training in the USSR.

After 1965, an Islamic movement gained influence among students and professors at Kabul University.[26] In 1973, the movement formed a leadership shura. Burhanuddin Rabbani, a lecturer at the Sharia (Islamic law) Faculty of Kabul University, was chosen as chairman of the council, which selected the name Jamiat-i Islami (Islamic Society). The deputy head was another lecturer, Abd al-Rabb al-Rasul Sayyaf. The main student leader was Gulbuddin Hikmatyar, a member of the Engineering Faculty.

Daoud's coup against Zahir Shah was the first time the government in Afghanistan was overthrown not by a rural-based tribal uprising but by profes-sional military officers. These officers, trained in the Soviet Union, some of them Parcham members or sympathizers, constituted part of the first generation of the newly educated. Daoud's coup thus signaled the entry into the political arena of this previously powerless group created by foreign aid–funded state building.

Daoud repressed the Islamic movement. Some of its leaders (including Sayyaf) were arrested, and the rest fled to Peshawar, capital of the predominantly Pashtun Northwest Frontier Province of Pakistan. There they received aid from the Pakistani government, with help from the CIA. The government of Zulfiqar Ali Bhutto did not share the Islamists' ideology but wanted to use them to pressure Daoud over the Pashtunistan issue. The Islamists also served Pakistan's security interests, as they were the only group in Afghanistan that had opposed the breakup of Pakistan and had supported that country against India during the 1971 war. The exiled movement collaborated closely with the Pakistani Islamist party, Jamaat-i Islami, which delivered aid provided by the Saudi-based and -funded organization, the Muslim World League (*Rabitat al-Alam al-Islami*, or Rabita).

In 1975 Pakistan used the Islamist exiles to stage a brief uprising in several areas of Afghanistan. Hikmatyar's efforts in the Pashtun province of Paktia came to naught, but former Polytechnic Institute student Ahmad Shah Massoud captured a government office in the Persian-speaking Panjsher Valley, north of Kabul. The army put an end to the "Panjsher Valley incident" in a day or two, and Massoud escaped back to Pakistan, where he began a serious study of guerrilla tactics and strategy.

After the failure of this uprising, staged against Rabbani's advice, the Islamic movement also split, into the Jamiat-i Islami, still led by Rabbani (which Massoud eventually joined), and the Hizb-i Islami (Islamic Party), led by Hikmatyar. Both of these groups recruited from the newly educated of rural background. Jamiat's leaders included Islamic scholars from different ethnic backgrounds, including several educated at the al-Azhar Islamic University in Cairo, where they had come in contact with the Muslim Brotherhood (*Jamaat al-Ikhwan al-Muslimin*). Its cadres, however, largely consisted of young men like Massoud, Tajiks with secular educations from the northeast of Afghanistan. Rabbani, an Azhar-educated scholar from the Tajik heartland, linked the two groups. Hizb, the more radical of the two, mainly attracted Pashtuns with secular educations from outside the tribal social system, as exemplified by its leader, a former engineering student born in a Pashtun settlement in the north, outside the tribal homelands.

None of these factions was ethnically homogeneous, and all denied (and still deny) that ethnicity played any role in their politics. Nonetheless, Pashto was the main language within Hizb and Khalq, whereas Persian was the main language within Parcham and Jamiat. Some groups, moreover, were notably underrepresented in these revolutionary organizations. Durrani Pashtuns from Qandahar tended to support the royal regime. Uzbeks participated little in national politics. Radical Hazara youth joined either Maoist or separate Shia Islamist organizations. Some Tajiks and Uzbeks also joined Maoist groups, as the Soviets supported the Pashtun nationalist government.

In 1978 a shakily reunited PDPA seized power in a military coup in which

Daoud was killed. The Soviets did not plan the coup in advance, but they quickly seized on the opportunity to expand their influence in the country, thus disquieting all its other neighbors. The PDPA-established Democratic Republic of Afghanistan (DRA) became unilaterally dependent on Soviet aid. The United States ended aid to the state in February 1979, after ambassador Adolph Dubs, who had been taken hostage by Maoist guerrillas, was killed when Afghan police with Soviet advisers attacked the hotel room where he was being held. The Afghan state was now totally within the sphere of influence of the Soviet Union, as surely as it had been in the British sphere from 1879 to 1919. But whereas Abdul Rahman Khan kept foreigners and direct foreign influence out of Afghanistan, thousands of Soviet advisers now poured into the country.

Far from stabilizing Afghanistan, the PDPA regime fragmented, and its policies soon led to the breakdown of the state institutions built up over the past century. Within a few months the Khalqis expelled the more moderate Parchamis and announced a revolutionary program, which they attempted to impose by force. They began to arrest, torture, and execute real and suspected enemies. In response to the Khalqis' policies, scattered revolts broke out in the country, usually without any link to national political groups. These revolts were largely orchestrated by local religious or social leaders, though some were set off by Islamist militants who returned to their native areas or incited mutinies in their army units. The insurgents largely relied on local resources — Islamic taxes levied on harvests and livestock, contributions from the wealthy, and booty — but some managed to obtain weapons from Pakistan, either from the markets in the tribal territories or from the Islamists, thousands of whom had by now received Pakistani military training.

The Islamists in their Pakistani exile declared jihad against the communists. They were soon joined by representatives of the conservative clergy and the elites of the old regime, although most former high state officials, rather than joining the struggle, made their way to the West, where they had often been educated. Dozens of exiled leaders competed to form resistance organizations in Peshawar. One of the legacies of the old regime was a fragmented polity without any civil society or political parties, so the Islamists aided by Pakistan were the only organizations ready to take to the field.

In February 1979, the Shah of Iran, the principal pillar of Western security policy in the Persian Gulf, was overthrown by the Islamic Revolution. In March 1979, military officers led by Capt. Ismail Khan, a member of Jamiat, took over first the garrison and then the city of Herat for several days, killing Soviet advisers. The army and administration of the state seemed headed for collapse, as insurgents operated from bases in Pakistan. Moscow, meanwhile, expected a reaction from Washington to events in Iran. The Brezhnev Politburo feared that the United States would try to install a pro-American government in Kabul with Pakistani assistance.[27] This miscalculation was a classic "enemy image" generated in a security dilemma. The United States and Pakistan, increasingly fearful of Soviet expansion into Afghanistan, were giving no thought to a coup or military incursion there. The Soviet leaders, however, believed that only preemptive action could stop the collapse of the Afghan state and eliminate the opportunity for American expansion. Mirroring the nineteenth-century tactics of the British and Russian empires, the Soviets carried out a defensively motivated aggressive act. As Garthoff wrote, "The Soviet leaders decided to intervene militarily in Afghanistan not because they were unwilling to keep it as a buffer, but precisely because they saw no other way to ensure that it would remain a buffer."[28] Now, however, the buffer would be closely allied with them rather than nonaligned. In December 1979 the Soviets sent a "limited contingent" of troops to take control of Afghanistan.

Once again, the goal of protecting the borders of an empire seemed to require intervention in the buffer state's domestic politics. Once again, for Afghanistan to fulfill its international functions, its internal disorder had to be brought under control through violent military campaigns. The Soviet troops secured the capital as the KGB seized the Afghan government from the unreliable and brutal Khalqi leader, Hafizullah Amin, who was killed.[29] The Soviets used their military presence to force the PDPA to reunite under Karmal, the leader of Parcham. They elaborated a new program for the government and began a program of counterinsurgency. By 1981 the Soviet troop presence stabilized at about 105,000. The Soviet troops and the regime they protected carried out indiscriminate bombing of rural areas and massive repression, including systematic torture of thousands of detainees by the secret police, headed by Najibullah.

Both superpowers poured far more resources into Afghanistan in conflict than they had ever devoted to cooperation for development. The intervention cost the Soviet Union about $5 billion per year, compared with a total of about $2.5 billion of aid in the previous twenty-five years.[30] Their yearly expenditure thus averaged about fifty times more. The troops and the many Soviet advisers who followed them guaranteed more direct Soviet control over the party and government. After the withdrawal of Soviet troops Moscow conducted an airlift of weapons and other supplies to Kabul. As one Moscow diplomat said, "Arms, food, fuel, even the money for the army's paychecks comes from here." In 1990 alone Moscow supplied Najibullah, now installed as president, with "54 military airplanes, 380 tanks, 865 armored personnel carriers, 680 antiaircraft guns, 150 R-17 rocket launchers and thousands of tons of fuel." The weapons also included more than 500 SCUD missiles, estimated to cost $1 million each. The Soviets also supplied an average of 250,000 tons of wheat per year, slightly more than 100 percent of the total estimated consumption of the population of Kabul.[31]

The Soviets soon found, however, that, far from stabilizing the situation, their troops provoked national resistance and worldwide condemnation. In the

United States, President Carter's statement that the Soviet invasion constituted the "greatest threat to peace since the Second World War" set the tone. The image of an expansionist Soviet Union hardened.[32] The West, most of the Islamic world, and most of the nonaligned countries condemned the Soviet intervention, though most European statesmen rejected the American interpretation of the events. A few European diplomatic initiatives that were intended to prevent the conflict from harming détente quickly foundered. Both the Soviets and the resistance, with its supporters, settled into the brutal routine of low-intensity warfare.

Just as Soviet unilateral aid to the PDPA-controlled government now far exceeded the totals given when the United States and USSR competed peacefully in aid to the government, so eventually did the aid from the United States, Saudi Arabia, and China to the Islamic resistance, the mujahidin. American aid started at about $30 million in 1980, already more than the average of $20 million per year during the previous twenty-five years. Saudi Arabia and other Arab sources at least matched American aid. U.S. aid went up to about $50 million in 1981 and 1982. Under the Reagan administration this amount increased to $80 million in fiscal 1983 and $120 million in 1984. The U.S. Congress, increasingly pushing for more effective aid, took the initiative of doubling the administration's 1985 request, raising it to $250 million, plus an extra allocation for antiaircraft weapons.[33]

The American budget for aid to the mujahidin, reportedly still matched by Saudi contributions, climbed to $470 million in 1986 and $630 million in 1987. It remained at that level through 1989. Starting in September 1986, the United States also supplied hundreds of shoulder-held, laser-guided Stinger antiaircraft missiles to the mujahidin, the first time this ultrasophisticated weapon had been distributed outside of NATO. From 1986 to 1989, total aid to the mujahidin from all sources exceeded $1 billion per year. Like the Soviet expenditure, this amount was also about fifty times the average yearly expenditure by the United States on aid to Afghanistan from 1955 to 1978.

The cooperative security arrangements among great powers that had unsteadily furthered the consolidation of an Afghan state since the end of the second Anglo-Afghan war had completely broken down, and the two superpowers, engaged in the intense endgame of the Cold War, poured sophisticated weapons and massive quantities of cash into every social network they could recruit in this still-impoverished country. The breakdown of international cooperation made inevitable the breakdown of the state.

PART TWO

Negotiating the Geneva Accords

In the early 1980s few saw a way to replace international conflict with cooperation in Afghanistan. Nonetheless, the Office of the United Nations Secretary General, acting on a mandate from General Assembly resolutions, set about elaborating a cooperative agenda. According to the U.N. plan, the Soviet Union would withdraw its troops from Afghanistan in return for simultaneous termination of U.S. and Pakistani aid to the mujahidin.

In the face of seemingly insurmountable Soviet objections, the U.N. agenda omitted any mention of the internal government of Afghanistan. But cooperation over Afghanistan depended as much as in the past on creation of a state that could control the territory effectively enough to meet the security needs of the neighboring states. The failure of the U.N. accords to address the future of the Kabul regime enabled the negotiations to go forward while hindering a final conclusion.

After 1985 increased aid to the mujahidin under the Reagan doctrine improved their military strength, but domestic changes in the USSR were the primary motivation for the Soviet withdrawal. Gorbachev needed a cooperative relation with the United States to free him to pursue domestic reforms. As the tempo of superpower summits picked up, it became clear that withdrawal from Afghanistan was a test he would have to pass to prove the sincerity of his new policy. Gorbachev's determination to pass this test, however, ultimately weakened the Soviet bargaining position. Although the original deal was incorporated in the text of the Accords that were finally signed on April 14, 1988, the United States announced that it reserved the right to aid parties in Afghanistan — though it promised to "meet restraint with restraint." The Accords ignored the domestic conflict in Afghanistan and failed to reinstate superpower cooperation. They assured Soviet troop withdrawal on a fixed schedule while leaving in place a proxy war.

3 Structures of War and Negotiation: Aftermath of the Soviet Intervention

Aid to the Antagonists

The Soviet Union's effort to make Afghanistan a friendly buffer on its southern border required the creation of an effective state apparatus in the country. To carry out this goal, Soviet advisers tried to establish a Sovietized state in Kabul, with an Afghan Communist Party, equivalents of the KGB and the Red Army, a state industrial sector, tractor stations, Communist youth groups, women's groups, and the whole panoply of Soviet institutions.[1] Soviet power also forced Parcham and Khalq to cooperate, under the domination of the former.

The United States, Pakistan, and Saudi Arabia used aid to the mujahidin to block the Soviets from this goal, not to promote any alternative political plan for Afghanistan. The issue of what kind of government Afghanistan should have would have divided the United States from its partners and splintered the mujahidin groups as well. General Akhtar Abdul Rahman, the director of Pakistan's Inter-Services Intelligence (ISI), argued that "if political activities were initiated before the capture of Kabul it would so weaken the Jehad that a military victory might prove unattainable."[2] In any case, no one in the United States or Pakistan believed that they would drive the Soviets out of Afghanistan and set up a new government. Most policymakers considered Afghanistan "lost" to communism and some form of Soviet domination. U.S. policy aimed only to impose costs that might discourage the Soviets from further acts of aggression and to keep the Soviet Army from consolidating its position in Afghanistan and moving against Pakistan.[3]

The apparent threat from the Soviet presence enabled the United States to use its hegemony as a provider of financial aid and as a security presence to coordinate cooperation among partners in Southwest Asia. Washington concentrated on solidifying the alliance system through aid to Pakistan, consultations with Saudi Arabia, and elaboration of a cooperative system with these partners to provide aid to the mujahidin. The aid flows, reinforced by a common ideology of militant anticommunism, solidified relations among the Reagan administration, Gen. Mohammad Zia ul-Haq's military regime, the Saudi monarchy, and the mujahidin groups.

While the mujahidin kept the Soviet Army tied down in Afghanistan, the United States could improve defense cooperation with Pakistan. The Reagan administration undertook a five-year program of $3.2 billion in assistance to Pakistan's military in 1981. The administration willingly overlooked the Carter administration's concerns over Pakistan's nuclear weapons program and the human rights violations committed by General Zia's martial law regime.

Because support for the Afghan resistance was meant to impose military and political costs on the USSR, not to create a political alternative to the Kabul regime, the U.S. government devoted little attention to the politics of the Afghan resistance. The United States was particularly indifferent about which groups might have more popular support, be more amenable to a political settlement, or be more likely to form a stable government. Most officials assumed that the mujahidin would lose, and some debated whether it was ethical to supply them with the weapons to keep alive a lost cause. Most concluded, though, that if the Afghans were determined to fight and willing to die with or without aid, Washington should at least give them the means to inflict significant damage. Pakistan, which bore far more risk than the United States and provided a base for resistance leaders, could decide how to distribute the weapons. The United States was satisfied as long as the mujahidin were "killing Russians." The Soviet invasion occurred less than five years after the fall of Saigon in April 1975, and the memory of American soldiers killed by Soviet-supplied weapons was still fresh.[4]

General Zia's regime, which was trying to legitimate itself through a program of Islamization, took advantage of the latitude it received to create a system of aid that protected Pakistani security interests. It did so by weakening Afghan nationalism and favoring the most radical Islamist groups. Both Zia and the Saudis subcontracted much of the dealings with the mujahidin groups to the Pakistani Islamist group Jamaat-i Islami, which supported Zia's Islamization program. Many of the ISI officers who carried out the policy were members of Jamaat. Arab Islamist groups later played a similar role. The Saudi-based *Rabitat al-Alam al-Islami* (Muslim World League, or Rabita) funded participation by recruits of the various branches of the Muslim Brotherhood. These militants staffed the Saudi Red Crescent and the Islamic Coordination Council in Peshawar.

In 1981 Pakistani authorities in consultation with Jamaat and the Saudis recognized six mujahidin parties out of dozens clamoring for aid. Later a seventh (founded by Sayyaf) was added because of the strong support it had in Saudi Arabia, though it had virtually none in Afghanistan. All of these parties had a

Table 3.1 *Recognized Sunni Mujahidin Parties*

Party[a]	Leader	Ideology	Headquarters Staff	Commanders	International Links
NIFA	Sayyid Ahmad Gailani. Spiritual Leader (pir) of Qadiri Sufi order. Arab lineage traced to Prophet. Married into royal clan.	Traditionalist-nationalist (Royalist). Most pro-Western.	Leader's family; Western-educated Pashtuns of old regime.	Tribal khans; some of their educated sons.	Weak; some U.S. conservatives.
ANLF	Hazrat Sibghatullah Mujaddidi. Cousin of executed Pir of Naqshbandi Sufi Order. Long-time conservative Islamic activist. Religious lineage from India.	Traditionalist-nationalist.	Leader's family. Western-educated Pashtuns of old regime.	Too few to analyze; probably khans and some ulama.	Weak.
HAR	Mawlawi Muhammad Nabi Muhammadi. Traditional alim, head of madrasa. Ahmadzai Pashtun of Logar. Member of parliament under New Democracy.	Islamic traditionalist.	Leader's family. Western educated Pashtuns from Logar.	Privately educated ulama, mullahs. Mostly Pashtuns, some Uzbeks. Most Tajiks left for Jamiat.	Weak. Close to one weak Islamic party in Pakistan.

HIH	Gulbuddin Hikmatyar. Former student at Faculty of Engineering, Kabul U. Kharruti Pashtun from detribalized settlement in North.	Radical Islamist. Views Afghan society (not just communist regime) as un-Islamic. Favors party domination.	State-educated intelligentsia; mainly (not only) Pashtuns from outside tribal society.	State-educated intelligentsia; mainly Pashtuns, but from all Sunni groups.	Favored by Pakistan ISI, Pakistani and Arab Islamists.
HIK	Mawlawi Yunis Khalis. Militant alim educated in British India. From Khugiani Pashtun tribe of Nangarhar.	Islamist; no elaborate ideology. Favors rule by ulama. Very anti-Shia.	State-trained intelligentsia and ulama from Pashtun tribal families linked to the leader.	Some state-trained intelligentsia, but mostly militant tribal ulama. All Pashtun.	Well supplied by ISI and CIA because of high body counts.
JIA	Professor Burhanuddin Rabbani. Lecturer at Sharia Faculty of Kabul U. Trained at al-Azhar. Tajik from Badakhshan.	Moderate Islamist. Views Afghan society as corrupted but Muslim.	State-trained ulama, Tajik and some Pashtuns; Tajik secular-trained intelligentsia.	Best and most commanders. State-trained Tajik (and some Uzbek) intelligentsia, including ulama; Tajik Sufis; Alikozai tribal ulama of Qandahar.	Some links to ISI and Arabs; intermittent. Some top commanders favored by U.S.
ITT	Professor Abd al-Rabb al-Rasul Sayyaf. Lecturer at Sharia Faculty of Kabul U. Trained at al-Azhar. Kharruti Pashtun from Paghman.	Radical Islamist, Salafi. Very anti-Shia.	A few individuals linked to leader or Saudi Arabia. Mostly Pashtun.	Opportunist, responding to leader's command of Arab funds. Very few, but very well funded and armed. Base in leader's home town, Paghman.	Favored by Saudis, other wealthy Arab donors from the Persian Gulf.

Source: Rubin, *Fragmentation of Afghanistan*, 208–9.

[a]NIFA: National Islamic Front of Afghanistan (Mahaz-i Milli-yi Islami-yi Afghanistan); ANLF: Afghan National Liberation Front (Jabha-yi Milli-yi Islami-yi Afghanistan); HAR: Harakat-i Inqilab-i Islami (Movement of the Islamic Revolution); HIH: Hizb-i Islami (Islamic Party, Hikmatyar group); HIK: Hizb-i Islami (Islamic Party, Khalis group); JIA: Jamiat-i Islami-yi Afghanistan (Islamic Society of Afghanistan); ITT: Ittihad-i Islami bara-yi Azadi-yi Afghanistan (Islamic Union for the Freedom of Afghanistan).

religious rather than nationalist orientation. The Pakistani authorities, who had already provided military training to thousands of Afghan Islamists and who wanted to avoid at all costs the establishment of armed Afghan nationalist guerrillas in "Pashtunistan," refused to recognize parties and exiles associated with the nationalist mainstream of the old regime. Leaders of some nationalist parties, supported by tribal elders and some traditionalist clergy, tried to organize a national resistance through a Loya Jirga, but Pakistan, Saudi Arabia, and the United States refused to recognize or aid the Jirga. Instead, all refugees and resistance commanders had to join one of the seven Islamic parties to receive aid. Three of the parties represented conservative and Islamic sectors of the old regime; four, including Hizb and Jamiat, represented the Islamist movement. Table 3.1 provides capsule descriptions of the seven parties.[5]

The structure of the pipeline supporting the mujahidin provided incentives for cooperation between mujahidin commanders and their suppliers but also increased the fragmentation of social control in Afghanistan. Supplying the resistance demanded transnational cooperation, as it involved at least four states (the United States, China, Pakistan, and Saudi Arabia), wealthy private donors in the Arab countries of the Persian Gulf, and the Afghan mujahidin organizations and commanders. Promises of further aid and threats of a cutoff constituted the suppliers' principal if imperfect tool of control over commanders with sometimes conflicting interests. This control through patronage resembles an iterated cooperation problem of the type studied by Robert Axelrod.[6] Indefinite repetition (iteration) of interaction, such as occurred in Afghanistan until the announcement of a cutoff of arms aid at the start of 1992, is necessary to provide incentives for compliance. Control in this case as in others was frustrated by lack of accurate information on the actions of mujahidin commanders and the difficulty of linking specific reprisals to specific acts of misappropriation or resistance.

The arms pipeline consisted of three parts.[7] First, the CIA bought weapons, using Saudi as well as American funds. The CIA transported the weapons to Pakistan, mostly by sea to the port of Karachi, but occasionally by air to Islamabad. Second, the ISI took custody once the weapons had arrived in Pakistan. It transported the containers in much smaller quantities to warehouses near Rawalpindi (in Ojhri, where the headquarters of the ISI's Afghanistan unit was located) or Quetta. It then trucked the weapons to depots controlled by the mujahidin groups in the border region. The CIA paid for these transport expenses through monthly deposits into special accounts in Pakistan.[8] In addition to weapons, mujahidin needed food, clothing, and other supplies, also paid for from CIA accounts. When these funds ran short, private Arab money "saved the system" but benefited only the Islamists.[9]

Third, the parties distributed the weapons to commanders and oversaw their transport into Afghanistan by private entrepreneurs. To pay transport costs, the

Saudi Red Crescent, funded by the Saudi Afghanistan Support Committee, maintained offices in the border regions. These offices, staffed by Arab volunteers largely recruited by the Muslim Brotherhood, gave the Afghan Islamist parties 100 percent of estimated transport costs plus an extra 5 percent for contingencies, but they furnished traditionalist-nationalist parties only about 15 percent of total costs.[10]

The Islamist parties that had been supported by Pakistan's military since 1974 benefited from both Pakistani preference and large quantities of aid from the Saudis and other Arab supporters. The ISI distributed far more weapons to the Islamist groups than to the traditionalist ones, supposedly because the former were more effective in carrying out ISI military instructions. They were also politically more congenial to Pakistan, as they had opposed the Pashtunistan demand and had maintained relations with the ISI dating back to before the war. General Zia was also relying on their Pakistani homologue, the Jamaat-i Islami, in running and legitimating his military regime. The Arab donors who paid for transport of weapons and many other functions gave almost exclusively to the Islamist parties, especially those of Sayyaf, their favorite, and Hikmatyar.

Increased pressure from the Soviet troops forced the leaders of insurgencies inside Afghanistan to turn outward for aid. They needed more and better weapons to meet the military challenge, and they needed financial assistance to survive the damage done to the local economy by the Soviet counterinsurgency effort. Virtually all resistance commanders in Afghanistan became affiliated to one of the exiled parties, which acted as intermediaries for the international aid. This was the first time that political parties had penetrated the Afghan countryside. The recognition by Pakistan of seven parties and by Iran of several Shia parties intensified the existing social fragmentation. In each locality, up to seven leaders could compete for weapons from different sources.

Format and Agenda of the Geneva Talks

The major states involved in Afghanistan at first emphasized military activity in pursuit of victory or advantage. In spite of some proposals for a settlement, there seemed little hope of restoring cooperation regarding Afghanistan. The U.N. Secretary General's Office nonetheless began a series of consultations, authorized by General Assembly resolutions that advocated a political settlement. These resolutions, which called for the withdrawal of foreign troops and an opportunity for the people of Afghanistan to choose their own government, passed annually with increasingly large majorities. Though the Security Council was paralyzed by the Soviet veto, the General Assembly resolutions gave the Office of the Secretary General a mandate to seek a political settlement and a degree of autonomy in seeking it. The U.N. mediator, Under Secretary General Diego Cordovez, exploited this autonomy to take a number of initiatives in the negotiations.[11] Whenever the talks seemed to be moving toward a consequential agreement, however, the member states with strong interests in the outcome intervened to take direct control of the negotiations.

During the first years of consultations, 1981–82, the United Nations established the outlines of what later became the Geneva Accords. These Accords always bore the marks of their premature birth in the age of the Cold War; they were conceived before the advent of New Thinking and the development of common values brought about a more cooperative relationship between the superpowers, which culminated in a regime for the resolution of regional conflicts. The fatal if inevitable flaw of the Accords was their inability to address explicitly the link between the international and domestic aspects of the conflict in Afghanistan. This shortcoming, which favored the Soviet interest in legitimating the existing regime in Kabul, exacerbated a problem typical of international cooperation, the difficulty of agreeing on a definition of genuine reciprocity. Later an international regime facilitated cooperative resolution of regional conflicts by partly defining appropriate reciprocity in such conflicts. In the early 1980s, however, no such regime existed.[12]

Moscow and Kabul, denying that a genuine domestic conflict existed, claimed that "everything comes from outside."[13] The resistance was entirely the creation of "imperialism" (the United States), "regional reaction" (Pakistan, Iran, and Saudi Arabia), and "new hegemonism" (China). The Soviet troops had responded to an invitation of the legal government of Afghanistan to assist it in combating external interference. Once external interference ceased, the Afghan government would be able to consolidate its position, and the Soviet troops would leave — not as part of an agreement with those who were meddling in Afghan affairs, but because they would no longer be needed. Soviet officials insisted that they had no intention of keeping troops in Afghanistan permanently or of using them for regional expansion.

Hence they proposed direct bilateral negotiations between Afghanistan — as represented by the Karmal regime — and its neighbors to end the interference. Once the interference ended, the USSR and the DRA would agree on a suitable timetable for the departure of the Soviet troops. This departure, however, was a matter between those two sovereign states alone and could not be the subject of negotiations with other states. Because the Soviets were not willing to guarantee troop withdrawal in return for discontinuance of aid to the resistance, Moscow had to find something else to offer. When President Carter charged that the Soviet presence in Afghanistan posed a threat to U.S. vital interests in the Persian Gulf, Brezhnev offered to discuss regional security guarantees in the context of such a "settlement": if the West and regional states allowed the USSR to consolidate control of Afghanistan by its client regime, Moscow would guarantee that this control would be defensive rather than expansionist.[14] This proposal would have returned Afghanistan *de facto* if not *de jure* to the status it had from 1879 to 1919, but within the Soviet rather than the British (or Western) sphere of influence.

The exiting Carter administration and the succeeding Reagan administration both rejected these proposals, which they viewed as coercion to act as accomplices in Moscow's effort to stabilize the Karmal regime. Direct negotiations with Karmal, as well as agreeing not to "interfere" in Afghanistan without a linked commitment by the USSR to withdraw its troops, meant accepting the legitimacy of the occupation and the regime it buttressed. Some analysts in the United States and Pakistan were certain that the Soviet Union had entered Afghanistan in pursuit of expansionist goals. Regardless of verbal commitments, once the USSR consolidated its position in Afghanistan, it could then seek to break up Pakistan, especially by supporting Baluch and Pashtun separatism. The Soviets would then be well positioned to intervene in post-Khomeini Iran or elsewhere in the Gulf. Some assumed that this had been the Soviet intention all along; others, such as President Carter's National Security Adviser, Zbigniew Brzezinski, argued that regardless of Soviet intentions, which were unknowable and changeable, the presence of the Red Army in Afghanistan constituted a dangerous expansion of Soviet capabilities.[15]

Some diplomats from Western and Muslim countries proposed that international and domestic issues be explicitly linked. A stable government could restore Afghanistan to its status as a genuinely nonaligned buffer, respecting both the USSR's need for border security and the demand of the West and the regional powers that Soviet troops be removed from the Persian Gulf area. The European Community, the Organization of the Islamic Conference, and Pakistan Foreign Minister Agha Shahi all proposed two-stage peace processes that would first deal with the "international" issues and then establish a "broad-based" government in Kabul. These proposals anticipated the model for regional conflict resolution that emerged later in the decade. At the time, however, Soviet Foreign Minister Andrei Gromyko dismissed all such proposals as "unrealistic fantasies."[16]

Confronted by a military and political stalemate in Afghanistan and overwhelming condemnation in the U.N. General Assembly, however, the Soviets tried to reduce the pressure on them by showing willingness to find a settlement. They agreed that a "personal representative" of the U.N. secretary general could mediate among the parties. Secretary General Kurt Waldheim appointed Javier Pérez de Cuéllar to this position. After Pérez de Cuéllar was elected as secretary general in late 1981, he in turn appointed Diego Cordovez, under secretary general for special political affairs, as his personal representative on Afghanistan.

On his first shuttle to the region in April 1981, Pérez de Cuéllar sought agreement on both the format for negotiations and the substantive agenda for discussion. Discussions continued during the fall 1981 meeting of the U.N. General Assembly and Cordovez's first shuttle to the region in April 1982. Both of these seemingly technical questions posed difficulties that were anything but technical: underlying each was the issue of the legitimacy of the Kabul regime and of the resistance.

The DRA demanded direct bilateral talks with Pakistan and Iran and rejected any participation by the resistance. Iran refused to participate in any negotiations without representation of the mujahidin. Pakistan refused to accord the Karmal regime the recognition implicit in bilateral talks but did not demand participation by the mujahidin. At that time the resistance had no organization capable of engaging in any such negotiations, and Islamabad would not permit the formation of such an organization on Pakistan's territory.[17] The Reagan administration trusted General Zia enough to let Pakistan take this stance, despite reservations in Washington. The Soviets apparently pushed Kabul into accepting a proposal to begin negotiations with indirect talks in which Cordovez would shuttle between the two delegations in Geneva while keeping the Iranian government informed.

All sides agreed that the agenda should include ways to reinstate cooperation by removing the conflictual flows of power resources: the Soviet Union would withdraw its troops (ending "intervention") and other actors would halt aid to the resistance (ending "interference"). The discussions would also address the return of refugees, and any agreement would receive appropriate international guarantees. Pakistan also proposed that "self-determination" be on the agenda, meaning the establishment of a new, more representative government. The General Assembly resolution that defined the secretary general's terms of reference reaffirmed "the right of the Afghan people to determine their own form of government and to choose their economic, political and social system free from outside intervention, subversion, coercion or constraint of any kind whatsoever."[18] The State Department, the Pakistan Foreign Ministry, and many Afghans therefore proposed that the agenda include internationally supervised elections.[19]

Establishing and supporting a stable government not subject to undue influence by any of Afghanistan's neighbors had always been a component of cooperation regarding the buffer state. Faced with seemingly insurmountable Soviet objections, the United Nations persuaded Pakistan to drop the demand for the explicit inclusion of self-determination on the agenda, which would instead deal indirectly with the linkage between the external and internal elements of the conflict.[20] By 1990 the United States and the USSR, consistent with the emerging international regime on regional conflict resolution, would agree on precisely the agenda the Soviets had summarily ruled out a decade earlier. Had the negotiations started later, Moscow might have been willing to include the establishment of an interim government in a common agenda with troop withdrawal.

In the early 1980s, however, no item that explicitly addressed the domestic politics of Afghanistan appeared on the formal agenda. States frequently engage in confidential, tacit, or indirect bargaining over subjects that for one reason or another they cannot or prefer not to negotiate directly. International agreements vary along a continuum of formality from tacit bargains to elaborate written documents carrying the force of international law. The more tacit an agreement is, the more flexibility the actors have, which can be advantageous if they genuinely want to cooperate on similar terms but disastrous when conflicting expectations lead to contradictory interpretations and problems of implementation. Such a calamity becomes particularly severe when implementation requires the cooperation of actors who were not included in the tacit bargain and may have learned of it later.[21]

The decisions on the format and the omission of self-determination from the agenda engendered resentment toward the United Nations among the mujahidin and other Afghans. These decisions also aroused opposition to the talks among supporters of the mujahidin in Washington and Islamabad, who argued that the secretary general should have seen it as his responsibility to insist on inclusion of self-determination and on some representation for a broader spectrum of Afghan opinion.[22] At that time, however, the secretary general's autonomy was insufficient to overcome the firm opposition of the Soviet Union and the DRA's unchallenged recognition in the United Nations. Pakistan and the United States had decided not to challenge the credentials of the DRA, and both retained diplomatic missions in Kabul. Furthermore, as Cordovez put it a few years later, expressing a seemingly unalterable convention of the time, "The U.N. is not in the business of establishing governments." Cordovez emphasized that the situation differed from that of Cambodia, for instance, where the de facto government of Hung Sen was not recognized by major powers or accredited to the United Nations.[23] As long as the DRA remained a member of the United Nations, the secretary general's personal representative had to deal with that government as the representative of a sovereign entity called Afghanistan, especially in the absence of challenge to its credentials.

U.N. officials argued that an agreement reached within the proposed format and agenda would promote self-determination in accord with the General Assembly resolution. The negotiations would remove the main source of the "outside intervention, subversion, coercion or constraint" cited by the resolution as the obstacle to self-determination, the Soviet troops. And although the United Nations could not explicitly call for the establishment of a new government in a member state, tacit understandings — "second-track" negotiations — could achieve the same result. Cordovez claimed: "My negotiations are based on the presumption that [the Soviets] realize that if this is going to work, they will do certain things in Kabul."[24]

The negotiations, Cordovez told me in April 1986, would "promote parallel developments without which there will be no settlement. The agreement is just a piece of paper that promotes parallel effects."[25] He illustrated this argument by drawing two parallel lines on a piece of paper; as if to illustrate how sensitive such a discussion was considered, he refused to let me keep the piece of paper, which had no other markings.

Underlying the official negotiations was an analysis of how international cooperation among states would affect the domestic politics of Afghanistan. De-escalation of aggressive behavior and the emergence of greater cooperation would allow Afghan national traditions to reemerge. The traditions that the United Nations had in mind were the nationalist ones of the old regime, based in part on the tribal traditions of the Pashtuns. These traditions, however, did not exist in some society outside of politics. They had been developed and institutionalized to legitimate rulers and social strata whose power depended significantly on foreign aid that was provided to strengthen the buffer state. As the war continued the flows of aid to radical political groups on both sides eroded these traditions.

4 International Conflict and Cooperation: A Game Theoretical Model

The U.N. format for the Geneva negotiations defined a cooperation problem. As defined by Keohane, "intergovernmental cooperation takes place when the policies actually followed by one government are regarded by its partners as facilitating realization of their own objectives, as the result of a process of policy coordination."[1] This case demanded coordination for mutual benefit of Soviet policies on military presence in Afghanistan and U.S. and Pakistani policies on aid to the mujahidin. In game theory terminology, the agenda implicitly defined troop withdrawal and termination of aid to the resistance as cooperative strategies and their opposites as noncooperative or defecting strategies. Hence the bargaining problem can be analyzed in terms of the formal game models that have been developed in the theory of international cooperation. The results of the negotiation generally confirm realist and neorealist arguments about the difficulty of cooperation, especially on security issues. The principal obstacle, however, seems to have been the continuing ideological opposition and mistrust between the superpowers, rather than the balance of relative gains among states, which realists see as the principal obstacle to cooperation.[2]

Most of the literature that uses game theory to approach problems of international cooperation does not apply it to specific cases except for purposes of illustration. Snyder and Diesing have developed a methodology for the application of such games to the study of specific international crises. I amend Snyder and Diesing's method to take into account certain criticisms of their work, as well as elements that they discuss but do not explicitly incorporate into their models. Snyder and Diesing attempt to uncover the "true" structure of each crisis by determining the preference ordering of each side. They note, however, both that actors may misperceive the situation, including the preferences of the other side, and that each side may be split among groups with different preferences.[3]

In the case under study here, the two sides at the table included pairs of states — the United States and Pakistan on one side, the USSR and the DRA on the other — each of which also had various domestic divisions and conflicts. Some of these differences derived from bureaucratic constituencies, others from "epistemic communities," groups linked by a common paradigm for understanding the relevant political situation.

Furthermore, preferences changed over time as new leaders with different constituencies came to power, and individual actors learned from experience. Decision making was also affected by the actors' various images of their opponents.[4] Even then, each side might dissemble its preferences and make threats that it had no intention of carrying out, trying to project a false image to its opponents to obtain a better result. Gorbachev in particular tried, even after he had secretly decided to withdraw the troops, to exploit the Reagan administration's conception of an aggressive and warlike Soviet Union. He continued to pretend that he might delay or reverse the withdrawal in response to apparent U.S.-Pakistani backtracking on their commitments.

Rather than attempt to identify a single preference ordering for each actor, I identify four such orderings on each side, each of which reflects both different subgroups and different images of that side held by the opposing side. The negotiation analysis thus comprises sixteen two-by-two games defined by these preference orderings. The analysis explains how changes in one side can cause coalitions to shift on the other and alter other aspects of the bargaining process.

Players and Strategies

The two actors — players — are the Soviet government and its Kabul clients on one side (represented by Kabul in the Geneva format) and the United States and Pakistan (represented by Pakistan) on the other. The Geneva agenda defined cooperative and defecting strategies for each side. In the theoretical literature these are known generically as C and D, respectively. The outcomes resulting from the choices of both sides are referred to by the strategy pairs, CC, DD, CD, and DC. Because the strategy choices available to the two sides in this case are not identical, I have adopted case-specific labels for the strategies and outcomes. When necessary for the argument, I shall clarify in context the relation of the case-specific terms to the general theoretical ones.

The Geneva agenda defined the Soviet-Kabul strategies as withdrawing the Soviet troops (W, the cooperative strategy) or keeping the troops in Afghanistan (K, the defecting strategy) and the U.S.-Pakistan strategies as ending aid to the mujahidin (E, cooperative) or continuing to arm them (A, defecting). The return of refugees was essentially a side payment to Pakistan. International guarantees would assure that the negotiations were in fact a two-player game, because each superpower would be responsible for ensuring that its client carried out its obligations.[5]

The negotiations addressed the timetable for the withdrawal, the timing of ending aid to the mujahidin, and the linkage of the two concessions. But in the course of the negotiation it became clear that these were pseudoissues used to delay or accelerate an agreement. Both sides knew that a short timetable for withdrawal linked to a "simultaneous" end of aid to the resistance was the only feasible outcome of the original Geneva process. The actual outcome — Soviet withdrawal but continued U.S. and Pakistani aid to the resistance — differed as a result of events that no one foresaw in the early 1980s, the dramatic changes in the Soviet Union.

Outcomes

The combinations of these two pairs of strategies define four outcomes. The results produced by a pair of strategies could vary, depending on the number and effectiveness of the Soviet troops, the amount and effectiveness of the aid to the resistance, and many less unpredictable factors. Both sides had continuous rather than discrete strategies available — a partial troop withdrawal, for example, or reduced aid — and the simplification here abstracts from that reality. The payoffs from each outcome could also vary with endogenous changes in preferences or the development of linkages between Afghanistan and other arenas of negotiation between the superpowers. We will bear these imperfections in mind, but the simplified model of four outcomes developed here provides a useful starting point for a discussion of the strategic framework of the negotiations.

The strategy pair *KA* is the status quo of mutual defection, which I shall call *War:* the Soviet troops remain, and the aid continues to flow. The U.N. process implicitly aimed at reaching *WE*, the cooperative outcome I shall call *Geneva Accords* (GA) or simply *Geneva*. At least at the start of the negotiations, each side would have preferred a version of the outcome known in the literature as exploitation — *DC*. For the Brezhnev regime exploitative victory was represented by *KE*, which I shall call *American Capitulation* (AC), under which Moscow could maintain its troops in Afghanistan indefinitely and external aid to the resistance would end. The United States and Pakistan preferred *WA, Soviet Capitulation* (SC), wherein the Soviets would withdraw their troops and aid to the resistance would continue. At the beginning of the Geneva process no one considered either exploitative outcome feasible.

These labels are useful shorthand, but they should not be taken literally. The Soviets ultimately did withdraw their troops without a corresponding U.S. commitment to end aid to the resistance, but they did not capitulate; rather, they increased arms deliveries to Kabul. The Geneva agenda had not defined such deliveries as a strategy subject to negotiation, but the United States had raised the issue during the last round of negotiations, and it defined a different bargaining game over the next four years.

Preferences and Payoffs

When we look at several different preference orderings for each side, the games that the various combinations produce will provide a framework for understanding the negotiations and the policy debates on each side. These debates dealt with: the definition of national interest, or what the order of preference should be for the possible outcomes; the effects of troop withdrawal or termination of aid to the resistance on the political or military situation, and thus the effect of strategy pairs on the ultimate military-political outcome; and the "intentions" — the inferred order of preference — of the other side.

All those preference orderings for each side that satisfy certain conditions appear in Table 4.1. I assume, first, that each side will uniformly prefer the opponent's capitulation to its own. (The preference rankings of radicals or traitors did not affect foreign policy decisions.) I assume further that no one on either side loves war for its own sake: I consider only preference rankings where the capitulation of the opponent is preferred to war.[6] Finally, I assume that neither side has a martyr complex; each prefers the Geneva compromise to its own capitulation.

These symmetrical assumptions eliminate most of the twenty-four possible orderings among the four alternatives. Of the five possible preference orderings that remain for each side, one is the equivalent of the game of *Chicken,* in which War is the least preferred outcome for each side. Chicken provides a model of brinkmanship, but it can be eliminated from the analysis of "low-intensity" or regional conflict, which involves no risk of annihilation for the sponsor states. The preference orderings used in the analysis are derived deductively rather than by inference from each actor's actions, avoiding the problem of circularity that Snidal observed with regard to Snyder and Diesing's own applications.[7]

Table 4.1 shows the four preference orderings for each side, in order from most to least aggressive. The first position I have called *Expansionist* on the Soviet side and *Rollback* on the American. It corresponds to the preference ordering in the game of Deadlock, in which there is no possibility of cooperation. I have called the second ordering on each side *Dealer.* This ordering corresponds to the game of Prisoners' Dilemma, which has been exhaustively analyzed as the prototype of the cooperation problem. Both of these preference orderings embody classical notions of Cold War conflict: capitulation of the other side is the most preferred outcome and one's own capitulation the least preferred. The first, more aggressive, position prefers a continuing war to the mutual restraint of a Geneva agreement. Such a position typifies an unconditional preference for a forward policy, what Herrmann

Table 4.1 *Preference Orderings for Negotiators at Geneva Talks*

	Soviet-Kabul Positions				American-Pakistani Positions			
Ordinal Payoff	*Expansionist (Deadlock)*	*Dealer (Prisoners' Dilemma)*	*World Order (Stag Hunt)*	*New Thinking (Harmony)*	*Rollback (Deadlock)*	*Dealer (Prisoners' Dilemma)*	*World Order (Stag Hunt)*	*Fortress Pakistan (Harmony)*
4	AC	AC	Geneva	Geneva	SC	SC	Geneva	Geneva
3	War	Geneva	AC	AC	War	Geneva	SC	SC
2	Geneva	War	War	SC	Geneva	War	War	AC
1	SC	SC	SC	War	AC	AC	AC	War
Dominant Strategy	K	K	None	W	A	A	None	E

Note: Soviet strategies are: keep troops (*K*), withdraw troops (*W*). American strategies are: aid resistance (*A*), end aid (*E*). Outcomes are: War = (*KA*); Geneva = (*WE*); Soviet Capitulation (*SC*) = (*WA*); and American Capitulation (*AC*) = (*KE*). Preference orderings are labeled both by their meaning in this context and by the theoretical game that results when both players have these preferences.

calls a "rollback" strategy, of trying to advance onto the opponent's terrain.[8] As applied to Afghanistan from the Soviet perspective, such a preference ordering meant that the USSR must keep its troops in Afghanistan, whether for ideological reasons (to assure the future of the Kabul regime) or for geopolitical expansionism (to approach the warm waters of the Persian Gulf). As applied by those Americans whose opponents called them "bleeders," such a strategy demanded continued aid to the mujahidin, whether to inflict costs on — "bleed" — the Soviet Union, to roll back the ideologically abhorrent Kabul regime, or to build up intelligence assets for future intervention in Central Asia.

These positions also correspond to the "enemy image" posited by attribution theory. Although many factors, including security dilemmas, can inspire aggressive behavior, an actor tends to attribute an opponent's aggressive behavior to such innate characteristics as expansionism. Each side held such an image of the other at the beginning of the talks.[9]

The second position (Dealer) prefers victory to compromise and war to capitulation, but chooses a Geneva agreement, with its de-escalation and protection of both Soviet and Pakistani border security, to unending war. This preference ordering corresponds to the Prisoners' Dilemma game and Herrmann's "containment" strategy. It accepts realist conceptions of international conflict but still finds value in negotiation.

Each of these Cold War positions has a dominant strategy — an approach that a player prefers regardless of the opponent's strategy. Soviet Expansionists and Dealers prefer to keep their troops in Afghanistan (K) regardless of the American position (War > SC, and AC > Geneva); American Rollback proponents and Dealers prefer to keep aiding the mujahidin (A) regardless of the Soviet position (War > AC, and SC > Geneva).

The next preference ordering describes conventionally self-interested proponents of constructing a cooperative world order. This *World Order* hierarchy corresponds to the preference ordering in the game of Assurance or Stag Hunt.[10] It could parallel Herrmann's "pax superpower" or "détente" strategies, depending on the actor's perceived capability to affect events. World Order actors prefer the Geneva compromise to all other outcomes because it would be a step toward institutionalizing cooperation between the superpowers; they still prefer war to capitulation, however. This preference order has no dominant strategy on either side.

The fourth ordering corresponds to the game of Harmony that would result if both players had this preference order. These orderings resemble Herrmann's strategies of "disengagement" (if perceived threat is low) or "fortress" (if perceived threat is high).[11] Proponents of New Thinking in the Soviet Union decided that the war in Afghanistan was a mistake. Not only did they consider the war unwinnable, they considered withdrawal more desirable than victory, which would tie the Soviets to a regime promoting a "revolution" they no longer believed in themselves. New Thinkers wanted to withdraw the troops from Afghanistan, with American cooperation if they could, without that cooperation if they must. Withdrawal from Afghanistan (*W*, the cooperative strategy) is the dominant strategy in this preference ordering.

Corresponding views carried little weight in the U.S. policy debate. Immediately after the Soviet invasion some officials of the Carter administration wondered whether it was ethical to give military aid to the Afghan mujahidin, who might only be encouraged to persevere and die in a doomed struggle. Others suggested that the best policy would be to let the Soviets choke on Afghanistan without giving them any grounds to blame the United States for the consequences of their own misdeeds. Such arguments, which could reflect a preference ordering resembling *Fortress Pakistan* in Table 4.1, never received serious attention because the Soviet invasion was perceived as a threat to vital U.S. interests and a violation of basic norms. The Reagan administration — aided, in fact, by the Soviet invasion — was moving foreign policy debate to the right, and international opinion was firmly against the Soviet presence. Because Afghanistan was far from U.S. borders and no American troops were involved, the U.S. commitment seemed virtually risk free, if expensive. By the time the Geneva negotiations began, all American policymakers clearly preferred continued support of the resistance to acquiescence in the Soviet invasion. Congress voted unanimously to authorize such aid as long as the Soviet troops were present.

In Pakistan, however, a significant sector of the opposition argued that General Zia was pursuing "America's war in Afghanistan." Aiding the mujahidin exposed Pakistan to Soviet retaliation from which the United States neither could nor would defend it, and war would fail in any case, because the Soviets would defend the Kabul regime at all costs. The security of Pakistan could be assured, and the withdrawal of at least some Soviet troops ultimately obtained, only by recognizing the Kabul regime and ceasing provocations against Moscow. This position corresponds to Herrmann's "fortress" strategy, and I have so named it. It resembles the policy known as *bandwagoning* in international relations theory, in which a small power tries to protect itself from a larger one not by seeking allies against it (*balancing*) but by negotiating terms of protection. Anticipation of bandwagoning underlay the domino theory, which posited the need for firm U.S. commitment to the defense of such small states to prevent them from assimilation into the Soviet realm.[12]

The Games

Figure 4.1 shows the sixteen two-by-two games that result from the various combinations of the preference orderings. Down the positive diagonal — the one

U.S.-Pakistani Positions

Soviet Positions		Rollback (Deadlock)		Dealer (Prisoners' Dilemma)		World Order (Stag Hunt)		Fortress Pakistan (Harmony)	
		E	A	E	A	E	A	E	A
Expansionist (Deadlock)	W	2,2	1,4	2,3	1,4	2,4	1,3	2,4	1,3
	K	4,1	3,3	4,1	3,2	4,1	3,2	4,2	3,1
Dealer (Prisoners' Dilemma)	W	3,2	1,4	3,3	1,4	3,4	1,3	3,4	1,3
	K	4,1	2,3	4,1	2,2	4,1	2,2	4,2	2,1
World Order (Stag Hunt)	W	4,2	1,4	4,3	1,4	4,4	1,3	4,4	1,3
	K	3,1	2,3	3,1	2,2	3,1	2,2	3,2	2,1
New Thinking (Harmony)	W	4,2	2,4	4,3	2,4	4,4	2,3	4,4	2,3
	K	3,1	1,3	3,1	1,2	3,1	1,2	3,2	1,1

Note: Numbers are ordinal payoffs from 4 (most preferred) to 1 (least preferred). Pairs are (Soviet ranking, U.S. ranking). W (withdrawing Soviet troops) and E (ending aid to the resistance), the cooperative strategies, are on the upper left; K (keeping Soviet troops in Afghanistan) and A (arming the resistance), the defecting strategies, are on the lower right. Preference orderings are labeled both by their meaning in this context and by the theoretical game that results when both players have these preferences. Thus the four theoretical games mentioned are those that are found on the positive diagonal.

Figure 4.1 *Game Theoretical Model of Bargaining in Geneva Talks*

starting at the upper left — are the games of Deadlock, Prisoners' Dilemma, Stag Hunt, and Harmony. Within each game, the outcomes, arranged clockwise from upper left, are Geneva, SC, War, and AC. Table 4.2 summarizes the results of these games.[13]

Consider first the four games in the upper left-hand corner, among two types of Cold War antagonists on each side. In each of these games, not surprisingly, War is a stable equilibrium without coordination among the players, illustrating why the war broke out in the first place. In three of them — all of those in which at least one side has Deadlock preferences — there is no room for negotiation, and the game between Dealers is a Prisoners' Dilemma. Although war is a stable equi-

Table 4.2 *Results of Theoretical Bargaining Games for Geneva Talks*

		U.S.-Pakistani Positions			
		Rollback	*Dealer*	*World Order*	*Fortress Pakistan*
Soviet Positions	*Ideological Expansionist*	Deadlock. War is stable, preferred equilibrium of dominant strategies.	War is stable equilibrium of dominant strategies.	War is stable equilibrium as best U.S. reply to Soviet dominant strategy.	U.S.-Pakistani aid ends; capitulation is stable equilibrium of dominant strategies.
	Dealer-Realist	War is stable equilibrium of dominant strategies.	Prisoners' Dilemma. War is stable equilibrium of dominant strategies, but Geneva is mutually preferred. Both sides would defect from Geneva without sanctions.	War is stable equilibrium of best U.S. reply to Soviet dominant strategy, but Geneva is mutually preferred. Soviets will defect without sanctions.	U.S.-Pakistani aid ends; capitulation is stable equilibrium of dominant strategies.
	World Order	War is stable equilibrium of best Soviet reply to dominant U.S. strategy.	War is stable equilibrium of best Soviet reply to dominant U.S. strategy, but Geneva is mutually preferred. U.S. will defect without sanctions.	Stag Hunt. Coordination problem. War is stable status quo (not an equilibrium in pure strategies) if there is no communication, but Geneva is most preferred outcome for both and hence attainable by communication.	U.S.-Pakistani aid ends. Soviets respond by withdrawing troops. Stable Geneva result attained without communication.
	New Thinking	Soviets withdraw unilaterally. Soviet capitulation is a stable equilibrium of two dominant strategies.	Soviets withdraw unilaterally. Soviet capitulation is a stable equilibrium of two dominant strategies.	Soviets withdraw unilaterally. U.S. ends aid. Geneva attainable and stable without communication or sanctions.	Harmony. Both sides move unilaterally to stable Geneva result.

librium of the two sides' dominant strategies, both sides prefer Geneva to War. For each side, however, the initial move toward Geneva—troop withdrawal, ending aid—would leave it worse off if the other side did not cooperate. Furthermore, once Geneva was in place, each side could improve its position by violating the Accords unilaterally, which would induce the other side to reciprocate, leading to a resumption of the war. As in all noniterated Prisoners' Dilemmas, reaching the mutually preferred cooperative outcome and assuring its permanence requires confidence-building, coordination of the change of strategies, monitoring, or the establishment of rewards for compliance and/or sanctions for violations.

If several such regional conflicts exist, a stable, cooperative solution of one can increase the likelihood of cooperation in the others. Such "evolution of cooperation" in iterated plays of Prisoners' Dilemma is one route toward the creation of an international regime.[14] Afghanistan, however, as Gorbachev noted in his February 1988 speech, was virtually the first regional conflict to inspire the United States and USSR to approach a cooperative settlement, and no such regime yet existed.

Taken as a whole, Figure 4.1 shows how political alliances can change with shifts in perception of the enemy. As long as actors with the first three preference orderings on either side believe they face a Rollback or Expansionist opponent, all would favor continuing the war and would find no room for negotiation (top three cells of the left-hand column for Soviet-Kabul negotiators, left three cells of the first row for U.S.-Pakistani negotiators).

Rollback ideologists would find nothing to negotiate whatever views the other side held, but they might become concerned if the Dealers and World Order advocates on their own side began to see the opponents as Dealers or World Order advocates. American Rollback proponents became seriously alarmed when others on their side began to take seriously Gorbachev's advocacy of international cooperation. World Order advocates who saw Gorbachev as a kindred spirit might even accept a Geneva agreement with weak sanctions, for in their view the USSR would have no motivation to violate the Accords. Among the arguments the Rollback proponents used were that the Soviets were actually Expansionists who were feigning an interest in Geneva—dissembling their preferences to evoke commitments from the other side.

On the other hand, Soviet advocates of New Thinking who believed that they were negotiating with American Dealers had an incentive to appear more hard-line. The stable solution with full information on both sides was Soviet Capitulation. If the Soviet New Thinkers, however, could convince the American Dealers that they were also Dealers, they could drive a wedge between the American Dealers and the Rollback proponents. The former would then be induced to ally with World Order advocates by committing themselves to ending aid as part of a Geneva settlement, which all Soviet positions preferred to unilateral withdrawal. If the Americans discovered the Soviets' true preferences, however, the Rollback proponents and Dealers would reunite to resume aid to the resistance. The Soviets might threaten to stop withdrawing the troops — feigning a preference for War over SC — but would ultimately withdraw anyway, perhaps with some side payments or sanctions to make the result more palatable. This, in fact, is a reasonable account of what happened.

Bargaining Tactics

This model also enables us to analyze bargaining tactics, including various uses of force, threats, and signals. We must understand that a great deal of uncertainty surrounded what outcomes would result from each combination of strategies. One aspect of the outcome that concerned all sides, of course, was the shape of the future regime in Kabul. A Geneva settlement accompanied by the creation of a stable, neutral, interim government would have a different meaning from a Geneva settlement that left the Kabul regime in place with no agreement on a mechanism for replacing it, an approach that would consign the ultimate outcome to the fortunes of battle. In lieu of an agreement over the future government, each side negotiated the terms under which it would end flows of assistance that strengthened its own clients for the coming battles. Experts on both sides devoted much of their energy to forecasting the political outcome in Afghanistan of continuing the war, of escalating it, or of reaching one or another form of agreement.

The use of force and other signals of determination to continue the war were meant to demonstrate to the opposing side that success in the war was not likely. The strategy was designed to lower the perceived payoff from war for the other side. Ideological Rollback proponents or Expansionists sought a higher level of force, for they would not be satisfied until the other side concluded that capitulation was preferable to war; Dealers would apply force until the other side concluded that a Geneva agreement with acceptable terms was preferable to war. Until 1986, the Soviets launched a major military offensive before virtually every round of the Geneva talks. In an effort to persuade Islamabad to adopt the Fortress position and break its alliance with the United States, the Soviets also began a campaign of terrorism in Pakistan in 1984, killing hundreds of people in bomb explosions in Peshawar and other major cities. They also launched a few limited cross-border air attacks.

The United States and Pakistan responded in part by organizing a few covert attacks across the Soviet border in Central Asia. Although it was difficult, even impossible, for Washington to time mujahidin offensives precisely, U.S. negotiators usually assured that the opening of each session in Geneva was accompanied by a press leak that provided figures for the aid to the mujahidin and asserted that it would continue.

These uses of "coercive diplomacy" were often interpreted by the other side as evidence of aggressive intentions, especially by ideologists who opposed the Geneva agreement. Dealers, meanwhile, had to use signals of various sorts to convey pacific intentions while simultaneously pursuing the war. A cooperative signal is an indication of willingness to compromise that is vague enough to be disavowed and does not impose any obligation upon the signaler. It is a means of testing the intentions of the other side. If Dealers are not sure whether they are in conflict with other Dealers or with ideologists, they can emit a signal to gauge whether there is a cooperative response. A clever hard-liner, of course — and each side's hard-liners credits the other's with cunning — can emit such a signal hypo-critically, hoping to shift the onus of blame to the other side and to evoke an irreversible commitment. In an atmosphere of mistrust, a clear signal of desire to cooperate may be necessary to cut through noise, but such a signal may also suggest weakness and trigger more demands.[15] This is what happened when the Soviets made clear their intention to withdraw from Afghanistan during the endgame of the Geneva negotiations.

5 Progress and Stalemate: The Geneva Talks and the Soviet Succession Crisis

As the process of negotiation began, the U.N. mediator was virtually the only actor who saw any prospect of success. Under Secretary General Diego Cordovez considered the core of his task to be reconciliation of Dealers who suspected one another of being motivated by an aggressive ideology that precluded compromise. His role was to facilitate the solution to a Prisoners' Dilemma between sides separated by vast mistrust. All sides had agreed that the solution would be for the troops to withdraw and for aid to the resistance to cease. In a diagram he drew up at the very beginning of the process, Cordovez showed the entire structure to both sides and wrote in that withdrawal and the end of aid would be simultaneous.

Cordovez compared the problem to moving objects on a desk: "Suppose we agree that I will move this telephone, and you will move that box. Only I absolutely do not believe that you are going to move the box, and you absolutely don't believe that I am going to move the telephone."[1]

Few if any U.S. officials believed that the Soviets seriously aimed to negotiate their troops out of Afghanistan. Some American officials believed (accurately at the time) that although the Soviets were unswervingly committed to supporting and maintaining the Karmal regime, they might, if possible, prefer to maintain the Communist regime without committing their troops. Soviets believed that the Americans preferred to keep their troops tied down in Afghanistan by aiding the mujahidin.

This distrust derived in part from the exclusion of domestic political issues from the agenda, which exacerbated the problem of monitoring and enforcing compliance with any Geneva-type agreement — the two classic problems of a cooperative solution to a Prisoners' Dilemma. Most American officials suspected that the Soviets refused to discuss self-determination because they sought to ensnare the United States and Pakistan in an agreement that would enable them to crush the resistance and ensure Karmal's survival. The USSR did not acknowledge the existence of any indigenous resistance, and American and Pakistani officials feared that the Soviets would treat continuing resistance to their troops and the Karmal regime as evidence of continued "interference" and refuse to withdraw even after the end of aid to the mujahidin. Hence for American and Pakistani Dealers, who were willing to give negotiations a chance, the key test of the Soviets' sincerity was whether they would agree to a short time frame for a verifiable withdrawal of their troops, linked to the rest of the agreement in such a way that they could not renege regardless of internal Afghan developments. To satisfy this test, the timetable must be based not on political but on logistic considerations, which, according to the Pakistani delegation, allowed three to four months.

Soviet officials were also concerned with the possible defection of the other side. They argued that the United States did not really want the Soviets to leave but preferred to bleed them militarily and discredit them politically. The Soviet officials claimed that they were ready to withdraw their troops in return for credible guarantees that Pakistani attempts to install a radical Islamist government would stop. Just as the Americans took as evidence of Soviet bad faith their assertion that all resistance was external, so the Soviets took as proof of Pakistani (and American) insincerity the claim that Pakistan was not aiding the resistance militarily. Pakistan was covertly aiding the resistance; what guaranteed that it would not agree to end all such assistance, then continue to give aid while still denying it? This eventuality would be intolerable, Soviet Foreign Minister Andrei Gromyko told Cordovez, because "once we leave, we don't want to come back."[2]

Gromyko claimed the Dealer preference ordering: he preferred to withdraw the troops with credible guarantees of noninterference from the other side, but the USSR would have to send the troops back if the "interference" continued. The U.S. and Pakistani governments would not be satisfied with a Soviet troop withdrawal, the Soviets feared, unless they could also roll back the Karmal regime. The Soviets, although they planned to continue economic and military aid to the Afghan state, hinted that they might sponsor some political changes in Kabul or allow domestic political processes to follow their own course, but they could not acquiesce in the overthrow by foreign-sponsored guerrillas of a government to which they had committed themselves. Such hints, however, usually conveyed through Cordovez rather than directly, did not convince anyone with influence in Washington or Islamabad.

The nature of the political regime in Afghanistan, though it was not on the table — indeed, precisely because it was not on the table — blocked progress on negotiations, even at this early stage. The Soviets had not invaded Afghanistan to place their troops closer to the "warm waters" of the Persian Gulf but to meet an (exaggerated) threat to the security of their border. They were willing to withdraw their troops, but only if they were confident that a stable, friendly, and ideologically compatible regime was in place in Afghanistan. Only a Parcham-dominated

PDPA, they believed, could assure this goal. The alternative, they inferred from experience and from the U.S.-Pakistani policy of aiding the Islamists, was either a radical fundamentalist state or the type of disintegrating state that Afghanistan had become under Hafizullah Amin. But the Soviets' "defensive" goal of establishing a stable PDPA-controlled regime in Kabul appeared to the country's other neighbors, the United States, most of the Muslim world, and much of the world community as aggressive, expansionist, and a violation of Afghanistan's right to self-determination.

Brief Progress under Andropov

Leonid Brezhnev died in November 1982 and was succeeded as first secretary of the Communist Party of the Soviet Union (CPSU) by Yuri Andropov. During his brief tenure, Andropov anticipated many of Gorbachev's early measures but did not institutionalize them. Andropov gave considerable priority to seeking a politically feasible way out of Afghanistan. In 1983 some observers hoped that Andropov's succession might represent an opportunity for overcoming some of the mistrust, but such speculation proved premature.[3]

Important exchanges had nonetheless occurred in a number of venues. Andropov considered ending the Afghan adventure on acceptable terms an urgent necessity. Between December 1982 and May 1983 he made statements and proposals that convinced U.N. mediators and some in Pakistan and the United States that he was serious. At Brezhnev's funeral Andropov gave a conciliatory interview to President Zia and spoke of the need for a negotiated solution (a cooperative signal). Zia conveyed this message in discussions in Washington in early December 1982. According to Selig Harrison, Moscow informed Cordovez in the same month that the Soviet government would accept an agreement with an explicit time frame for troop withdrawal (a concession on enforcement).[4] In January–February 1983, Cordovez shuttled between Kabul and Islamabad, where he carried on discussions with Soviet and American officials. In February he traveled to Washington to meet Under Secretary of State Lawrence Eagleburger, and on March 28 both he and Pérez de Cuéllar met Andropov in Moscow. From April 11 to 22 the Geneva talks convened, and Cordovez had lengthy discussions as well with the high-level Soviet delegation that accompanied the Afghans for the first time.

In their Moscow conversation Andropov explicitly told Pérez de Cuéllar and Cordovez that the invasion was a mistake. According to Harrison, "he ended it by holding up his hand and pulling down his fingers, one by one, as he listed the reasons why the Soviet Union felt a solution had to be found soon to the Afghan problem. The situation was harmful to relations not only with the West, but also with socialist states, the Muslim world, and other Third World states. Finally, he said, pointing his thumb down, it was harmful for the Soviet Union internally, for its economy and its society."[5]

Cordovez, in an effort to convince his interlocutors that Andropov was serious about the negotiations, recounted this conversation to diplomats from the United States and Pakistan, journalists, scholars, and others.[6] Saying that the intervention was a "mistake" did not mean that Andropov was willing to withdraw troops unconditionally, but it was an ambiguous signal that he would prefer some negotiated solution based on the Geneva framework to war — that he had a Dealer preference ordering. Andropov did not indicate what precise terms would be required to make Soviet withdrawal preferable to the status quo.

As a result of his conversations in Moscow, Cordovez believed that if Pakistan sent some kind of "positive signal," the Soviets would be ready to offer a fixed timetable for withdrawal and link it to a coincident end of aid to the mujahidin. At Geneva, Yaqub agreed to work out a detailed text on ending interference to send such a signal. Many U.S. government officials, however, suspected that the United Nations might provide a cover for a sellout of the Afghan resistance. Some may have pressured Pakistan to stiffen its stand, in particular the demand that emerged as the key sticking point: a Soviet commitment on changing the regime in Kabul. As Eagleburger told Harrison in March 1983, U.S. objections focused on "the absence of a [domestic Afghan] political process, all of this uncertainty over the future of the regime and the resistance."[7]

In discussions at Geneva with both Yaqub and Andropov's special ambassador, Stanislav Gavrilov, Cordovez also discussed political changes in Kabul, the "parallel developments" that would make the agreement work and assuage the uncertainty surrounding the effects of a Geneva agreement for both sides. In view of the confusion that ensued about who said what to whom, it is difficult to dispute Riaz Mohammad Khan's assertion that these exchanges were "extremely fuzzy." Such fuzziness is an inherent risk of off-the-record, second-track negotiations, and it easily leads to misunderstanding and increased mistrust, as happened in this case.[8]

Pakistan had made one point clear, or so its diplomats thought: that it would not sign an agreement with Karmal, who in Zia's words "came in riding on Soviet tanks."[9] Cordovez seems to have interpreted this declaration as a commitment on the part of Pakistan to sign a satisfactory agreement with "A.B.K." — anyone but Karmal — though Pakistani officials dispute this interpretation. Gavrilov gave indications that Moscow was considering replacing Karmal, perhaps with Sultan Ali Kishtmand, another Parchami, who was then prime minister.

After the talks the Soviets gave what might have been intended as a signal that they would abandon support for Karmal and broaden the base of the regime: their military command in Kabul began to negotiate directly with Ahmad Shah

Massoud over a cease-fire in the Panjsher Valley. Massoud had returned in early 1979 from Jamiat's exile bureaucracy in Pakistan to organize resistance in Panjsher. By the early 1980s he had structured Panjsher as a classical guerrilla base that had withstood several Soviet offensives. Thanks to his accomplishments and to his French connections (he had attended the French high school in Kabul), he was emerging as the most famous resistance commander inside Afghanistan. At Massoud's insistence, the Soviets excluded the Kabul regime from the Panjsher negotiations, which concluded in May. This signal seemed to make little or no impression on Islamabad or Washington, where it was interpreted mainly as evidence of Massoud's military prowess. According to Mohammad Es'haq, a close adviser of Massoud's who participated in the negotiations, the Soviet negotiators never indicated that the agreement with Massoud was linked with the Geneva talks or with a political settlement.[10]

Toward the end of the Geneva round in April 1983, Cordovez told Gavrilov that because the progress on the text on noninterference constituted a signal from Pakistan, the next step was up to Moscow. The Soviets had to offer (technically, have Kabul offer) a timetable for troop withdrawal at the next round, now scheduled for June. According to Cordovez, Gavrilov "promised" to bring a time frame of eighteen months to the June round.[11] Eighteen months was short enough to be a serious negotiating position, although longer than Pakistan and the United States were likely to accept. (Cordovez had penciled in a six-month timetable in an early draft.) After the April round Cordovez announced that the agreement was "95 percent completed."

In May a severe stroke left Andropov incapacitated. According to Cordovez, Andropov was living in a hospital-like room and working one hour a day at most, the figurehead leader of a "government by proxy."[12] Control over Soviet policy reverted to hard-liners — Foreign Minister Gromyko, the military, the KGB. Yaqub traveled that month to Riyadh and Washington, where he encountered lack of enthusiasm or worse over the agreement that seemed to be taking shape. He then traveled to Moscow and met Gromyko on June 8. According to Harrison, Yaqub told him that following Cordovez's overoptimistic statement, he came under pressure to pull back.[13] The Pakistanis never gave a signal comparable to the Soviets' truce with Massoud that they would be willing to stop aid to the mujahidin.

The real explanation for the lag in the talks, however, seems to lie not in the realm of international politics but in Soviet domestic affairs. At later stages of the negotiations, when Gorbachev was determined to withdraw the troops, he refused to allow far more serious reversals in the United States and Pakistani position to halt progress. Andropov, however, had not consolidated a power base within the party and the government, as Gorbachev would. He had conducted his negotiations with Cordovez through people like Gavrilov who were accountable to him personally outside the formal state and party structure. When he became incapacitated, he left no apparatus to continue the effort to find a way out. He died in February 1984 and was replaced by an aging, conservative time-server, Konstantin Chernenko.[14] The old-guard leadership that reasserted itself did not consider the war to be as damaging to Soviet interests as Andropov had, and they refused to take the ideological and security risks of abandoning Karmal. Gromyko harshly rebuffed Yaqub and charged the United States and Pakistan with reneging on previous agreements. He refused not only to give a timetable for withdrawal but even to make a firm commitment to provide one in the future, and he stated that the timetable could not be included in a U.N. document signed by Pakistan. The June round quickly stalled, and Afghanistan entered the deepest freeze of the Second Cold War.

Escalation: 1984–86

Each side, with some justification, interpreted this result as evidence that the other was pursuing an aggressive strategy. The only alternative in a conflict between two hard-line sides was to use military force to alter the other side's perceived benefit from continuing the war. In game theoretical terms, rather than make *CC* more attractive through confidence-building measure, each side tried to increase the costs to the other of *DD*.

After the death of Andropov, Soviet foreign policy in Afghanistan as in Europe entered its last defiant and aggressive stage, which lasted through Gorbachev's first year. In April 1984, once the snows had melted in the Hindu Kush, the Soviet army launched a 20,000-man offensive against Panjsher. For the first time this offensive included saturation bombing by high-altitude Tupolev bombers based in Central Asia. This offensive signaled not only renewed military aggressiveness but a reversal of the implicit political recognition extended to Massoud and by extension the internal resistance.

Other such offensives followed, especially along the Pakistan frontier. The Soviets introduced units of helicopter-borne troops, giving their army greater mobility and the ability to operate behind enemy lines and interdict some supply convoys from Pakistan. The Soviet-Afghan forces also increased the number of symbolic violations of the Pakistan border, while the KGB and KhAD (the Afghan secret police, headed by Najibullah, a former student activist of Parcham) escalated bombings and assassinations in Peshawar and the tribal territories. These tactics were calculated to raise the costs to Pakistan of acting as a conduit for U.S. support for the resistance and to increase domestic pressure against General Zia's pursuit of "America's war in Afghanistan." By raising Pakistan's cost of war (*DD*), the Soviets hoped to change that country's preference ordering. If Pakistan could be convinced that static defense (*CC*) or even Soviet exploitation (*CD*) was better than war, it could be split from its superpower patron. The Soviets also seemed to signal their long-range intentions by increasing the number of Afghans educated in the USSR and in particular by establishing a program of sending first-graders to the USSR for ten years of education.[15]

Nonetheless, this escalation observed strict limits. Unlike the Americans in Vietnam, the USSR did not increase its troop commitment. Moscow never transferred troops from other commands (in Eastern Europe or the Far East) to join the 40th Army, which was based in Termez, Uzbekistan. It maintained the size of its contingent, then estimated at 115,000, far short of the minimum (about 500,000) that counterinsurgency specialists estimated was necessary to mount a serious military challenge to the resistance.[16] Nor did the USSR stage an aerial bombing campaign against mujahidin sanctuaries in Pakistan, as the United States had against North Vietnam and Cambodia.

Hard-line analysts in the United States and Pakistan interpreted these tactics as evidence that the implacable Soviets were patient enough to pursue a long-range plan rather than a quick military solution. They were planning, analysts speculated, to absorb Afghanistan within several decades by building up the Kabul regime, creating new elites, and subverting Pakistan.[17] In retrospect it appears that many of these tactics in fact resulted from the extended succession crisis and political vacuum in Moscow, which left the military and the KGB on autopilot.

Whatever their source, Soviet counterinsurgency tactics had brutal results, and in 1984 the destruction of Afghanistan's people and land received more international attention. The United Nations Commission on Human Rights voted to appoint a Special Rapporteur on Afghanistan, the first time this body had ordered such an investigation of a Soviet client state. The report that Felix Ermacora of Austria presented to the Human Rights Commission in February 1985 corroborated accounts by private human rights groups of massive killing of the civilian population and systematic torture of prisoners.[18]

These reports coincided with efforts by conservative lobbies, many members of the U.S. Congress, and some officials (mainly Reagan political appointees) to increase the level of aid to the mujahidin. Some mujahidin commanders had also become effective lobbyists, regaling Washington with amazing (and often true) tales of diehard resistance, and complaining (less convincingly) that no aid was reaching them.[19] Liberals and most Democrats opposed aid to the guerrilla groups in Nicaragua and Angola, but support for aid to the Afghans, who had suffered an unprovoked attack by the Soviet Union, crossed the political spectrum. Democrat Paul Tsongas of Massachusetts sponsored the first Senate resolution calling for effective aid to the Afghan resistance in the fall of 1982. In the fall of 1984 Congress by unanimous vote took the initiative of doubling the administration's request for "covert" aid to the mujahidin, raising it to $250 million.[20]

The policy debate in Washington included three typical positions, approximately equivalent to the first three preference orderings described in Chapter 4. Selig Harrison of the Carnegie Endowment for International Peace adopted the World Order position, arguing for a negotiated settlement that would recognize the Soviets' predominance in Afghanistan, even at the price of leaving a slightly modified Kabul regime in place "as part of a broader improvement in U.S.-Soviet relations."[21] Few advocated this view in Ronald Reagan's Washington, but many Pakistani opponents of the Zia regime embraced it or the even more accommodationist policy of Fortress Pakistan.

A second camp in Washington (Dealers) lobbied essentially for staying the course: maintain the pressure on the Soviets without provoking them through excessive escalation into an overt reaction against Pakistan. This position, which predominated in the State Department, opposed hasty concessions at Geneva but did not rule out future negotiations. In any case, its proponents argued for continuing to impose costs on the Soviets for their aggression.

The third (Rollback) view, which ultimately won out, was the Reagan doctrine: extend maximum support to "freedom fighters," enough to enable them not just to die or exert pressure but to win. Proponents of this view argued that negotiations leading to a settlement rather than a sellout could occur only after the Soviets paid much greater military costs in Afghanistan, forcing them into an unacceptable choice of withdrawing or shifting forces from elsewhere in their overextended empire.[22]

Some analysts conflated the second and third positions, calling their advocates "bleeders" collectively. But the Rollback proponents considered the Dealers in the State Department "bleeders": they wanted to use the Afghans to damage the Soviets without giving the mujahidin the means to defeat them. The Dealers portrayed the Soviets as unsuccessful and "bogged down" in Afghanistan, hence potentially willing to compromise, whereas both Harrison and the hard-liners claimed that the Soviets were consolidating their position and would not be easily dislodged. Both ends of the spectrum, in other words, argued that the United States gained little by continuing the war under the current policy. World Order advocates, for whom $CC > DD$, argued for concessions that would entice Soviet Dealers or World Order advocates toward Geneva, whereas Rollback advocates, for whom $DD > CC$, campaigned for escalation to shift the balance of military advantage and compel the Soviets to withdraw under unfavorable terms.

The Reagan doctrine won in April 1985, when the president signed National Security Decision Directive 166, which outlined a strategy to drive Soviet forces from Afghanistan "by all means available."[23] NSDD 166 authorized an increased supply of higher-quality weapons. It approved expanded efforts to supply the resistance with air defense weapons as well, which, in the words of an aide to Rep. Charles Wilson, would be "the cure-all for the whole thing."[24] It was not until a year later, however, that a directive authorized the supply to the resistance (and therefore to Pakistan) of shoulder-mounted, laser-guided Stinger antiaircraft missiles. The Stingers were so technologically advanced that they had not previously been shared even with some members of NATO. They were the first U.S.-manufactured equipment supplied to the mujahidin; their supply amounted to a break with the fiction of "deniability." Allocation of the Stingers constituted a strong signal of American commitment to the mujahidin. The ISI first test-fired the Stingers in Paktia Province of eastern Afghanistan in August 1986, and the missiles began entering Afghanistan by the hundreds in late September.[25] Meanwhile, the American budget for aid to the mujahidin, reportedly matched by Saudi contributions, climbed to $470 million in 1986 and $630 million in 1987.

The new allocations required more involvement by the CIA. Director William Casey traveled frequently to Pakistan, where together with Gen. Akhtar Abdul Rahman, director of ISI, he planned military strategy for the Afghans. They decided to escalate the conflict beyond the hopes even of some supporters of NSDD 166 by sponsoring ISI-planned attacks across the Amu Darya into Soviet Central Asia. Hikmatyar readily agreed to such activities, but Massoud considered them unwise. The war had to remain a foreign adventure for the Soviets, Massoud argued, lest it arouse patriotic feelings. This became one of many points of contention between Massoud and the ISI.[26] The mujahidin and in particular Hikmatyar thus gained even greater importance for those in the CIA Operations Division who wanted to break up the USSR through attacks on what they considered the most vulnerable republics, those in Central Asia.

The decision to increase the quantity and quality of aid to the resistance was scarcely opposed by either Dealers or World Order advocates, for the Soviets under Chernenko, who had died only a month before NSDD 166 was signed, had been behaving aggressively and inflexibly on all fronts. U.S. analysts who took some version of the two middle positions endorsed increased military pressure so long as it was combined with diplomatic initiatives to gauge the intentions of the new Soviet leadership. Criticism focused less on the aid itself than on the way it was distributed. Because the main goal of the CIA and the ISI was to inflict enough military damage on the Soviets to force them to withdraw, they gave aid readily to parties that they considered militarily effective in that limited sense. The ISI and the CIA promoted Hikmatyar's party as the most militarily effective. The ISI in particular endorsed this evaluation, which legitimated their policy of channeling the most support to the group whose organization and ideology were most compatible with Pakistan's security interests. Those who considered military aid a means of pressing for a negotiated solution urged that it be given to more moderate groups, in particular to nationalist groups affiliated to the old regime, which would be better partners for a negotiated political solution. These critics also questioned Hikmatyar's military effectiveness.

The escalation strategy also had a political dimension that appealed to the Dealers, although a State Department official charged with implementing that element complained that "people in this town don't take political stuff seriously. They think if we just got enough of the right equipment there it would solve the problem. But the experience of the whole twentieth century shows that every guerrilla war is won politically."[27] The political dimension addressed again the problem of the domestic politics of Afghanistan and a successor regime, but without contradicting the support for the Islamists of the ISI-CIA-Istakhbara triangle. The first priority, the State Department official said, was to pressure the resistance into cooperating politically so that it could become a "viable partner for negotiation." Negotiations between a restructured and militarily successful resistance and the USSR would ultimately bypass or supplement Geneva. Second, the United States would initiate a program of humanitarian assistance for Afghans living in resistance-controlled areas of Afghanistan, enabling the resistance to organize genuine base areas. And third, the United States would engage in a campaign of public diplomacy that would increase the diplomatic costs to the Soviets, especially in their bilateral relations with Third World countries. Some State Department officials, for example, wished to portray the conflict as "East-South" rather than "East-West" and felt that statements by members of Congress and some administration officials linking Afghanistan to Nicaragua or the Cold War were counterproductive.[28]

By "unity of the resistance" both the United States and Pakistani governments now meant an alliance of the seven recognized parties, with the balance of power in the hand of the Islamists.[29] About a month after NSDD 166 was signed, General Zia invited all seven leaders to a dinner at which he and Prince Turki, head of the Saudi intelligence service, ordered them to join an alliance, the Islamic Union of Mujahidin of Afghanistan.[30] Membership in this alliance was henceforward a condition for receiving aid. The seven leaders rotated in three-month terms as "spokesman" for the alliance. The alliance sent delegations every fall to the meeting of the U.N. General Assembly. In 1986 the delegation, then led by Burhanuddin Rabbani, met President Reagan at the White House — a meeting that Hikmatyar had refused the previous year despite a long telephone call from General Akhtar.[31] Dissension among the parties, however, precluded their opening a single office abroad.

The alliance also founded a leadership council of three members from each party and a set of committees — embryonic ministries — for health, education, agriculture, refugee affairs, and other matters. Committees on military and political affairs remained meaningless, for military assistance continued to go either through the parties or directly to favored commanders, with Hikmatyar continuing to receive a disproportionate share.

Cross-border assistance programs were already providing some civilians living in areas controlled by mujahidin with food, cash for food, and support for health care, educational, and agricultural programs. European groups had pioneered these operations, but spending by the U.S. Agency for International Development (USAID) soon dwarfed their budgets. During 1986–90 USAID spent $60.6 million on health, $30.2 million on education, and $60 million on agriculture, as well as additional money on engineering projects, training in various fields, medical care for wounded in the United States, road building, demining, direct food supplies, and other programs.[32] The United States used the cross-border humanitarian assistance program to build up the Peshawar-based bureaucracy of the Islamic Union.

The mostly European organizations, like the Swedish Committee for Afghanistan, that had pioneered the delivery of assistance to Afghans in resistance-controlled areas had developed a complex and flexible methodology based on direct relations with commanders. This method was effective in delivering the aid to those in need, but it not only failed to create a national political center, it contributed to political fragmentation by strengthening the autonomy of commanders. USAID was the implementing agency for this part of the program. USAID was accustomed to seeing its aid as "nation building," an end that it accomplished by building up the counterpart local institution that was its implementing partner. The committees of the Islamic Union, together with a group of American and Afghan nongovernmental organizations (NGOs), were to become these implementing partners. The foreign aid–funded bureaucracy of Peshawar developed into a crude caricature of the foreign aid–funded bureaucracy of the old regime in Kabul. A bureaucracy without a political center, a territory, or a population, financially independent of its own people, accountable to no one but foreign donors, it proved an obstacle rather than a means to mounting a challenge to the Kabul regime.

In spite of political failures and vast waste and corruption in the military program, the mujahidin did achieve military successes. They downed more than two hundred Soviet aircraft. In 1987 civilian casualties decreased significantly, and supply lines became more secure. But the Stinger missiles were not the only reason — or even the main reason — that Soviet troops became less aggressive. As the United States, Pakistan, China, and Saudi Arabia poured billions of dollars and the most advanced weaponry into rolling back the Afghan outpost of an inflexible, expansionist, ideologically committed Soviet empire, the leaders they were fighting, who had fought in the name of Stalin to defend the Soviet Motherland in the Great Patriotic War, were falling one by one to a weapon more surely guided than Stingers and more implacable than mujahidin. As the old leaders died, a new generation took command.

6 New Thinking and the Geneva Accords

In March 1985, a month before President Reagan signed NSDD 166, which authorized a policy of driving Soviet forces from Afghanistan "by all means available," Konstantin Chernenko died. Mikhail Gorbachev, who succeeded him as first secretary of the Communist Party and chief of state of the Soviet Union, came to power determined to end the state's open-ended entanglement in Afghanistan. Reform of the crisis-ridden Soviet system was the top priority for Gorbachev and his close associates. Even as hard-liners in Washington and Islamabad prepared an escalation to weaken the Soviet commitment to the PDPA regime, new leaders in Moscow saw little benefit in continuing the hemorrhage of blood and treasure required to save the Afghan revolution. Nonetheless, Gorbachev's group needed time to develop the details of their policy. Above all, they had to win the internal battles with those who were still convinced that the war in Afghanistan could and should be won.[1]

To carry out this policy, Gorbachev also needed a generally more cooperative relationship with the United States, a goal for which withdrawal from Afghanistan proved to be a necessary condition. Diminished international tension would enable Gorbachev to rebuild the Soviet economy and society by redirecting resources away from wasteful military spending. The timing of Soviet decision making on Afghanistan became more closely linked to Soviet-American summits than to the military or political situation inside Afghanistan.

The simple realist model that dominated official U.S. analysis deemed the Soviet Union's willingness to withdraw a measure of the worsening military situation that increased aid to the mujahidin had effected. In terms of game analysis, the change in the military situation raised the costs of DD to the point where even CD was preferable. That analysis also suggests that, in a negotiation between two Dealers, mediation that enabled two sides with unchanged preferences to find a superior solution might also have brought about the decision to withdraw under the Geneva Accords. Withdrawal could also have resulted from changes in Soviet preferences as a result of leadership succession and domestic transformation.[2]

In the analysis presented below, I argue that all of these factors played a role, but that the domestic change in the Soviet Union was the fundamental condition that allowed the other two factors to work. Gorbachev and Foreign Minister Eduard Shevardnadze came to power convinced that they must extricate the USSR from Afghanistan, though they had not yet decided what concessions would be necessary. To implement this policy they needed to overcome considerable internal resistance. The increased aid that enabled the mujahidin to withstand the continued onslaught of the Soviet military in 1985 and 1986 — the most violent years of the war — helped New Thinkers argue that no military solution was possible. The Accords, as Cordovez had crafted them, helped them argue that the cost of withdrawal would be acceptable. Nonetheless, the effect of the military pressure was limited: the mujahidin never captured a single Soviet base. In the end, when the Reagan administration insisted on a noncooperative solution, Gorbachev withdrew the troops because he had concluded it was in his interest to do so — not only or even mainly because of the situation in Afghanistan, but because Afghanistan had become a test that he had to pass to advance his broader agenda of building a more cooperative relationship with the United States.

Concessions on Coordination, Enforcement, and Monitoring

As Gorbachev came to office, Soviet military commanders were planning their most aggressive year of the war. Gorbachev allowed them to go ahead, but at the same time he prepared the ground for an eventual change in course. Most fundamentally, he began to revamp the party-state apparatus, putting his sympathizers in key positions. The replacement of Andrei Gromyko as foreign minister with the Georgian party chief Shevardnadze brought a key ally into the inner circles of Soviet foreign policy. Immediately upon taking power, Gorbachev ordered the Central Committee to begin a review of Soviet policy in Afghanistan.[3] He notified the United Nations that he wished to revive the Geneva talks, moribund since August 1983; a new round was set for June.

Gorbachev quickly offered new ideas — conforming to the model of how to resolve a Prisoners' Dilemma between Dealers — that eased the deadlock in the talks. The new Soviet leader first made a series of concessions on the coordination of change of strategies and enforcement of cooperation: he proposed that the Soviet withdrawal be linked more tightly to the end of "interference" and explicitly included in a legally binding international agreement. He then made unprecedented concessions on monitoring, allowing a U.N. body to inspect the troop withdrawal.

In May 1985 Cordovez shuttled again between Islamabad and Kabul, where

Gorbachev's emissary conveyed to him a new proposal for the format of the settlement. Previously the Soviets had insisted that withdrawal was a bilateral matter that would be dealt with in an agreement between them and Kabul alone. The United Nations had proposed a bilateral agreement between Kabul and Islamabad on ending "interference," combined with a statement of understanding or a set of letters signed by the U.N. secretary general, which would include texts on the return of refugees, international guarantees, and the relationship of the troop withdrawal to the other aspects of the agreement. Such a statement by the secretary general, however, would not be legally binding on the USSR. The Soviets had previously told Cordovez that they would never abrogate their sovereignty by giving a commitment to third countries—Pakistan or the United States—to withdraw their troops. The new Soviet leadership swept aside these inhibitions.[4]

The agreement the Soviets now proposed would consist of four legally binding agreements: two bilateral agreements between Afghanistan and Pakistan that would end interference and provide for the return of refugees; an agreement on international guarantees, to be signed by the Soviet Union and the United States; and an agreement on "interrelationships," including a timetable for troop withdrawal, to be signed by both of the regional parties and the two guarantors. The Soviets would thus commit themselves to withdrawing their troops from Afghanistan in a legally binding document also signed by both Pakistan and the United States.

The Accords would not be enforceable by a court in the same way as a legal agreement in a law-bound society. But as Lipson notes, "The more formal and public the agreement, the higher the reputational costs of noncompliance." In a world of imperfect information, reputation has a value.[5] An agreement more binding in form would entail a higher level of commitment by the Soviets, and violating it would entail a greater loss of the capital of trust that Gorbachev was trying to build up and that was essential to his foreign policy.

At the June 1985 talks, the Soviets forced the Afghan delegation to affirm their acceptance that the proposed settlement's two major events—the end of the aid and the start of the withdrawal—would occur simultaneously on the day that the agreement took effect. Although American supporters of the mujahidin later attacked this "Day One" bargain as a sellout of the resistance, it had been strongly resisted by Kabul. Cordovez had persuaded Pakistan Foreign Minister Yaqub Khan to accept a draft including "simultaneity" at the August 1984 round, but the Afghans, who had earlier accepted Cordovez's general diagram of the negotiations, including simultaneity, rejected the provision. Karmal had told Selig Harrison that such an agreement would amount to "suicide" for his regime.[6] Soviet and Afghan officials had insisted that confirming that aid to the mujahidin had ended was a prior condition for beginning the withdrawal.

The June 1985 talks also produced agreement on another element of enforcement, international guarantees. The agreement between the superpowers gave the United States a recognized role in enforcing the withdrawal of Soviet troops from a sensitive area on the USSR's border. When Cordovez sent the proposed text on guarantees to both Moscow and Washington for comment, the Soviets immediately sent a detailed, mainly positive, reply. Middle-level State Department officials, meanwhile, gave verbal assurances of support but supplied nothing in writing, perhaps for fear of arousing opposition from the Rollback faction in the CIA or the White House.

At the August 1985 round in Geneva, the negotiators virtually completed the texts of the first three instruments, on ending "interference," the return of refugees, and international guarantees. The omitted agenda item, the status of the government in Kabul, remained an obstacle. The Kabul government insisted that it would discuss the fourth instrument or give a timetable for withdrawal only in direct talks with Pakistan, a demand for symbolic recognition that Islamabad continued to refuse.

The dominant view in Washington was that this demand supplied further evidence that Moscow was orchestrating the talks in order to consolidate the DRA and legitimate the Soviet presence. Cordovez, however, believed that the demand for direct talks came from the PDPA, not the Soviets. "After all," he said, "the Karmal people [were] in a way negotiating their own demise," and they wanted to extract the maximum amount of recognition from these talks.[7] In return for giving up the security of the Soviet troops, they insisted on another type of support, international recognition. The Soviets would solve this problem in due time, Cordovez argued, but they would make no further concession on the legitimacy of the government that they were supporting until they received an indication that the United States would act as guarantor of an agreement calling for an end to aid to the resistance. The Soviets would risk the stability of the regime that had made Afghanistan into a friendly buffer only when they received assurances that the United States would cease trying to destabilize that friendly buffer. Gorbachev's conception of legitimate cooperative reciprocity over Afghanistan was embodied in this condition, but Afghans who were suffering under the occupation regime and their foreign supporters rejected it.

The Agenda of U.S.-Soviet Summitry

Linking issues to create an iterated problem also promotes cooperation. According to many analyses, strategies of reciprocity evoke cooperative behavior in iterated cooperation problems, and reciprocity constitutes a general, though often vague, norm in the international system. For both the new Soviet leadership and the Reagan administration, Afghanistan became linked to both the broader agenda of regional conflicts and the broadest agenda of reduced U.S.-Soviet tensions. The two sides, however, defined cooperation in Afghanistan differently and ultimately could not agree on what constituted legitimate reciprocity.

Meetings among middle-level officials with regional responsibilities could not produce effective linkage to other issues. The linkage between Afghanistan and other issues was articulated, rather, at the increasingly frequent dialogues between counterparts at higher levels — meetings between foreign ministers or deputy foreign ministers and even superpower summits. Important personal relationships developed between U.S. Secretary of State George Shultz and Soviet Foreign Minister Shevardnadze and between Presidents Gorbachev and Reagan. As Gorbachev met repeatedly with Reagan over the next few years, Afghanistan became a sensitive indicator of the state of U.S.-Soviet relations. Soviet tanks rolling across the border to crush resistance in a neighboring country had provided the most visible recent symbol of the expansionism of the "evil empire." As relaxation of tension in Europe and strategic disarmament became the centerpieces of Gorbachev's foreign policy, progress toward disengagement from Afghanistan became vital not only in itself but as a confidence-building measure that advanced other negotiations as well.[8]

By the August 1985 round of the Geneva talks, preparations were already under way for Gorbachev's first summit meeting with Reagan, to be held at Geneva in November 1985. At the Geneva summit Reagan reiterated that Soviet withdrawal from Afghanistan was necessary for an improvement in relations. Gorbachev vigorously argued that he wanted to withdraw the troops through the U.N. negotiations, but that the United States had not been cooperative. No reply had been received from the State Department about the willingness of the United States to guarantee an agreement. American assent to its role as guarantor was necessary for progress toward an agreement on withdrawal. The Soviets wanted to withdraw from Afghanistan, Gorbachev argued, but only if the United States provided credible guarantees of its willingness to stop fueling the war.

Back in Washington, where the Geneva talks had not been taken very seriously thus far, Secretary Shultz asked a State Department task force to devise a way to test Gorbachev's intentions.[9] This is a standard negotiation tactic for a Dealer who is trying to learn whether the opponent is also a Dealer or merely a dissembling aggressor. This task force recommended a highly hedged offer to guarantee, coupled with a public challenge to the Soviets to respond by setting a date for the withdrawal of their troops.

On December 8, 1985, Deputy Secretary of State John Whitehead wrote to Cordovez that "the United States could accept the draft guarantee, provided, of course, that the central issue of the withdrawal and its relationship to other elements of the settlement is effectively addressed and resolved."[10] Whitehead then challenged the Soviets in a public speech to pass the test that the United States had posed: "On December 16, a new round of U.N.-sponsored negotiations will begin in Geneva. . . . The way is thus open to tackle, once and for all, the prompt and final withdrawal of the Soviet army from Afghanistan. If, as General Secretary Gorbachev indicated in Geneva, the Soviet Union supports the U.N. process, and if, as the Soviet Union continues to claim, it is sincerely interested in achieving a political settlement, then this next round of talks will provide them a forum to demonstrate their sincerity."[11]

The meaning of Whitehead's letter later became controversial. The Soviets and the United Nations understood it to mean that the United States would accept an accord structured as described in the existing draft, on the condition that the outstanding issues were resolved to Washington's satisfaction. The major issue left unresolved in the draft was the duration of the troop withdrawal. The letter appeared to embody the Dealer preference ordering. The United States voiced no objection to either the existing agenda or to the draft condition that the termination of aid to the resistance coincide with the start of the withdrawal. The United States, however, could later point to the language in Whitehead's letter — referring to the withdrawal and "its relationship to other elements" — to indicate that it had never promised to accept simultaneity in isolation from the issue of the timetable. No State Department official to whom I spoke in 1986 or 1987 offered such an interpretation, however.

This apparent decision to guarantee an agreement that included a cutoff of aid to the resistance at the beginning of the withdrawal — before all Soviet troops had left and while the Soviets could still aid Kabul — occasioned charges of a sellout by some supporters of the mujahidin. They claimed that appeasers (Dealers, in our terms) in the State Department, who would be satisfied with a strategic compromise with Moscow rather than victory over the Communists in Kabul, had made a secret deal behind the back of President Reagan. The decision was vetted and approved by an official of the National Security Council who died soon after, but it was never seen by Reagan himself, who did not like to be bothered with details and seemed to be unaware of the content of the draft Accords. No one in the administration had objected at the time to the conditional promise to guarantee. Reagan administration groupthink still held that Gorbachev was a slicker and more dangerous expansionist Communist who would never negotiate withdrawal from Afghanistan or anywhere else. U.S. agreement to guarantee was a harmless "psychological war gambit" that would help expose the Kremlin's true intentions.[12]

Gorbachev could not respond immediately to Whitehead's challenge. Discussion of a timetable for withdrawal set off factional conflicts between dealers and ideologists in both Moscow and Kabul. In Moscow the military felt they were making progress and wanted to continue. In Kabul, Babrak Karmal resisted a change in policy, warning Gorbachev, "If you leave now, you will have to send in a million soldiers next time."[13] Karmal assumed, of course, that the Soviets remained committed to the defense of his revolution and that they would have to send the soldiers back to save his regime.

Karmal dug in his heels and refused to authorize his diplomats to offer a timetable in indirect talks. In the December 1985 round to which Whitehead had referred, the Afghan foreign minister, Shah Mohammad Dost, placed a folder on the table before Cordovez. He claimed that it contained a proposed draft of the fourth instrument, including a timetable for the withdrawal of Soviet troops, but he said that he would open it only when a date was set for direct talks with Pakistan.[14]

General Zia, meanwhile, was coming under increased domestic pressure to agree to direct talks. He had decreed an end to martial law on December 31, 1985, after the election — in polling that excluded political parties — of a civilian government, led by Prime Minister Mohammad Khan Junejo. Although Zia had institutionalized many of martial law's authoritarian features through constitutional amendments promulgated by decree, the opposition could now protest against his policies more openly. Many adopted the Fortress Pakistan stance, advocating disengagement from Afghanistan. Like the Reagan hard-liners, they argued that the Soviets were firmly committed to maintaining a Communist regime in Kabul. Conservatives in Washington, however, did not have to endure the presence of thousands of well-armed guerrillas and millions of refugees or acts of terrorism by the KGB-trained Afghan secret police. General Zia also provided military training to some Pakistani Islamists alongside the Afghans and used both against liberal and leftist Pakistani opposition groups. The latter groups called for direct talks with Karmal even at the cost of recognizing his government — no more illegitimate in their eyes than that of their own military dictator — to induce Gorbachev to withdraw the troops that menaced their borders. Gorbachev himself, however, soon rendered such concessions unnecessary.

The Soviet Decision to Withdraw

By the twenty-seventh congress of the CPSU in February 1986, where Gorbachev consolidated his hold on the Party, he had in hand what he thought was an American commitment to guarantee an accord that provided for the termination of aid to the resistance. This assumption provided part of the context in which he reviewed the internal CPSU report on Afghanistan prepared during the year since he came to power. At the time, no one revealed the content of that review. After the signing of the Geneva Accords, however, the Central Committee outlined its internal critique of previous Afghan policy in a circular to all party units. The assessments that only later became public reveal the preferences that guided Soviet policymakers at the time.

This May 1988 circular characterized the sending of Soviet troops to Afghanistan as the result of a series of miscalculations and errors.[15] The Soviet analysts drew three main lessons from Afghanistan. First, it was difficult if not impossible to establish a stable socialist-oriented state in an underdeveloped country by imposing the rule of a militarized Marxist-Leninist party. Thus the ideological justification of the intervention was invalid. Second, the failure of overwhelming force to subdue a seemingly weak, disorganized opposition provided a sober lesson in the limits of military power. Hence the means used to pursue the invalid ideological goal were ineffective. Finally, foreign policy decision making had to be opened up to wider participation. The domestic and global foreign policy of the Soviet Union required withdrawal for reasons that transcended the situation in Afghanistan itself. Gorbachev believed that the reduction in both expenditure and international tension that would result from withdrawal were necessary for *perestroika*.[16] In effect, withdrawal from Afghanistan constituted a goal of Soviet foreign policy, not simply a concession that might be offered the United States in return for something else. Withdrawal of the troops from Afghanistan had become a "dominant strategy" of the Soviet leadership, though they took care not to reveal this change of preferences and had not yet won over all key actors.

Resistance to a change in Afghan policy was still sufficient to keep the item off the official agenda of the Party congress, but in his February 26 address, Gorbachev described Afghanistan as a "bleeding wound" and stated that he wanted to bring the troops home "in the nearest future."[17] The results of this declaration soon became evident in both Kabul and Geneva. Karmal had to be removed; he refused to carry out his part of the new policy, and Pakistan would not sign an agreement with him. During Cordovez's subsequent trip to the region (March 8–18, 1986), Soviet diplomats in Kabul gave him a formula that deferred the demand for direct talks to some unspecified future point, after the indirect negotiations had progressed.[18] Pakistan accepted the compromise, correctly surmising that it could limit direct contact with Kabul representatives to the signing ceremony. Immediately after the visit by Cordovez, Karmal was invited to Moscow, where he was informed that he would be replaced. On May 5, on the eve of the next Geneva round, Kabul radio announced Karmal's resignation as general secretary of the PDPA and the "election" of Najibullah under the guns of Soviet tanks.

In Geneva, as promised, the Afghan delegation produced a timetable as part of a complete draft of instrument four. The draft and the timetable indicated that the Kabul government was still far from accepting the consequences of Soviet withdrawal. Cordovez had penciled a six-month time frame into the draft, but

DRA Foreign Minister Dost proposed a withdrawal over four years, on condition of verification that aid to the resistance had been terminated. Cordovez persuaded the Afghans to reduce the time frame to three and a half years, then three at the next round in August. It was clear, however, that this proposal was designed to keep the troops long enough after the aid cutoff to wipe out the resistance as a military force and secure the future of the PDPA.

Cordovez saw these proposals as evidence not of bad faith (the leading interpretation in Washington) but of a shift in the focus of negotiation away from Geneva and toward the second track. The Soviets had decided to withdraw but wanted to leave a stable buffer state behind. After the May round Cordovez observed, "At the last talks the Russians were excellent. This is something hard to explain to outsiders. It was not just a question of the time frame. All issues were settled in the direction of Pakistan by the initiative of the Soviets." He argued that "the Soviet Union will not come to decide the time frame until other issues are settled." Cordovez predicted, "Now the agreement must start a catalytic effect. What will produce the settlement will be outside the agreement."[19] What produced the withdrawal, however, was neither the agreement nor a domestic political settlement in Afghanistan, but the continuing transformation of the Soviet Union.

The Soviet leaders now set about working on the second track. In a speech in Vladivostok on July 28, Gorbachev for the first time publicly hinted at Moscow's plans for negotiations "outside the agreement" toward a domestic settlement. In a major address on policies in Asia, Gorbachev alluded to the decision at the Party congress to "bring home Soviet troops stationed in Afghanistan at the request of its Government." As a signal of his seriousness, he announced the unilateral withdrawal of six regiments before the end of 1986 and called for a corresponding "curtailment of outside interference in the affairs of Democratic Afghanistan." He then announced: "We support the course taken by the present Afghan leadership towards national reconciliation, a widening of the social base of the April national-democratic revolution, *including the setting up of a government with the participation in it of those political forces which found themselves outside the country's borders but which are ready to play a sincere role in the nation-wide process of constructing a new Afghanistan*" [emphasis added].[20] The good relations the Soviet Union had enjoyed with Afghanistan's "kings" and "tribal leaders" became a staple of Soviet pronouncements.[21]

The Soviets carried out the symbolic troop withdrawal in October, before the November summit in Reykjavik, but both Washington and Islamabad derided it as a mere troop rotation designed to manipulate world opinion — a fair assessment of the act's purely military significance. Far from signaling a willingness to reciprocate with even a symbolic reduction of aid to the mujahidin, the United States and Pakistan began shipping Stingers into Afghanistan in the months immediately after Gorbachev's speech. In Reykjavik discord also erupted over the

United States' Strategic Defense Initiative (Star Wars), a major setback in the progress toward more cooperative relations. Gorbachev and his advisers came to believe that completing the troop withdrawal from Afghanistan was key to convincing the Reagan administration that New Thinking constituted a genuine change in Soviet foreign policy.[22]

As a result, the Soviets continued their unreciprocated concessions. Whereas their previous compromises at Geneva had made the cooperative solution more enforceable, they now proposed means of monitoring their withdrawal. When Cordovez traveled to the region in November and December, Soviet officials in Kabul accepted a proposal to set up a U.N. body to monitor the implementation of the agreement, including a count of Soviet troops as they withdrew. The Soviets had previously told Cordovez that no great power would accept such monitoring.[23]

With the acceptance of the draft on the monitoring mechanism as an annex to instrument four, Cordovez announced publicly, "It [is] now true for the first time that the only issue remaining [is] the question of the time-frame."[24] But the time frame was a surrogate for the central question that the Geneva talks did not address: who would control the Afghan state?

Domestic Settlement and Second-Track Diplomacy

The Soviets (through the now more amenable Kabul delegation) offered a timetable of twenty-two and then eighteen months at the Geneva round of February 25–March 8, 1987. Pakistan, which had demanded a time frame of three to four months, moved to six and then seven months. The latest Soviet-Afghan offer, the same eighteen-month figure that Cordovez had expected from Gavrilov in 1983, signaled willingness to reach an acceptable solution provided all other conditions were met. The main subject of negotiation was these other conditions, the "parallel developments" that Cordovez had expected the negotiations to spark. From mid-1986 to late 1987 the Soviets insisted that decisive progress on the timetable depended on "national reconciliation."

Since Gorbachev's Vladivostok speech, Soviet and PDPA spokesmen had spoken of "national reconciliation" and the need for a coalition government. The Soviets confirmed this key shift in position at a CPSU Politburo meeting on November 13, 1986.[25] Gorbachev declared that continued military pressure by the Red Army had not produced any positive results and that, because of increased aid to the mujahidin, the situation on the ground had in fact worsened. The Soviet leaders decided to withdraw their troops from Afghanistan under a Geneva agreement by the end of 1988. They were willing to do so partly because they assumed that the United States, by offering to guarantee the agreement, had agreed to sign and abide by an accord that would end aid to the resistance.

Gorbachev crafted a compromise between those in Moscow who wanted to try to secure the PDPA's future and those who were willing to withdraw the troops with minimal conditions. The Soviets would delay offering an acceptable time-table for one year while they attempted to form a transitional government in Kabul. This decision was kept confidential within the Soviet establishment, con-cealed at first even from some members of the Central Committee. As late as the following July, some Soviet officials were still telling Najibullah that he could rely indefinitely on Soviet support.[26] As analysis of the bargaining games in the previous chapter suggests, secrecy was vital to the Soviet Union's negotiating posture, for if the United States and Pakistan knew that Moscow intended to withdraw by a certain date, Dealers in those capitals, lacking incentive to offer further concessions, would join the hard-liners.

For one year the Soviets insisted in negotiations that formation of a transi-tional government in Kabul was a prior condition for troop withdrawal. They emphasized their wish to prevent a massacre of their clients, as well as the impossibility of ignoring an organized political force such as the PDPA. Almost exactly one year after the Politburo meeting, however, the Soviets dropped the demand for a transitional government and pressed forward toward an agreement on withdrawal that was linked neither to a domestic settlement nor, ultimately, even to the end of aid to the mujahidin. Moscow continued to lobby for a domestic settlement with some participation of the PDPA but no longer made it a condition for withdrawal.

At the beginning of the yearlong Soviet push for a transitional government, Moscow put pressure on Kabul to negotiate with the mujahidin and also asked both the United Nations and Pakistan to help convince some resistance figures to participate. Although the Geneva talks had progressed, U.S.-Soviet relations were entering a tense phase following the confrontation between Gorbachev and Reagan at Reykjavik, where the conflict over "Star Wars" had prevented them from discussing a "bracketed" text for a joint statement on Afghanistan.[27] Mistrust of the Soviets in the Reagan administration had not yet been mitigated by any positive changes, and any prior conditions placed on withdrawal were viewed as ways of avoiding the principal test — withdrawing Soviet troops from Afghanistan.

Soon after Gorbachev's speech in Vladivostok the Soviets had begun to make increasingly public declarations that they no longer insisted on a Communist-dominated regime in Kabul or even one with any Marxist characteristics. They told Cordovez that Najibullah would establish a new government in Afghanistan with "nothing Marxist about it — lots of landlords."[28] The official position of the mujahidin leaders in Pakistan was that they would never negotiate any agreement or join any coalition with the Soviet puppets in Kabul, but the Soviets asked Cordovez to explore the possibility of bringing elements of the resistance into the Kabul government.[29]

The emphasis on landlords in the national reconciliation policy signified the Soviets' interest in forging an alliance between their clients and the tribally based state elite that had guaranteed security in the area for a century. Moscow hoped that such an alliance would prove a bulwark against the Islamic elites that were favored by the policies of Pakistan, Saudi Arabia, and the United States. But the tribal and traditional forces, although they were willing to engage in local alliances for local reasons, never agreed to any broad political cooperation with the PDPA regime.

After the November 1986 Politburo meeting the Soviets eased the way for Cordovez to promote such an internal settlement. The implications of this initiative went beyond Afghanistan. Not only had the Soviets accepted that a "revolution" led by a Marxist-Leninist vanguard party could be reversed, but U.N. involvement marked a shift in operating rules regarding the domestic sovereignty of member states. This latter change was key to the subsequent development of an international regime in which the United Nations repeatedly mediated domestic conflicts to steer antagonists toward some form of national reconciliation, culminating in internationally monitored elections.

Until this time, the U.N. Secretary General's Office had felt inhibited from communicating with the mujahidin or other antigovernment forces, for the DRA was the official representative of Afghanistan. During his November 20–24 shuttle to Kabul, however, following hints from the Soviets, Cordovez asked Afghan Foreign Minister Dost for permission to contact the mujahidin leaders. Dost refused, but when Cordovez spoke to Soviet officials, they told him to ask again in two days. This time, Dost gave an "incomprehensible" reply. Giandomenico Picco, an assistant to the secretary general for special political affairs, leaned over and addressed Cordovez in Spanish: "No lo empuje" — Don't push him. Cordovez confirmed his permission later with the Soviet embassy in Kabul.[30] Upon his return to Islamabad in the next stage of the shuttle, Cordovez asked to meet the seven leaders. He was informed that several of them were out of the country and that they could not be assembled on such short notice; some, moreover, refused to meet him.

In December, Soviet Deputy Foreign Minister Yuli Vorontsov invited Pakistan Foreign Secretary Abdul Sattar to Moscow. Vorontsov emphasized the importance to the Soviets of finding a "respectable end of their misadventure." He explicitly stated that the Geneva process would remain on hold pending an internal political settlement and asked for Pakistan's assistance in setting up a transitional government.[31] He did not mention any time limit for the effort.

On December 11, Najibullah and the entire PDPA leadership were summoned to Moscow. Upon his return four days later, Najibullah announced the plan for national reconciliation: a cease-fire, a coalition with political leaders in Kabul, and recognition of the local power of commanders. Confused PDPA rhetoric reflected continuing factional struggles in both Moscow and Kabul. In his speech to the Central Committee announcing the policy Najibullah said that only those who supported the "revolution" could join the government; at the same time he sent letters to the seven mujahidin leaders offering them cabinet positions.

The mujahidin alliance rejected these proposals. They did not believe that Najibullah's offer to share power was sincere, and former PDPA and Russian sources have confirmed their suspicions.[32] The mujahidin preferred to continue the war rather than being left in the field without further aid to fight a well-armed Kabul regime. They felt that increased aid, particularly the arrival of Stingers, was changing the military situation in their favor, and they were encouraged in this view by the ISI and CIA. A political settlement would also be likely to marginalize them in favor of figures from the old regime. The leaders announced the formation of a commission to draft statutes for an Islamic interim government that would hold elections and establish the framework of an Islamic state.[33] They rejected the Geneva format and demanded direct negotiations between the Soviets and the mujahidin.

The Pakistan Foreign Ministry, home to a certain number of Dealers, wished to respond to the Soviet position more positively.[34] (Recall the model's prediction that a Dealer's offer to negotiate splits Rollback proponents and Dealers on the other side.) Because the mujahidin leaders adamantly opposed negotiations or dialogue with Najibullah, let alone coalition, the Foreign Office began to explore the idea of a neutral transitional government organized around the exiled former king, Zahir Shah, and excluding the major antagonists of the war. In January, Yaqub Khan mentioned this plan to the mujahidin leaders in several meetings. He traveled to Rome, where he met Zahir Shah's son-in-law and nephew, Gen. Abdul Wali, who recommended that Pakistan support the convening of a Loya Jirga. Such a council, Wali predicted, would turn to the former king.

The three nationalist parties also favored a Loya Jirga, but the Islamists, supported by the ISI, vetoed it. Moving forward with this option would have split the Islamic Union and required a break with the Islamists, whom the ISI and the CIA considered the main effective military force of the resistance. The essence of the U.S.-Pakistani policy remained exertion of military force on the Soviet Union to compel it to withdraw, and makers of that policy still did not take seriously the internal changes in the USSR. The ISI, the CIA, and anticommunist militants sought to draw the Dealers away from the negotiations by portraying Gorbachev as an expansionist who was feigning interest in negotiation to entice the naive into concessions. As in the model, when confronting an expansionist USSR, Rollback proponents, Dealers, and World Order advocates agreed on supporting armed resistance.

In any case, in 1987 the Soviets showed little interest in the Zahir Shah option or in a government of neutrals. Yaqub raised these alternatives in discussions with Soviet Foreign Minister Shevardnadze and other Soviet diplomats, who continued to insist that the PDPA, because of its organizational strength and control of the state apparatus, had to play a major role in the transition. Soviet officials refused to consider alternatives to the official policy of national reconciliation. Yaqub responded that if the PDPA was so strong, the Soviets should simply propose a short timetable for withdrawal, and the State Department took the same position. No Afghans would enter into a coalition or negotiations with a government propped up by Soviet troops. National reconciliation could come only after withdrawal.

Far from signaling interest in a political settlement, the CIA under the personal supervision of Director Casey, together with the ISI, accelerated cross-border attacks by Hizb-i Islami (Hikmatyar) forces into Soviet Tajikistan in early 1987.[35] The Pakistan Foreign Ministry was also more reluctant than usual to pursue options that might alienate the Reagan administration, for the U.S. Congress was due to consider a package of renewed aid to Islamabad. On March 5, 1987, the administration announced that it intended to request $4.02 billion dollars for Pakistan over six years, a bid to maintain the U.S.-dominated alliance by continued aid flow.[36]

Soviet rigidity may have resulted less from policy in Moscow than from the difficulties the Soviets were having in Kabul, where they tried to induce the PDPA to make genuine concessions to other political forces. By May, Cordovez reported that "the Russians are very upset with their Afghans. They can't get them to move. They wanted to pull out 50,000 troops in April for the anniversary of the Sawr Revolution, but the Afghans wouldn't let them." The United Nations was also having troubles with "its" Afghans: Zahir Shah refused to make any decisive move.[37] Najibullah, who had a very small base of support in the PDPA (in contrast to the Kremlin and the Lyubyanka), was engaged in a difficult balancing act between two enemy factions, the Khalqis and the pro-Karmalites. He was also receiving contradictory signals from the factions then battling for control in the Soviet leadership.

Cordovez decided to take a more active role at devising a form for the second track. In July 1987 he drafted a proposal for a U.N.-sponsored meeting of representatives of all Afghan parties. The meeting was to include the seven major Sunni parties who belonged to the resistance alliance in Peshawar, resistance commanders, refugee and tribal leaders, the former king and his supporters, and the PDPA. The participants would choose an interim government in which "no party would be assured a predominant role."[38]

Cordovez recognized that a genuinely broad-based Afghan government would deny a major role to the PDPA — the party might expect no more, he said, than to have an unknown official designated "minister of sports."[39] Because Cordovez realized that the resistance would not recognize the Kabul regime as a government, he proposed that the PDPA participate as one Afghan party among many. The DRA itself would not formally participate. Delegations would not have to sit in the same room or even the same hotel, as long as they were in the same city.

The Soviets did not formally assent to Cordovez's proposal, but they encouraged him to use it as a basis for discussion. The United States and Pakistan did not oppose the proposal but saw it as premature. And because this was the first regional conflict in which the United Nations had involved itself to this extent, there was no precedent on which to base trust. The United States and Pakistan worried that the Soviets, by making agreement among Afghans a condition for their withdrawal, might shift the onus for their continued presence onto the mujahidin.[40] In Pakistan the Foreign Office and the new civilian prime minister, Mohammad Khan Junejo, saw merit in the Cordovez proposal. But the ISI, which controlled Pakistan's relations with the mujahidin, argued that the resistance was winning on the battlefield, and that there was therefore no reason to retreat from the Islamic Union proposal to establish an alliance-led interim government.[41]

Cordovez nevertheless tried to circulate the proposal. Blocked by the Pakistani government from direct access to the Afghan leaders in Peshawar, he brought the proposal to their attention through intermediaries and through informal talks with some members of the delegation of the resistance parties that attended the U.N. General Assembly session in the fall of 1987. Responses ranged from negative to noncommittal. The participation of the PDPA in the meeting (if not in the subsequent government) was the major obstacle. In addition, even moderate forces open to some form of compromise saw no reason to jeopardize the tenuous unity of the resistance before the Soviets had committed themselves to withdrawing their troops. In any case, it was impossible for the leaders to break with the ISI and the CIA, on whom they depended for aid and even survival.[42]

Because Pakistan and the United States continued to insist that a short timetable was key to progress on a settlement, the Soviets made one last attempt to use this card to induce progress on national reconciliation. On August 29 the DRA suddenly asked that the Geneva talks be reconvened, and Soviet officials hinted to Cordovez that they would offer a twelve-month timetable. During the September 7–9 meetings, however, the Soviet clients in Kabul apparently resisted. They lowered their offer from eighteen to sixteen months, although the day after the end of the round an article in *Pravda* stated that twelve months was an acceptable timetable.[43] Pakistan raised its proposal to eight months.

Delinking Withdrawal from Change of Government

The Soviets decided that the only way forward was to send the U.S. government a clear signal of their intention to withdraw regardless of changes in government. They deliberately shifted the focus of the negotiations away from the

U.N.-mediated talks between Islamabad and Kabul to bilateral superpower negotiations.

The week after the September 1987 Geneva round, Soviet Foreign Minister Shevardnadze came to Washington for a ministerial meeting. On September 16, before the working session on regional issues, he asked to speak to Secretary Shultz privately. Shevardnadze "opened with a quiet directness," Shultz recalled, saying " 'We will leave Afghanistan. . . . It may be in five months or a year, but it is not a question of it happening in the remote future. I say with all responsibility that a political decision to leave has been made.' "

Shevardnadze asked for American cooperation in limiting the spread of "Islamic fundamentalism." Shultz, though he reiterated that the United States insisted on a short timetable, affirmed American interest in "a neutral, nonaligned Afghanistan." He observed:

> This meeting was a private sharing of critical information. Gorbachev and Shevardnadze had both said publicly on earlier occasions that the Soviets would withdraw from Afghanistan, but we saw no evidence on the ground to lend credence to their statements. This private assurance was different. I had enough confidence by this time in my relationship with Shevardnadze that I knew he would not deliberately mislead me.
>
> We then joined our waiting working group and listened, on Afghanistan, to the same old arguments. I said nothing, but I looked over at Shevardnadze and he at me as we shared a knowing glance.[44]

Although he trusted Shevardnadze, Shultz attributed the decision to withdraw not to change in the Soviet Union but to military pressure alone: "There was no doubt why the Soviets wanted to leave: the war was bloody, and the resistance by the Afghan mujaheddin was fierce." Increased U.S. aid had made the difference: "The tide of the conflict [had] shifted."[45] The lesson to be drawn was that military pressure worked. This conclusion is consistent with attribution theory, according to which one tends to attribute desired outcomes to one's own efforts and undesired outcomes to objective conditions or the actions of others. Schultz declared general sympathy with Shevardnadze's concern with "fundamentalism," but there is no sign in his memoirs — or in any of my interviews or discussions with officials at high levels of the Reagan administration — of serious consideration that the political nature of the forces receiving U.S. aid in Afghanistan might affect Soviet decisions.

Moscow soon conveyed through normal channels its decision to propose a short timetable not conditioned on progress on the second track. On October 30, 1987, Soviet Deputy Foreign Minister Yuli Vorontsov confirmed this decision to U.S. Deputy Secretary of State Michael Armacost in Geneva. The Soviets apparently did not immediately convey this decision to Pakistan. Political relations between the two superpowers and personal relations between their two presidents were warming as negotiations on medium-range missiles advanced. As the super-powers prepared for the Washington summit scheduled for December 8–10, Gorbachev wanted above all to remove Afghanistan from the U.S.-Soviet agenda.

The previous July, Gorbachev had finally told Najibullah of the Politburo's decision: Soviet troops would leave Afghanistan in 1988, he told the Afghan leader, "whether you are ready or not."[46] As the date approached, Najibullah hurried to prepare. He continued the purge of his enemies (and the opponents of national reconciliation) from the PDPA leadership. In November he called a "Loya Jirga" that adopted a new Constitution of the Republic of Afghanistan — a consti-tution written by four Soviet advisers.[47] On November 29, during the Loya Jirga, Gorbachev told the Afghan leader by telephone that he was going to offer a twelve-month timetable to Reagan in Washington. The next day Najibullah an-nounced the same offer to the Loya Jirga.

In Washington the two presidents confirmed the warming of U.S.-Soviet relations as they signed a treaty to limit intermediate-range missiles. Gorbachev announced that Soviet troops would leave Afghanistan within twelve months of the effective date of the Geneva Accords. Shultz and Armacost believed him, but the CIA still argued that "the Soviet talk was political deception; we were foolish to take them seriously." In the CIA's estimation, any withdrawal that took less than eighteen months would lead to the collapse of the Najibullah regime, a develop-ment that the Soviets would not countenance.[48]

For Gorbachev, Afghanistan had become both an irritant in his developing relationship with the United States and a deeply unpopular commitment at home. During the December 1987 summit in Washington the two leaders agreed to meet six months later in Moscow. Gorbachev was determined to start the Soviet pullout before then regardless of obstacles raised by Kabul, Islamabad, or Washington.

Signing the Accords with "Positive Symmetry"

Hard-line elements in both the U.S. and Pakistani governments attributed Gorbachev's decision entirely to a supposed reversal of the military situation as a result of increased aid to the resistance, especially the introduction of Stingers. The perpetuation of a military stalemate had indeed played a role in Soviet decision making, but Gorbachev had already shaped the major components of his decision before any Stingers entered Afghanistan.

Whatever underlay the decision, by the end of 1987 Gorbachev had publicly committed himself to withdrawing Soviet troops from Afghanistan. His words made such an agreement conditional on the implementation of the Geneva Ac-cords and thus to the end of aid to the resistance. But the political reality was that any backtracking on this apparent commitment, whatever legalistic justification might be provided for it, would severely damage other negotiations on which Gorbachev was counting. Furthermore, the Soviet leadership had concluded that the presence of Soviet troops in Afghanistan served no Soviet foreign policy interest. In terms of the game theory model, the Soviet leadership had adopted and revealed the New Thinking preference ordering. As predicted by the model, U.S. and Pakistani Dealers and Rollback proponents reunited on a policy of continuing aid to the resistance as the Soviet troops withdrew, to the dismay of World Order advocates and the intense but impotent outrage of Moscow.

The process through which this happened was more complex than a simple model can describe. At the summit President Reagan, still apparently unaware of the content of the Accords his administration had agreed to guarantee, told Gorbachev he would not cut off aid to the Afghan "freedom fighters." He called on Gorbachev to set a "date certain" for the troop pullout. Midlevel State Department officials, who had supported the Geneva deal, "clarified" to their Soviet counterparts that aid would be halted at the start of the withdrawal. Even if they might have preferred to continue aid to the resistance, they assumed that the agreement of both sides to guarantee the Accords, combined with Gorbachev's commitment to a timetable of twelve months or less, had locked both sides into the commitments they had made to each other and to the United Nations.[49]

Mujahidin supporters in Washington, however, refused to accept the codification of the deal, which had been worked out in secret negotiations. They began to mobilize against the Accords. During the course of the war the proponents of military escalation had marshaled a great deal of public support for the "covert" program of aid to the resistance, but the diplomats working on the negotiations had massed no political support for the "secret" text of the Accords.

Both Secretary Shultz in Washington and President Zia in Islamabad saw that the newly revealed Soviet position gave them more bargaining leverage. Realists all, they behaved like egoistic actors under anarchy and sought maximum advantage. Although some State Department officials argued that Whitehead's December 1985 letter had left the acceptability of the entire framework open, Shultz acknowledges that "our negotiators in Geneva had taken the position that upon Soviet withdrawal from Afghanistan, our support for the mujaheddin, having served its purpose, would cease."[50]

Severance of ties to the resistance was unacceptable to both the Reagan administration and Zia, but each responded in a manner that reflected its national interests. This divergence was a foretaste of increasingly troubled U.S.-Pakistani relations as the Soviet threat declined.

The United States and Pakistan faced a choice between two strategies for affecting the future balance of power in Afghanistan, each exploiting the Soviet commitment to withdrawal. One approach, favored by Zia, was to push for explicit negotiations over an interim government. The other, favored by the State Department, was to demand various safeguards in the Accords to affect the flow of external resources to the contending parties in ways favorable to the mujahidin. The Soviets readily accepted — even offered — some such safeguards regarding the length and structure of the withdrawal process. Far more controversial was the U.S. proposal that the resistance and the Kabul regime should receive "symmetry" of treatment; aid to the mujahidin would not stop unless aid to the PDPA-dominated state apparatus ended as well. This proposal in essence added Soviet aid to the Kabul government to the diplomatic agenda, although no one had even proposed its inclusion during the consultations in 1981 and 1982 that set the agenda for the Geneva negotiations. The new proposal embodied the different conceptions in Washington and Moscow of what constituted reciprocity in Afghanistan.

In Islamabad, General Zia had been caught unawares by the announcement in Washington of the Soviet decision to drop linkage between the withdrawal timetable and formation of an interim government. He worried that the superpowers had reached a deal behind his back, ignoring the interests of Pakistan and the resistance. In Pakistan's view, the United States' main interest was simply the withdrawal of Soviet troops, whereas Pakistan also required the establishment of a stable (or, even better, friendly) Afghan government and the return of the refugees. In other words, the United States, which had no direct interest in the region as Britain had had, was interested primarily in weakening the Soviet Union, but Pakistan had an immediate stake in the stability and political complexion of its neighbor. Pakistani strategists, like Soviet ones, wanted secure borders and a friendly Afghanistan; for Islamabad that scenario was likeliest if Islamists had significant power.

Zia suddenly announced in an interview that the Geneva Accords should be signed after — not before — the formation of a tripartite coalition government of mujahidin, prominent exiles, and members of the current government in Kabul.[51] In his view, the Soviets' previous insistence on forming a transitional government before they committed themselves to a withdrawal timetable had been a delaying tactic. Now that the withdrawal commitment was in hand, however, the Soviet position in Afghanistan would begin to deteriorate. The United States and Pakistan could use the leverage that this commitment provided to insist on a new government more to their liking.

Cordovez shuttled to the region during January 18–February 9, 1988, to prepare for the last round at Geneva, scheduled to begin March 2.[52] In Pakistan the government scrambled to pressure the Islamic Union into making a proposal for an interim government. The Foreign Office and the civilian government proposed a version of the Zahir Shah option, the establishment of a small interim State Council, to be led by the former king as an interim authority pending elections.

The ISI supported the proposal of the Islamists for elections organized by the alliance in eighteen months, an unrealistic schedule in view of the momentum in the relations between the superpowers (not to mention the limited capabilities of the Peshawar parties).

Virtually all factions in the Pakistan government agreed that Cordovez should meet leaders of the alliance, but Hikmatyar, Sayyaf, and Khalis resisted. Relations among the parties became so tense that Mujaddidi, a vocal supporter of cooperation with the United Nations, tendered his resignation (soon withdrawn) from the Alliance. Khalis, who was then spokesman, finally agreed to met Cordovez on February 6, explaining that he was doing so only because of a personal request from Zia.[53] Zia and some American officials in Islamabad suggested to Cordovez that he postpone the Geneva round to allow these efforts to come to fruition.

Gorbachev acted to preempt these efforts. Not only Zia but also Najibullah was resisting the terms of the final agreement. While in Kabul, Cordovez finally pressured Najibullah into dropping a demand for assurances of his survival in a transitional government. When Cordovez communicated this concession to Gorbachev, the Soviet leader preempted television programming for his dramatic surprise speech of February 8, 1988, in which he proposed that the troop withdrawal begin on May 15 and last ten months. Gorbachev thus met Washington's demand for a short timetable and a "date certain" for withdrawal. He also said: "There is a need to make clear our position on yet another aspect — whether the withdrawal is linked with the completion of efforts to set up a new, coalition government in Afghanistan, i.e., with bringing the policy of national reconciliation to fruition. We are convinced that it is not."[54]

Following his speech, Gorbachev dispatched Vorontsov to Islamabad on February 10 to follow up on Cordovez's visit. Zia still proposed that the Geneva round be postponed pending formation of an interim government, but Vorontsov insisted that the talks should go forward and reach an agreement on withdrawal. As Pakistani government pressure mounted on the alliance to articulate a proposal for an interim government, gunmen assassinated Professor Sayd Bahauddin Majrooh in Peshawar on February 11. Majrooh was a revered poet and philosophy professor whose Afghan Information Centre Monthly Bulletin had become an indispensable source for journalists, human rights monitors, and other foreigners covering the war. Majrooh came from a family of sayyids — a religious descent group supposedly descended from the Prophet Muhammad — with long links to both the Afghan monarchy and the Pashtun tribes of the Kunar valley. He had studied in France and Germany, and his father (still living in 1995) had been the principal author of the constitution of New Democracy in 1964. The previous July, Majrooh had published results of a survey in which more than 70 percent of Afghan refugees who responded said that they supported Zahir Shah rather than any of the mujahidin leaders as the future leader of Afghanistan.[55] The assassination of Majrooh was widely interpreted as Gulbuddin Hikmatyar's riposte to the Pakistan Foreign Office's advocacy of the Zahir Shah option or an interim government of old regime intellectuals like Majrooh.

Under strong pressure from Zia, the alliance presented a proposal for a transitional government two weeks after Vorontsov's departure. The alliance envisioned what it called a broad-based government, but it was too narrow to satisfy even most mujahidin. Under the proposed formula, the seven leaders would constitute a leadership council. The council would appoint a cabinet consisting of two members from each of the seven parties of Peshawar, seven exiles, and seven "Muslims presently serving inside Afghanistan." The party leaders could not agree on even part of the cabinet until June 19, after the start of the Soviet pullout. Gen. Hamid Gul, the director of ISI, reportedly drew up the list in exasperation and imposed it on the leaders after they had repeatedly failed to agree. The list showed considerable deference to Saudi sensitivities, for Saudi princes had agreed to pay the "government" $1 million per month. The prime minister was a "Wahhabi," a member of Sayyaf's party. The cabinet contained no resistance commanders from inside Afghanistan, no representative of the Shia resistance parties, and no important independent intellectuals or technocrats. The proposal met with a cold reception from the Afghan refugees and resistance commanders, to say nothing of exiles or the Kabul regime.[56]

Pakistan, faced with both American and Soviet determination to press ahead with agreement on withdrawal and with the inability of the Islamic Union — or the unwillingness of the ISI — to present any remotely plausible proposal for a domestic political settlement, eventually abandoned insistence on a transitional government. When the Soviets acceded to Cordovez's request for a "single-digit" timetable and came down to nine months, with half of the troops to leave in the first three, the United States and Pakistan agreed. The Accords themselves were complete, but the United States refused to sign without an agreement on "symmetry."

Congressional opponents of the Accords claimed that to guarantee an agreement that provided for termination of aid to the mujahidin while Kabul continued to receive Soviet aid contradicted the policy of military and political support for the resistance. The Accords, as these critics saw it, placed the resistance at a military and political disadvantage, recognized the Kabul regime as party to an agreement with the United States, and ignored the question of the nature of the government of Afghanistan — the issue at the heart of the conflict. Intensive lobbying in Washington culminated in a February 29 Senate resolution that called for aid to continue until the Soviets had completely withdrawn.[57]

Such a course, however, would have required rewriting the laboriously prepared text of the Accords. Instead, the United States suggested that the agenda be amended to include what would have in effect constituted a fifth instrument, consistent with the other four. In a Washington meeting with Foreign Minister Shevardnadze in mid-March, Secretary Shultz proposed that the United States and the USSR sign a separate agreement to refrain from providing military aid to any party, with a detailed protocol that would specify what forms of assistance were prohibited.[58] The terms of this proposal came to be known as "negative symmetry." Such an agreement would have constituted a unilateral concession by the Soviets, who had already agreed to withdraw their troops from Afghanistan in return for the United States' agreement to end aid to the resistance; now Washington wanted more from Moscow without giving any more in return. The Soviets refused, citing their treaty commitments to the government of Afghanistan. The Soviet authorities wanted to assure that the Kabul government would remain stable as they pulled out their troops, not collapse like the Saigon government.

The decisive break with the Geneva framework for cooperation, which signaled the renewed alliance between Dealers and Rollback ideologists, came with the next American proposal. In lieu of negative symmetry, the United States proposed "positive symmetry," under which Washington asserted its right to aid the forces it supported regardless of the text of the Accords. Shultz opposed making this right conditional on anything, including, as an early draft by an aide had specified, continued Soviet supply to Kabul. According to the Schultz version: "The United States has advised the Soviet Union that the United States retains the right, consistent with its obligations as guarantor, to provide military assistance to parties in Afghanistan. Should the Soviet Union exercise restraint in providing military assistance to parties in Afghanistan, the United States similarly will exercise restraint."[59] This proposal, which in effect vitiated the agreement at the heart of the Geneva Accords, infuriated the Soviets. Nonetheless, they preferred it to the risk of withdrawing their troops from Afghanistan without giving military aid to the Kabul regime. After a series of empty threats — to sign the Accords with Kabul and Islamabad alone, to withdraw unilaterally (perhaps not completely) on their own terms, even to postpone or halt the withdrawal — Moscow acceded.

This course of events created strains in several quarters. Zia had opposed signing the Accords without an interim government, but Prime Minister Junejo outmaneuvered him by calling a round-table conference of all Pakistani political parties. Nearly all parties, especially Benazir Bhutto's Pakistan People's Party, endorsed signing the agreement even without an interim government. This decision led Zia, supported by the ISI, to support positive symmetry, with the aim of overthrowing Najibullah and installing a mujahidin government by military means. According to Schultz, when President Reagan asked Zia how Pakistani leaders would handle their commitment to violate the agreement, "Zia replied that they would 'just lie about it. We've been denying our activities there for eight years.' Then, the president recounted, Zia told him that 'Muslims have the right to lie in a good cause.' "[60]

The breakdown of apparent understandings over the Geneva Accords illustrates how cooperative agreements among opponents can be undermined by lack of a common conception of reciprocity, aggravated by the misperceptions posited by attribution theory. Shultz insists in his memoirs that "we had sharpened our position, but only in the light of Soviet insistence on continuing their own supply operations [to the Kabul regime]." Despite Shevardnadze's appeal for cooperation against "fundamentalism," Shultz apparently did not consider the possibility that Soviet supply operations at this point might be motivated at least in part by concern that the United States, Pakistan, and Saudi Arabia were transferring hundreds of millions of dollars worth of sophisticated weapons to radical Islamist parties who opposed not only the Kabul regime but any negotiated political settlement.

Each side had a technically defensible definition of reciprocity, but each definition depended as much on a notion of legitimacy as on counting troops and weapons. Reciprocity, Keohane argues, "refers to exchanges of roughly equivalent values in which the actions of each party are contingent on the prior actions of the others in such a way that good is returned for good, and bad for bad."[61] From the Soviet point of view, even though sending troops to Afghanistan had been a mistake, removing them was a major and difficult decision, which deserved an appropriate response from the Americans. Regardless of the character of the Afghan regime (which they were in any case trying to improve), Soviet state-to-state aid to Afghanistan was consistent with international agreements that dated back decades and served legitimate state interests. It could not be equated with aid to guerrilla movements mostly led by Islamic radicals. From the U.S. perspective, the presence of Soviet troops in Afghanistan was totally illegitimate, and the USSR should not be rewarded for withdrawing them.[62] America's legitimate aid to the resistance could not be equated with the Soviet invasion.

Once the Soviets withdrew, a situation of rough equivalence prevailed for the first time: both sides were aiding and arming their clients, though the Soviets were giving more. Reciprocity could take the form of either negative symmetry (mutual restraint) or positive symmetry (both sides giving aid). Keohane notes that power ultimately determines what amounts to reciprocity (or symmetry), and so it did here. U.S. bargaining leverage assured that Washington's conception of reciprocity prevailed. This agreement turned out to contain the seeds of further escalation.

Najibullah feared what positive symmetry might mean for him, and he threatened not to sign the agreement under such conditions. On April 6, 1988, Gorbachev "unexpectedly and suddenly" flew to Tashkent to join Shevardnadze and Najibullah, who had been meeting in Kabul. Through a combination of threats and offers of future military aid, Gorbachev persuaded Najibullah to accept the new realities. The promises of full support necessary to convince Najibullah to sign the agreement with positive symmetry may have been the source of increased Soviet aid to Kabul that U.S. officials later saw as evidence of bad faith.[63]

The foreign ministers of Pakistan, Afghanistan, the United States, and the USSR met to sign the Accords in Geneva on April 14. Secretary Schultz stated that the United States did not recognize the Kabul regime as the legitimate government of Afghanistan and reserved to itself the right to arm Afghan parties it supported, but he called for "balanced restraint" by all parties. Shevardnadze asserted that the Soviet Union limited the obligations of the Accords to those enumerated in the text of the four instruments.[64]

The Accords forbade both Afghanistan and Pakistan from undertaking a whole range of actions aimed at "intervening or interfering in the internal affairs" of the other. Acts that were proscribed ranged from "hostile propaganda" to the "organizing, training, financing, equipping and arming of individuals and political, ethnic and any other groups for the purpose of creating subversion, disorder or unrest in the territory of the other High Contracting Party."[65]

The Soviet Union promised to withdraw its troops from Afghanistan within nine months, with half the troops to depart in the first three months. Both obligations entered into force on May 15, 1988, so half of the Soviet troops were to be withdrawn by August 15.

As guarantors, both the United States and the USSR agreed to "undertake to invariably refrain from any form of interference and intervention in the internal affairs" of Afghanistan and Pakistan "and to respect the commitments" on noninterference. Another document provided a framework for the "voluntary and unimpeded repatriation" of the Afghan refugees in Pakistan, including an official role for the United Nations High Commissioner for Refugees (UNHCR).

The Accords established the United Nations Good Offices Mission in Afghanistan and Pakistan (UNGOMAP) to monitor the implementation of the Accords. Ungomap included a military section under a Finnish general and a political section under Benon Sevan, an Armenian from Cyprus and veteran U.N. diplomat. The mission was empowered to receive and investigate complaints from both sides that the Accords were not being properly implemented.

The Accords said nothing about the future government of Afghanistan. Gorbachev wanted above all to assure that the Kabul regime remained stable enough to assure an orderly withdrawal of all Soviet troops by February 15, 1989. At the signing ceremony, however, all parties to the Accords stated that they had asked the secretary general of the United Nations, through his personal representative, Diego Cordovez, to use his good offices to help the Afghans to form a transitional government.

PART THREE

Afghanistan After the Cold War:
From Regional Conflict to Failed State

In the immediate aftermath of the signing at Geneva, cooperative understandings broke down, and the proxy war escalated. After the fall of the Berlin Wall in November 1989, however, trust increased between the superpowers, leading them to reach a series of agreements on both arms control and regional conflicts. The U.S.-Soviet dialogue, in conjunction with ongoing U.N. efforts, brought the two sides close to an accord by the end of 1990, but the resurgence of hard-line opposition in Moscow prevented a final agreement.

The growth of trust between the superpowers corresponded to a fraying of the bipolar coalitions pursuing the Afghan war. Both the regional powers — Pakistan, Saudi Arabia, Iran, and later the Central Asian republics — and the Afghan protagonists felt freer to pursue their own goals, which were not always identical to those of the superpowers that had more or less sponsored them. As the United States and USSR moved closer, they experienced increasing resistance from their own allies, without whom they could not implement any agreement they reached. The emergence of multiple, independent actors complicated the problem of cooperation.

By the end of 1991, with the failure of the restorationist Soviet coup and the breakup of the USSR, one of the superpowers had disappeared and the other had disengaged. The Afghan problem was turned over to the U.N. Secretary General's Office, but good offices alone, here as elsewhere, were insufficient to resolve a conflict among heavily armed forces with different ethnic and regional bases. Deprived of Soviet aid or any other form of international support, the Kabul regime disintegrated. The mujahidin and remnants of the regime's armed forces and militias fought to seize the capital, while the rest of the country remained under the control of local groups. Regional states and ideological movements supported various protagonists. Afghanistan reverted to the status of a lawless borderland that threatened the security of surrounding states, but now its warlords possessed billions of dollars worth of modern weapons and access to millions of dollars in cash from the drug trade.

7 Cooperation Between the Superpowers

Eighteen months elapsed between the signing of the Geneva Accords and the fall of the Berlin Wall. Both the United States and Pakistan went through leadership transitions during this period, which led to some delay before new policies could be adopted. Both Washington and Islamabad thought that Gorbachev had withdrawn the troops because of a military defeat, so both prepared to carry the war home to Kabul and set up a mujahidin government rather than work out a negotiated transition.

The departure of Soviet troops, however, by reducing the common threat that had held together the United States, Pakistan, Saudi Arabia, and the disparate groups of mujahidin, revealed the divergence of interests among them. The withdrawal also reduced the pressure for unity among the factions of the PDPA, and dissension on the other side reduced the direct threat to the regime. Both sides of what had appeared to be a bipolar conflict began to fragment.

Pakistan's military saw the possibility of gaining "strategic depth" against India by implanting a friendly Islamic regime in Kabul, whereas the United States wanted to weaken the Soviet empire by replacing Najibullah with a stable, "moderate" regime. Iran and Saudi Arabia increasingly used the various mujahidin forces as proxies for their rivalry within the Islamic world. The Soviet Union and the Afghan regime increasingly engaged mujahidin leaders in direct or indirect negotiations in an attempt to incorporate them into some transitional arrangement. The commanders and party leaders played on these rivalries to increase their independence, frustrating the designs of the external powers as local strongmen have often frustrated the policies of the central state.[1]

Although the international system still retained a structure of bipolarity, the abating threat eroded the coherence of the allies and created a more complex multilateral cooperation problem. Cooperation against a common threat can succeed without a common ideology — witness the allies of World War II — but cooperation for political goals beyond self-defense requires greater ideological commonality than existed among these powers and greater organizational capacity than existed among the mujahidin.[2]

The end of the Cold War in Europe, the failure of the mujahidin to win a military victory, and increasingly strained relations with Pakistan and Saudi Arabia led the United States to pursue a more cooperative relationship with the Soviet Union in Afghanistan. During 1989–91, in this and other negotiations, the United States and the USSR worked out elements of an international regime for the resolution of regional conflicts. The norms and institutions of such a regime included termination of foreign military presence and aid, a cease-fire, and the creation of a new government through free and fair elections. Agreements of this type were concluded on Nicaragua, El Salvador, Cambodia, Angola, Namibia, and ultimately Afghanistan. Implementing such agreements turned out to be much more difficult that negotiating them; the structure of the transition was a constant sticking point.

Starting in late 1989, the U.S. and Soviet negotiators contrived to apply this developing regime to Afghanistan. Paradoxically, however, the growth of a cooperative relationship and the diminution of antagonism between the superpowers enabled them to disengage from areas that derived their strategic value from their location as buffers between antagonists. As Katz pointed out, "although disengagement improve[d] Soviet-American relations, it also result[ed] in the superpowers' losing leverage over their Third World allies."[3]

As the United States and the USSR worked out a cooperative solution to Afghanistan, their capacity to implement such a solution declined. The United States lost hegemonic control over its partners, though this drift was temporarily and partly reversed during 1991, when hard-liners in Moscow seemed to pose a renewed if reduced threat and the Gulf War provided the United States with an opportunity to reassert its strategic interests. The ISI also lost control over many of the mujahidin, who were no longer subject to the pressures of the Soviet military presence and benefited from an economic revival, notably in the drug trade. On the other side, the Soviets lost the direct coercive control that the Red Army had exercised over the Kabul regime. Factional, ethnic, and tribal conflict reemerged in both the regime and the resistance. The government's armed forces increasingly relied on locally raised militias that came to resemble the mujahidin in structure and tactics. As long as aid kept flowing from both sides, however, defection from cooperation within each alliance kept within clear limits.

Tacit Understandings Collapse, Escalation Ensues

In spite of the United States' insistence on its continuing right to aid the mujahidin, negotiations at Geneva concluded with some hope still alive for cooperation between the United States and USSR. Although the powers had agreed on an explicit policy of positive symmetry, many sources reported that they had agreed on implicit negative symmetry.[4] Neither side put such an agreement in writing, but both sides would show restraint. Soviet diplomats told Americans that they would not insist on retaining Najibullah and would let "nature take its course" after the departure of their troops.[5] The implication seemed to be that the Soviets would not reintroduce military forces to Afghanistan and would recognize a successor government if Najibullah was overthrown. They even began to shape public opinion to anticipate such an eventuality; one senior military official predicted in an interview that Najibullah would not last.[6] The Soviets also apparently promised that they would withdraw without attacking any mujahidin if allowed to leave without interference. The United States, for its part, promised to meet Soviet restraint with restraint. To the extent possible, the United States and Pakistan would deter mujahidin from attacking the remaining Soviet troops and allow the Red Army a dignified retreat.

But this cooperative arrangement became a classic case of a failed tacit agreement on reciprocity. Because each side had a different understanding of what had been promised and of what actions were equivalent to actions on the other side, the agreement broke down and led to escalation. The degeneration of the Geneva Accords into a document that legitimated a proxy war without Soviet troops illustrates the danger of "understandings" without explicit agreements on what activities are proscribed. Several international relations theorists have pointed out that without clear definition of *cooperation,* solutions to Prisoners' Dilemmas based on reciprocity can lead to an "escalating feud."[7]

When an explosion in a depot destroyed weaponry that was to have been transferred to the mujahidin days before the Accords took effect, the United States and Pakistan undertook a supply effort that continued after the Accords' implementation date. The Soviets may have taken this as an uncooperative signal. The Soviets also transferred large amounts of their departing troops' equipment to Kabul's forces; Moscow may not have considered this as new aid, but Washington did. The Soviets also seem to have expected the mujahidin to remain in place and observe a cease-fire during the withdrawal. When the mujahidin instead overran several provincial capitals and government bases, the Soviets responded harshly. They charged Pakistan with violations of the Geneva Accords and rushed additional aid to shore up Najibullah, including such sophisticated weapons as SCUD-B missiles, which had not previously been introduced into Afghanistan. The United States had apparently interpreted the Soviets' promise to "let nature take its course" as assurance that they would not come to Najibullah's rescue, whereas the Soviets believed that they had asserted their right to continue to provide such assistance, especially while their own troops were still in the country.[8]

The exchange on positive symmetry and the disintegration of any agreement on implicit negative symmetry put the United Nations in a difficult position. Contrary to the fears of the opponents of the Accords in Washington, UNGOMAP proved quite effective in monitoring the Soviet withdrawal. It was caught in a bind, however, about monitoring the cutoff of aid. The United Nations was not privy to the U.S.-Soviet exchange on positive symmetry, but it concluded that it now had no effective mandate to carry out one of the tasks the Accords required of it. UNGOMAP made a political decision implicitly to accept the U.S. interpretation and not try to enforce the ban on aid to the resistance. Kabul repeatedly charged Pakistan with violations — lodging hundreds of complaints — and the United Nations went through the motions of investigating them, but despite open discussion in the press of U.S. and Pakistani aid to the resistance, the United Nations never announced evidence of a single violation.

The Soviet withdrawal coincided with political changes in the United Nations, Pakistan, and the United States that presented obstacles to new initiatives and facilitated the retention of control over policy by the intelligence agencies. The personal prominence of Diego Cordovez in mediating the Accords — which he occasionally referred to as "my agreement" — had led to friction with Secretary General Pérez de Cuéllar. Cordovez left the United Nations midway through the Soviet withdrawal, in August 1988, to become Foreign Minister of Ecuador. Despite the somewhat different efforts of some other officials, notably Giandomenico Picco in the Secretary General's Office and Benon Sevan in UNGOMAP, Afghanistan never again received the same degree of high-level attention in the Secretariat.

In any case, the United States and the Soviet Union had seized the initiative from the United Nations in the last stages of the negotiations. The Reagan administration, departing after 1988, had already declared victory in Afghanistan and was not about to take any risky new initiatives. The CIA estimated that the Najibullah regime would collapse before the onslaught of the mujahidin within a year, probably less.[9]

The incoming Bush administration took a cautious view of the warm relations that had developed between Presidents Reagan and Gorbachev. Powerful figures in the administration, in particular Deputy National Security Adviser Robert Gates, Casey's former deputy at the CIA, remained ultraskeptical of Gorbachev's intentions. As late as January 1988, after Gorbachev had publicly announced in Washington that he would withdraw Soviet troops from Afghanistan on a twelve-month timetable, Gates had bet Secretary Shultz that the troops would not leave.[10] Upon taking office in January 1989, as the Soviets were completing their withdrawal, President Bush ordered a "reassessment" of policy toward the Soviet Union, including Afghanistan policy. The Bush administration formally decided in February 1989 to pursue the formation of a government of "self-determination" in Afghanistan, meaning one dominated by the recognized resistance parties.[11]

During the first half of 1989, U.S. supplies to the mujahidin slacked off, apparently in response to intelligence estimates that the Kabul regime would fall soon after the Soviet withdrawal and the expectation that Moscow would not give extensive aid to Najibullah. By mid-1989, however, the United States and Saudi Arabia agreed each to supply $600 million by the end of the year; the United States also found another $100 million, for a total of $1.3 billion. The weapons included Stingers, heavy artillery, and other arms considered appropriate for a shift from guerrilla tactics to more conventional warfare.[12]

In Pakistan, meanwhile, a struggle over institutional prerogatives between the military and civilian politicians left the ISI with little or no high-level political supervision by the fall of 1988.[13] Military dominance of Pakistani policy on Afghanistan continued to fit well with Washington's goals.

On April 10, 1988, four days before the signing of the Geneva Accords, a shocking incident had brought the conflicts in the government of Pakistan to a crisis. A munitions dump exploded in Ojhri, near Islamabad, raining missiles and shrapnel on the population. Hundreds died, the opposition protested, and the Junejo government initiated an investigation. This "munitions dump" turned out to be the headquarters of the ISI's Afghan operations. Weapons and munitions had always been stored in Ojhri in a manner that violated all rules of safety and security.[14] The United States and Pakistan had prepared to flood the mujahidin with weapons just before the Accords were signed, and Ojhri had become even more heavily — and haphazardly — stocked than before. A civilian investigation, which found the highest military and intelligence officials guilty of gross negligence, convinced Prime Minister Junejo to dismiss Gen. Akhtar Abdul Rahman (the former director of ISI, whom Zia had promoted to chairman of the Joint Chiefs of Staff Committee) and Gen. Hamid Gul (director of ISI). Junejo even intended to deprive Zia of his position as chief of army staff (COAS).[15] As prime minister and minister of defense, Junejo had formal jurisdiction over the COAS, but Zia had institutionalized military prerogatives in the constitutional amendments that he had promulgated precisely to deprive politicians of such powers. Junejo's government served at the will of the president, who happened to be the about-to-be-dismissed COAS. On May 29, 1988, before Junejo could issue the orders, Zia dismissed the government, dissolved the parliament, and called for new elections.

At first, the military reasserted direct control over the government. Zia announced new elections but specified that they would again be held without political parties. This matter was still before the Supreme Court of Pakistan when on August 17, 1988, a plane carrying Generals Zia and Akhtar, U.S. ambassador Arnold Raphel, and several other Pakistani generals exploded in an incident that remained unexplained in 1995. Virtually all the officials responsible for formulating Pakistani policy on Afghanistan perished in the crash. The new COAS, Gen. Mirza Aslam Beg, announced support for the constitutional process, according to which Ghulam Ishaq Khan, a veteran bureaucrat and the president of the Senate, succeeded to the presidency. The new president announced that elections would be held with the participation of political parties.

The November 1988 elections brought the populist Pakistan People's Party (PPP) to office, if not to power. The party's leader, Benazir Bhutto, became prime minister on December 2 only after protracted negotiations with the military over its institutional prerogatives. Among other conditions, the military insisted on maintaining control over Afghanistan policy and on the continuing tenure of Yaqub Khan, whom Zia had reinstated as foreign minister after dismissing Junejo. The military also insisted on full control over military promotions and appointments.[16] The result of these agreements was a divided government incapable of taking any coherent initiatives. The military now had less political supervision than under President Zia. Diplomacy and military policy ran on separate tracks with little if any coordination.

This was the unpromising context in which the United Nations tried to complete its mission by brokering the formation of a transitional government in Kabul. Even before the Soviet withdrawal, Cordovez renewed the effort he had started in 1987 to plan for a transitional government of "neutrals." All parties to the Geneva Accords had agreed to grant the U.N. secretary general the authority to use his good offices to promote the formation of a broad-based government in Afghanistan. On May 8, 1988, a week before the start of the troop withdrawal, Cordovez published an article in the *Washington Post* that proposed a solution based on "Afghan traditions." At a press conference in Islamabad on July 9, he called for the establishment of a National Government of Peace and Reconstruction to oversee the transition, which would be completed by a Loya Jirga. This proposal differed very little from the one that the United States and the USSR finally agreed to in September 1991, after thousands more lives had been lost and billions more dollars spent.[17]

After the departure of Cordovez in August, and while political changes were taking place in the United States and Pakistan, these efforts stalled. Cordovez reports that Gen. Zia had promised support for the U.N. effort in a meeting just before his death. Whether or not Zia would have fulfilled that commitment, his successors showed no interest. The United States rather coolly decided that Cordovez's efforts "were not to be opposed."[18] Only President Zia might have been able to convince both Washington and mujahidin hard-liners to cooperate with such a plan. Even if he had done so, how the Soviets would have responded is equally a matter of speculation. Cordovez had just left Pakistan for consultations in Moscow when Zia was killed.

Other U.N. officials later continued these consultations, but their efforts were circumscribed by what the great powers would allow. After a lapse of several months, Secretary General Pérez de Cuéllar assumed overall responsibility for the effort in November. Over the next several years Benon Sevan, the political officer of UNGOMAP, and Giandomenico Picco in the Secretary General's Office in New York consulted with representatives of the five external governments who continued to be involved: the United States, USSR, Pakistan, Saudi Arabia, and Iran.[19] Sevan shuttled constantly between Kabul, Pakistan, and Iran, where he met with both government officials and mujahidin leaders based in Peshawar and Tehran. The United Nations also met with Zahir Shah and other Afghan émigrés connected to the old regime, but this effort focused more on the leaders supported by the USSR, Pakistan, and Iran, whereas Cordovez had concentrated on strengthening moderates from the old regime unaffiliated to the warring parties.

When the U.N. effort to form a new government faltered, the Soviets moved on their own, even trying to replace the United Nations as an intermediary among the Afghan parties. Some analysts have argued that powerful states that can offer threats and incentives are more effective mediators than the U.N. Secretary General's Office.[20] On October 13, 1988, Gorbachev appointed Deputy Foreign Minister Yuli Vorontsov as ambassador to Kabul, with a mission to create a coalition government that would include the PDPA, the mujahidin, and representatives of the old regime and would take power after the Soviet withdrawal. First the Soviets had to bring their own Afghans into line, for both the Khalqis and pro-Karmal Parchamis opposed this policy. Before the convocation on October 19 of a several-times-postponed PDPA Central Committee Plenum to discuss this issue, at least seventeen Central Committee members were arrested, including Karmal's top supporters. One month later, without being formally dismissed from the Politburo, Khalqi Interior Minister Sayyid Muhammad Gulabzoy was bundled onto a plane at night and told of his appointment as ambassador to Moscow.[21]

In December, Gorbachev presented a new diplomatic proposal in a speech to the U.N. General Assembly. He supported the formation of a transitional government based on an "intra-Afghan dialogue." He urged negative symmetry — an end to the delivery of weapons to all sides — as a component of a settlement, and he proposed a cease-fire in place and a U.N. peacekeeping force between the sides. The cease-fire in place meant that the Najibullah regime would control the central government at least at the beginning of the transition.

Seeking agreement on Gorbachev's proposal, Vorontsov opened direct negotiations between the USSR and the mujahidin, just as the State Department had hoped in 1985. But by now the intelligence agencies had effective control of policy in both countries, and both thought that a military victory was at hand. Vorontsov met representatives of the Peshawar alliance in Taif, Saudi Arabia, and in Islamabad. He also met the Shia leaders in Tehran and Zahir Shah in Rome. He urged the Afghan parties to negotiate some form of power sharing in an interim government, with a minority share even for the PDPA. But he confronted the problem that had blocked a political solution for years: the mujahidin parties refused any negotiation or cooperation with the Kabul government under any terms. This radical rejection of the legitimacy of one side of the war, which had no parallel in any other regional conflict, led to the use of complex forms of inter-mediation that ultimately failed. Concerted cooperation of strong leaders in Wash-ington and Islamabad with Vorontsov's effort might have led to a settlement, but both Washington and Islamabad had lame-duck regimes that were incapable of making political decisions on Afghanistan.

The principal intelligence agencies of both the United States and Pakistan predicted that the DRA would not long outlast the Soviet withdrawal. Neither they nor the mujahidin saw any reason to seek a political settlement. They rejected any immediate agreement on negative symmetry, citing the new supplies of sophisti-cated weapons to Kabul but in fact expecting a quick military victory by the resistance. The United States, Pakistan, and the mujahidin regarded Gorbachev's proposal for a cease-fire monitored by a U.N. force as a way to use international forces to protect the Kabul regime.

Washington and Islamabad concentrated their efforts on creating a form of unity that was imposed by leaders and created an artificial coalition to take over the state after a military victory by the mujahidin. At the insistence of their foreign sponsors, the seven recognized Sunni mujahidin parties chose an Interim Islamic Government of Afghanistan (IIGA) at a shura in Pakistan as the last Soviet troops left Afghanistan in February 1989. Soviet Foreign Minister Shevardnadze arrived in Islamabad as the shura was about to convene and told Pakistani Prime Minister Bhutto that his government would remove the entire "upper echelon" of the PDPA from Kabul in return for minimal representation of the party at the shura.[22] Bhutto's government was too weak to make any meaningful response, especially in view of the CIA and ISI estimate that Kabul would soon fall without compromise or negotiation.

The seven parties appointed all 519 representatives to the shura, excluding all participation by the Kabul regime, the officials of the old regime who had fled to the West, and the Shia parties. The council was composed almost entirely of Peshawar-based party officials, mostly Pashtuns from eastern Afghanistan. The IIGA it chose was the result of ISI and Saudi manipulation of the shura's electoral process. According to U.S. diplomats in Riyadh, the Saudi intelligence service spent $26 million per week during the shura. Others claim that each delegate received at least $25,000.[23] ISI Director Hamid Gul promised the presidency to Mujaddidi to keep him from walking out in protest. Sayyaf became prime minister in deference to the Saudis, who had promised to fund a conventional Islamic Army for the government if their Wahhabi sect was adequately represented.[24] A plan to make Hikmatyar the defense minister and the commander of this army collapsed in the complex deal making that ended the meeting. The shura's domination by one subethnic group (Ghilzai and eastern Pashtuns) intensified ethnic resentments, and the obvious manipulation of the Peshawar bureaucrats by Saudis and Pakistanis increased nationalist sentiment among commanders. The IIGA never succeeded in establishing itself in Afghanistan or in organizing the elections it promised. In fact, it was a government in exile rather than an interim government.[25]

The United States did not recognize the IIGA, but it shifted some of its "humanitarian" aid to that putative government's ministries of health and education to build up the IIGA as a credible political alternative to the Kabul regime.[26] Military aid continued to go separately to the parties. This policy, maintained in the interest of military "efficiency" — the need to keep building up Hikmatyar — effectively nullified all political attempts at unification. The ISI organized a mujahidin offensive in March that was intended to install the IIGA in the eastern Afghan city of Jalalabad, but lack of effective coordination as well as unexpectedly stiff government resistance prevented any significant advance.[27]

The influx of Soviet aid and the successful resistance at Jalalabad boosted the morale of the regime and wounded that of the mujahidin. An attempt by Massoud to recover failed in the summer of 1989. Plans to capture the important northern center of Kunduz had to be called off when forces of Hizb-i Islami (Hikmatyar) captured and massacred ten of Massoud's senior commanders and about twenty others as they returned from a strategy meeting on July 9. In the resulting furor, Mujaddidi called Hikmatyar a criminal and a terrorist, and Hikmatyar suspended his participation in the IIGA.

U.S.-Soviet Dialogue and Cooperative Conflict Resolution

The global strategic situation was changing, however, and not only in Afghanistan. With the advance of the Eastern European revolutions of middle to late 1989, the Brezhnev doctrine was clearly dead and the Cold War over. The Bush administration was also elated over advances in conflict resolution in Central America, especially Nicaragua, where elections were planned for February 1990, elections in which the Sandinistas would be defeated. Nicaragua was Washington's top priority on the U.S.-Soviet agenda of regional disputes.[28] The outlines of the regime for regional conflict resolution were being set.

By the fall of 1989, both the dramatic improvement in U.S.-Soviet relations and the evident failure of the mujahidin on the ground led the Bush administration to explore a more cooperative approach in Afghanistan. The goal of U.S. policy was redefined as the procurement not only of Afghan "self-determination" but of a negotiated political settlement with the Soviets that would lead to the "sidelining of extremists," including Najibullah, Hikmatyar, and Sayyaf. The United States engaged in a two-track policy, beginning a diplomatic dialogue with the USSR on a political settlement while trying to improve the military performance of the mujahidin to keep the pressure up.

The supposed lesson of the Soviet withdrawal from Afghanistan was that military pressure was required for diplomatic success, which is sometimes true, but not invariably so. Success in coercive diplomacy requires coordination of diplomacy and coercion by a common center, generally the executive of a single state. The unopposed American military entry into Haiti in September 1994 — whatever the outcome of this effort — illustrates this principle. The president himself simultaneously examined the terms of the negotiations in Port au Prince and authorized the dispatch of the military forces. In the negotiations with Moscow over a political settlement in Afghanistan, however, an essential contradiction constantly undercut the ability of the United States to coordinate the military track with the political one.[29] In the view of the U.S. and Pakistani agencies that actually implemented the coercive component of the effort — the CIA and the ISI — the Afghan groups most effective in pursuing the military track were those that most staunchly opposed the political track. This split was hardly surprising, for one of the goals of the political track was to marginalize Hikmatyar, on whose military the CIA and the ISI depended.

In the fall of 1989, the State Department tried to address this problem by challenging the large share of aid that went to Hikmatyar and Sayyaf, as well as the Peshawar parties' exclusive status as conduits for assistance. Congressional supporters of the mujahidin also charged the CIA with incompetence and acquiescence in ISI policies, and the head of the CIA's Afghan Task Force was dismissed in September 1989. The Bush administration decided that no weapons paid for by its funds would be given to Hikmatyar or Sayyaf but would go instead primarily to regional or local military shuras inside Afghanistan.[30] This policy made little if any difference on the ground, however, because Saudi and other Arab funds took up the slack in aid to the mujahidin "extremists," although the State Department kept pushing Pakistan and the Saudis to cooperate. The operations wing of the CIA, which maintained close links with the ISI and the Saudi Istakhbara, regarded the new policy with skepticism if not hostility. In practice, U.S. maintenance of the arms pipeline continued to strengthen the Afghan groups that U.S. policy allegedly had abandoned.

With the departure of the Soviet troops and increased publicity about the share of weapons that Hikmatyar was receiving, the previously unshakable support for the policy in the U.S. Congress began to waver. By November 1989, U.S. fiscal 1990 had begun, and the Congress allocated only $280 million, a 60 percent reduction of the previous year's outlay. Saudi Arabia came up with another $435 million, and Saudi and Kuwaiti princes contributed $100 million from their "private" funds. This $535 million worth of weapons would be distributed through February 1990 — one year after the end of the Soviet withdrawal — by which time, the CIA had predicted, the mujahidin would win. When this did not happen and U.S. funds ran low, Saudi and Kuwaiti government and private sources supplied another $1 billion in 1990 before Saddam Hussein invaded Kuwait. Hikmatyar also received funds from Libya and Iraq.[31]

While trying to make its military aid more effective, the United States began a dialogue on Afghanistan with the USSR. This dialogue involved the two powers in a cooperation problem different from that of the Geneva talks. During the Cold War hostility and mistrust that were based on genuine conflicts of interest and radically different goals constituted the main obstacles to superpower cooperation. Powerful groups on both sides saw no potential for cooperation in what they perceived as a zero-sum conflict. Now, however, both governments recognized a common interest in ending the war in Afghanistan. Furthermore, they had elaborated elements of a regime that enabled them to agree quickly on the basic goal: a transition to a new, more legitimate and representative government in Afghanistan.[32]

The obstacles this time were twofold. First, the negotiators had to design a transition process that took into account both realities on the ground and the remaining differences of interest; the conflict resolution regime gave relatively little guidance on this score. Second, whereas the Geneva Accords had involved actions of the superpowers themselves, in 1990 they were negotiating over a process that would require accord among actors over whom the superpowers now had less leverage. A successful transition would require cooperation among five states (the superpowers, Pakistan, Saudi Arabia, and Iran) — some of whom had no relations with each other (the USSR and Saudi Arabia, the United States and Iran) — and numerous political actors in Afghanistan itself. In effect it was a multilateral transnational cooperation problem.

The theoretical literature on international cooperation has analyzed such problems in, for instance, studies of the management of the debt crisis.[33] Theories of cooperation generally predict that the more actors there are the more difficult it is to overcome security dilemmas and other collective action problems. One tool for managing such problems is the assumption by hegemonic actors of responsibility for sets of smaller actors — the strategy by which the superpowers managed the international system during the Cold War. Each superpower could rely on the threat of the other to help discipline its own allies. But as the United States and Soviet Union became better able to cooperate with each other on Afghanistan, they became less able to deliver the cooperation of their allies and clients, whose defection ultimately derailed the process that the superpowers agreed upon.

The U.S.-Soviet dialogue formed the center of the public political process. During the Geneva talks, the United Nations had taken center stage until the endgame, but U.N. involvement now mainly complemented the principal sphere of negotiations, assuming greater prominence only after the superpowers had disengaged. As in the Gulf War, which overlapped with these negotiations, the Bush administration used the United Nations not to pursue a genuine multilateral policy but to advance U.S. interests while giving the Soviets a face-saving out. The United Nations accepted this approach and concentrated efforts on the Peshawar parties, as Washington demanded. Cordovez, in contrast, had argued that moderates not affiliated to the belligerents would be more likely to form an effective interim government. The State Department and the United Nations at times worked together closely, even to the point of holding joint or parallel meetings with the heads of the intelligence agencies of Pakistan and Saudi Arabia. The U.N. Secretary General's Office, which was authorized by General Assembly resolutions to use its good offices to broker a settlement, argued that the external dependence of all political forces in Afghanistan was so great that they would never reach agreement until their sponsors developed an "international consensus" on means to bring peace to Afghanistan.[34] The issues standing in the way of such a consensus were those on the agenda of the U.S.-Soviet discussions, including the nature of a transitional period and the cessation of military aid to Afghan parties to the conflict.

According to participants, these negotiations came to resemble what the literature calls "integrative" rather than "distributive" bargaining. The United States and USSR continued to have different interests, but their basic outlook was increasingly similar. The negotiators began to feel that they were engaged in a partnership to find a way out of a problem that both wanted to escape. Threats, charges, countercharges, and dissembling of preferences played little if any role. Instead, discussions focused on finding language and procedures that would satisfy needs of both sides. Hence game theory does not provide a useful framework for analyzing these interactions.[35]

The U.S.-Soviet Negotiation Process, 1989–90

The first U.S.-Soviet discussions on Afghanistan after the withdrawal took place at the working level in Stockholm at the end of July 1989. In a September 1989 meeting between Secretary of State James Baker and Shevardnadze at Baker's ranch in Jackson Hole, Wyoming, both sides agreed that "a transition period is required, as well as an appropriate mechanism to establish a broad-based government."[36] Talks continued during the succeeding months at several levels and venues. The discussions of Afghanistan focused on the nature of the transition, soon defined, according to the international regime for conflict resolution, as the holding of free and fair elections or their equivalent in Afghan terms; the termination of weapons supplies; and the withdrawal of sophisticated weapons, which the United States claimed created an imbalance.[37] The mujahidin, however, now received over half of their aid from sources other than the United States, an issue that the Soviets repeatedly raised. The United States maintained that it could still halt most of the aid; others paid for many of the arms, but only the United States had the logistic capability to organize and carry out such a massive program of distribution.

The United States, which hoped that military victories by the resistance would make possible a transition largely under the control of the mujahidin parties, insisted in any case that a prerequisite for any transition was the removal of Najibullah.[38] Furthermore, in order to assure that the Afghan government could not use its control of the security forces and mass media to affect the outcome of an election, the United Stated argued that the "transition mechanism" should be an interim government with full powers, which would replace Najibullah. The Soviets countered that Najibullah had to remain in place during the transition to provide stability. They pressed for a transition administered by the incumbent (the "Nicaraguan model"). Eventually they introduced the idea of an independent commission that would oversee the election while the government remained in power.

The United States began to back away from its insistence that Najibullah's removal was a prerequisite for the transition and to explore a number of compromises between the two positions. As a first step, at the first summit meeting between Presidents Gorbachev and Bush, in Malta on December 1, 1989, the United States agreed that Najibullah could remain in power at the beginning of the transition, provided that the Soviets guaranteed his removal by the end of it. The discussions now focused on a transition mechanism. The United States at first proposed a set of procedures, including elections in Kabul and refugee camps, accompanied by shuras in resistance-held areas to be organized by the IIGA. After the Soviets rejected this proposal as unworkable, discussions shifted to the formation of a body of relatively nonpartisan dignitaries who could oversee a transition, however it was conducted.

In March 1990, Khalqi Defense Minister Shahnawaz Tanai allied with mujahidin extremist Hikmatyar in an abortive coup, which further discredited both the ISI and the military option. After the coup attempt, the United States began to explore the linkage of negative symmetry to the transition. The United States wanted a "date certain" for negative symmetry, whereas the Soviets demanded prior assurance that Saudi Arabia and Pakistan would comply. The United States argued that domestic political constraints prevented those countries from announcing a cutoff but that they would be unable to proceed without U.S. support.

After July 1990 the two sides discussed a new proposal by Vorontsov, now Soviet U.N. representative, for explicit power sharing between the existing government and the transition mechanism. The United States and the United Nations consulted with the mujahidin and Kabul over which ministries would be controlled by the transition mechanism and which by the government. The United States insisted that elections could not be free and fair unless the security forces and mass media were under impartial control during the transition.[39]

Moscow raised concerns over the enforcement of negative symmetry. An end to U.S. aid might merely provide cover for aid from other sources. Soviet negotiators insisted on a simultaneous end to military aid by all parties — including Pakistan and Saudi Arabia — as well as a cease-fire. The United States argued that it could not deliver a cease-fire, for it had no direct operational control over the mujahidin, but that an aid cutoff would produce de facto de-escalation.

By the end of the summer of 1990, the continuing stalemate provided both sides with further evidence that neither the military option nor Kabul's attempt to co-opt the mujahidin politically was working. Both sides were also under domestic pressure to produce results. In Washington the consensus that had existed during the Soviet occupation disintegrated. The Bush administration wanted to get Afghanistan off the U.S.-Soviet agenda without antagonizing the Republican right, and congressional resistance to continued allocation of such large funds grew. The Senate-House conference committee on the intelligence appropriations bill for 1991 cut the allocation by $30 million to $250 million and held half of it in reserve — "fenced" it — so that disbursement of the appropriated funds would require further congressional approval. The Soviets, preoccupied with their own domestic problems, do not seem to have exploited this weakness.[40] The Soviet leadership under Gorbachev and Shevardnadze was also coming under increasing pressure from hard-liners in Moscow. After extensive negotiations (about twenty sessions over a period of three months) between Under Secretary of State Robert Kimmitt and the Soviet ambassador to Washington, Alexander Bessmertnykh, the two powers finally approached an agreement. The two foreign ministries had prepared a joint statement to be issued after Shevardnadze and Baker met in Houston on December 11, 1990. Both sides had agreed to support the establishment of a U.N.-sponsored transitional organ that would replace the current government, to end all weapons supplies, and to leave the precise structure of the transition to U.N. consultations with the Afghan parties.

At the last minute, however, Shevardnadze, under apparent pressure from hard-line officials, refused to agree to a date certain by which weapons supplies would be cut off. At his joint press conference with Secretary Baker on December 13, Shevardnadze stated that the two sides had agreed on "the idea of free elections and the formation of a transitional body that would supervise those free elections. We also support cease-fire and a cutoff in arms deliveries. As to exact date, that is still a subject of further consideration."[41] Back in Moscow, he resigned on December 21, warning the public against "reactionaries." The hard-liners were staging a comeback. In January they staged a coup in Vilnius, a rehearsal for the

August events in Moscow. Among their leaders was KGB chief Vladimir Kryuch-kov, former head of international operations, who had sponsored Najibullah's rise to power.[42] The U.S.-Soviet dialogue stalled.

The Gulf War

During this period the rising power of hard-liners in Moscow and the Iraqi invasion of Kuwait combined temporarily to reverse some of the cooperative trends that had begun with the end of the Cold War. The resurgence of some old guard policies in Moscow briefly reignited bipolar antagonism between the United States and the USSR. Washington's leadership in the Gulf War reasserted hege-monic control over at least part of the United States' Cold War alliance system — in particular Saudi Arabia, the part most relevant to Afghanistan. The CIA and the ISI argued that with the hard-liners in ascendance in Moscow, further military action was necessary in Afghanistan.[43] Immediately after the Gulf War, at the end of March 1991, the CIA and the ISI threw their resources, including many Pakistani advisers on the ground, into the battle for the perennially besieged Afghan garrison town of Khost, in Paktia.

Tribal forces led by commander Jalaluddin Haqqani of the Jadran tribe finally took the garrison, but this policy ultimately backfired when the coalition that had taken the town broke apart. Although Hikmatyar's forces had played only a minor role in the fighting, Hizb-i Islami managed to seize the radio station and most of the garrison's heavy weapons, and the ISI prevented Haqqani from recovering Hikmatyar's spoils. Hikmatyar, Gen. Asad Durrani (the director general of ISI), and Qazi Hussein Ahmad (the leader of the Pakistani Jamaat-i Islami) all paid well-publicized visits to Khost, broadcasting the Pakistani role to an increasingly nationalist Afghan public.

The cost in Pakistani effort and the inability of the Pashtun tribal mujahidin to establish a government even in this small town — instead, they pillaged it — ultimately aggravated the credibility crisis for proponents of the military option. Saudi Arabia, resentful that some mujahidin clients had opposed its position in the Gulf War and increasingly dependent on the United States, became more amenable to a political settlement. The president and prime minister of Pakistan also decided that it was time to promote negotiations.

After the Gulf War, the Bush administration approved one off-budget transfer by the CIA of $30 million worth of captured Iraqi weapons to the mujahidin. But the administration's 1992 budget proposal incorporated the assumption that a negotiated settlement would lead to a termination of military aid to the Afghan resistance: it contained no budget line for that program. A contingency allocation elsewhere provided funds that could be transferred to the mujahidin if the negotiations fell through. Under an agreement with the Soviet and Russian governments, aid was terminated as of fiscal 1992. Private sources in Arab countries of the Gulf, however, continued to provide an estimated $400 million in aid per year.[44]

As a result of the Soviet-American dialogue, the Pakistani and Saudi decisions after Khost and the Gulf War, and Iranian support for a political settlement, in May 1991 the U.N. secretary general could finally issue a statement that summarized an "international consensus" on Afghanistan in five very generally worded points, which closely paralleled the language of the joint statement drafted but not released the previous fall by the United States and USSR.[45] According to the U.N. statement, the political settlement would begin with the establishment of a "transition mechanism" in Afghanistan. In conjunction with the beginning of the transition, all external parties would stop supplying weapons to Afghanistan, and all internal parties should adopt a cease-fire. The interim authority would organize "free and fair elections, in accord with Afghan traditions," to choose a "broad-based government." The specification of "Afghan traditions" referred to the possibility that a Loya Jirga or another form of tribal representation might replace elections in some areas. The Iranian government objected to this phrase, insisting instead on "Western-style" elections, including the participation of women.[46]

The remaining disagreements between Washington and Moscow were resolved after the abortive August 1991 coup that led to the dissolution of the USSR. Najibullah resisted pressure from hard-liners in the PDPA to congratulate the Moscow coup leaders, but the ultimate defeat of the uprising meant the loss of his patrons, most notably in the KGB and the Red Army. On September 13, 1991, Soviet Foreign Minister Boris Pankin and Secretary Baker agreed to the text that had been prepared for Houston the previous December, this time with a date certain for the implementation of negative symmetry. The United States and the USSR agreed that the transitional authority should have "independent authority with all powers required to prepare for, conduct and implement" elections. The transition mechanism should be worked out through intra-Afghan dialogue sponsored by the United Nations. Both sides would cut off all weapons supplies at the end of the year and work toward the "withdrawal of major weapons systems," namely the SCUDs and Stingers.[47] The United States terminated all deliveries as of September 30, the end of fiscal 1991, despite opposition from the CIA.

8 Decline of Hegemonic Control

Even as the more cooperative relationship between the superpowers enabled them to reach an agreement, other actors were becoming less compliant to the pressure needed to implement it. The decline in hegemonic control had both international and domestic consequences. The regional powers that had supported the mujahidin no longer shared a common aim of expelling the Soviet troops, and their differences with the United States and with each other led them to pursue divergent strategies. The mujahidin were less dependent than before on outside supplies, for military pressure had lessened. They began to pursue varying individual and group interests, giving rise to ethnic claims and an increase in smuggling and the drug trade. On the other side, Soviet troops could no longer prevent factionalism from breaking out within the Kabul regime. To defend his power, Najibullah increasingly used Soviet aid to build up military forces outside the normal chain of command, creating a patchwork of tribal and ethnic militias with competing goals. Only continued aid flows enabled him to bargain for their allegiance.

Pro-Mujahidin Regional Powers

Once the Soviet troops were out of Afghanistan, Washington found that its interests increasingly diverged from those of Pakistan and Saudi Arabia. The radical change in relations between the great powers was most strikingly symbolized by the Bush administration's decision in September 1990 to terminate all aid to Pakistan — military and economic, including the delivery of F-16 fighters for which Pakistan had already paid. Under the Pressler amendment to the Foreign Assistance Act, the president could authorize aid only if he issued a finding that Pakistan was not making nuclear weapons. Contrary evidence had been available for years, but in the spring and summer of 1990 the administration finally declined to certify Pakistan's nonnuclear status. This decision derived in part from new intelligence, in part from the rapid decline in Pakistan's strategic importance. Congress showed no inclination to consider the administration's tepid requests to reconsider the Pressler amendment.

This decision was the culmination of a process that had been under way for some time. Since early 1988, when the Soviets made it clear their troops would leave (and especially after the assassination of National Endowment for Democracy grantee Majrooh in February), the State Department had been complaining to Pakistan and the Saudis about excessive support for Hikmatyar. In an attempt to separate Afghanistan from Pakistan policy, in June 1989 the U.S. government appointed Peter Tomsen as an ambassadorial-level special envoy to the Afghan resistance who did not report through the embassy in Islamabad.

After the death of Zia, Pakistan's divided government lacked a coherent policy. Almost as soon as Benazir Bhutto took office in December 1988, conflict broke out between her government and the military, ostensibly over Afghanistan, but largely over the domestic prerogatives of the military and the ISI. The ISI used military successes in Afghanistan to justify its domestic prerogatives; Bhutto used its failures in Afghanistan to reduce those prerogatives. After the Jalalabad debacle, ISI director, Gen. Hamid Gul, tried to pin the blame on Bhutto in an April 24 leak to the *New York Times*.[1] A month later, on the eve of her first trip to Washington as prime minister, Bhutto fired Gul. She followed this up by ignoring the list of serving generals from which General Beg asked her to pick a successor and instead appointed Gen. Shamsur Rahman Kallu, who had resigned from the military in protest when Zia became president.[2] By the following fall, however, General Beg had shifted Afghanistan policy to his own office, and he treated Gul as his adviser on Afghan affairs. Kallu was never able to assert control over the ISI's activities in Afghanistan.

The Pakistani generals aimed to place Hikmatyar in power in Afghanistan in order to assure themselves of a friendly government that would give them strategic depth against India. Their Saudi and other Arab allies wanted to expand their own version of Sunni Islam and stop the spread of Iranian influence by strengthening Sayyaf. Both began to fear that a deal between the superpowers with the connivance of the Bhutto government would sideline the more militant Sunni Islamist forces.[3] Just when the State Department began to try to turn U.S. policy away from the support for Hikmatyar that the CIA still urged, Saudi Arabia increased its aid to Hikmatyar as the strongest Sunni force while Arab volunteers continued to flock to both him and Sayyaf. The ISI had made a tremendous investment in Hikmatyar over the years and regarded him as the key guarantor of Pakistani interests in Afghanistan. Both the ISI and the CIA considered him a useful tool for shaping the future of Central Asia. Hikmatyar also received aid from Middle Eastern Sunni Islamists, Muammar al-Qaddhafy, and, later, Saddam Hussein.

The ISI used both Saudi support and operational control over the distribution of much of the U.S. aid to seek a military victory dominated by the forces of Hikmatyar. Reports from the field alleged that CIA officers were directly involved in at least some of these efforts, which contradicted Washington's official policy. The CIA did not support Hikmatyar's brand of Islamism — "Of course, he is not a Jeffersonian democrat," was the formula acknowledgment of objections — but it endorsed the ISI's evaluation of his military effectiveness, discounted the possibility of a negotiated settlement, and promoted the benefits of cooperation with the Saudi and Pakistani intelligence organizations.

In the fall of 1989, as the U.S.-Soviet dialogue began, a Pakistani military mission came to Washington to promote an "action plan" for a new mujahidin political and military offensive. According to this plan, the now-discredited IIGA would convene another shura, this time with representation from around the country, and would hold elections to command greater legitimacy. The State Department incorporated this plan into the first proposal for a transition during the U.S.-Soviet dialogue. At the same time, Pakistan and the United States would concentrate on turning the mujahidin guerrillas into a conventional force by improving their command and control capabilities and by increasing their supplies of rockets and other heavy weapons. The heart of the military strategy was the creation of a conventional mujahidin army that would consist of eight battalions based in Pakistan, most under the command of Hikmatyar. Hikmatyar's conventional force was known as the Army of Sacrifice (*Lashkar-i Isar*). ISI- and CIA-sponsored military activity increasingly took the form of encouraging individual commanders to fire rockets into Kabul city, where they mainly killed civilians. Commanders with greater power and a strategic vision resisted this policy, but those who followed it, including Hikmatyar's commanders, were paid for each rocket fired.[4]

The ISI tried to use Hikmatyar's militia several times in pursuit of a military victory that would preempt the U.S.-Soviet negotiations and prevent the ISI's client from being sidelined. The first attempt was in March 1990. As part of an ethnic realignment of Afghan politics after the Soviet withdrawal, Hikmatyar had begun to negotiate an alliance with his fellow Pashtuns in Khalq. The ISI and the Saudis seem to have supported these efforts. In December 1989 Najibullah announced the arrest of Khalqi officers who, he charged, had been plotting against him in cooperation with Hikmatyar. On March 7, 1990, the day the accused were to go on trial, the Khalqi defense minister, Shahnawaz Tanai, launched a coup. He bombed the presidential palace while trying to break the security cordon south of Kabul to let Hikmatyar's battalions into the city. Najibullah barely escaped the bombs, but he defeated the coup. Hikmatyar announced the formation of a Revolutionary Council with Tanai, and the ISI and Saudi intelligence pressured other mujahidin leaders to join, reportedly paying commanders as much as $15,000 to support the coup. As long as the United States continued to give aid, however, it had enough leverage to block these offensives. U.S. diplomats, including the ambassador to Pakistan, Robert Oakley, and Special Envoy Peter Tomsen, intervened forcefully to support Peshawar mujahidin leaders who refused to join the Revolutionary Council.[5] Tanai fled to Pakistan, where Hikmatyar appointed him commander of the Army of Sacrifice.

Pakistan's Afghanistan policy became increasingly confused as conflicts intensified among Bhutto, the army, and the president. The Pakistani military regained full control when President Ghulam Ishaq Khan, at the behest of the generals, dismissed the Bhutto government on August 6, 1990, a few days after Iraq invaded Kuwait. Without interference from the caretaker government, whose sole mandate from the president was to crush Bhutto's PPP, the ISI tried to reorganize the IIGA in Peshawar with Hikmatyar as minister of defense, the position that they had intended him to receive at the February 1989 shura. At the same time, as the U.S.-Soviet dialogue seemed to approach agreement, the ISI tried to coordinate a massive assault on Kabul city by Hikmatyar, to whom they transferred forty thousand rockets and seven hundred trucks of ammunition.[6] The planned assault, which like the earlier uprising was short-circuited by the U.S. State Department, intended to precipitate chaos that would facilitate a coup from within. The attack would have included an indiscriminate shower of inaccurate rockets on the city, causing thousands of civilian casualties, a strategy that foreshadowed Hikmatyar's actions in 1992.

The conflict in the Islamic world over the approaching Gulf War in late 1990 and early 1991 temporarily resurrected U.S. hegemony and weakened the ISI. Hikmatyar and other radical elements of the Afghan mujahidin, as well as their supporters in the Pakistani military and ISI, joined the international Islamist opposition to the U.S.-led coalition operating from Saudi Arabia. The civilian government of Pakistan, along with the nationalists and moderates among the mujahidin, supported the U.S.-Saudi position. The Saudis had made arrangements to transport two thousand mujahidin to Saudi Arabia to offer symbolic support to the U.S.-led coalition, but the project was repeatedly held up by objections from radical mujahidin groups and Pakistani military officers, including Chief of Army Staff Mirza Aslam Beg. Beg's faction in the military was deeply resentful of what they saw as American inconstancy, exemplified by the decision to cut off aid to Pakistan but not to other nuclear proliferators, like India and Israel. Beg argued that the United States would be defeated in the Gulf when Iran came to the aid of Iraq, and that Pakistan should align itself with Iran and China in opposition to the emerging U.S.-Soviet joint hegemony. In February, Saudi Istakhbara chief Prince Turki made a special trip to Pakistan to remonstrate with his counterparts, and five hundred mujahidin from the leading nationalist groups (Gailani and Mujaddidi), whom the Saudis had hardly assisted, finally made the journey. The Saudis at least temporarily cut off official funding to Hikmatyar and some other groups, though wealthy individuals maintained their aid unimpeded. The United States amplified its insistence to the ISI that Hikmatyar and Sayyaf be cut off. Most U.S. funding for ministries of the IIGA was also halted in March. The rapid victory of the U.S.-led coalition in the Gulf discredited General Beg.[7]

The exit of Soviet troops and the end of the Iran-Iraq war also freed the Iranian government to pay more attention to Afghanistan. Tehran had opposed the presence of Soviet troops in a neighboring Muslim land, but its government now became increasingly concerned with the rise of Pakistani and particularly Saudi influence over the Sunni Islamists in Afghanistan.

Even before the end of the Iran-Iraq war, the second-track discussions in 1987 inspired the Iranian government to organize the Shia groups that they supported to challenge the hegemony of the Pakistan-based Sunni groups. On June 18, 1987, eight groups based in Iran announced the formation of an alliance. It was probably not a coincidence that this group had one more party than the alliance of Sunni groups in Pakistan. Iran insisted that this alliance be included in all negotiations.

Iran accelerated its activity after the withdrawal of Soviet troops. Immediately after the end of the troop withdrawal in February 1989, Soviet Foreign Minister Shevardnadze visited Tehran. There he received the singular honor of being the only visiting foreign minister ever received by the Ayatollah Khomeini.[8] Khomeini died in June 1989, leaving a last will and testament that denounced the Saudis' Wahhabi sect in the bitterest terms, making it even more difficult for Iran and the groups it supported to collaborate with the Saudi-supported IIGA, which enjoyed the strong support of Riyadh. Iran's Afghan policy moved closer to Gorbachev's government in an attempt to balance the increasing pressure from the U.S.-Pakistan-Saudi coalition. In the summer of 1989 President Hashemi Rafsanjani told the Shia parties that the jihad was over and that they should seek a political settlement with Kabul. Tehran similarly signaled its support for a political settlement to the Soviet government and the United Nations. The Iranian strategy was to block a takeover by the U.S.-, Saudi-, and Pakistani-backed groups. Iran preferred Najibullah without Soviet troops to the mujahidin backed by rival states.[9]

In order to strengthen its clients for negotiations, Iran in 1990 induced the Shia parties to go beyond an alliance of parties by uniting into a single party, the Hizb-i Wahdat (Unity Party). Unlike Pakistan, which still gave aid separately to seven parties and their commanders, Iran now gave all aid only to this single center. It also gave some humanitarian and economic aid to Najibullah, whom it preferred to the Saudi-supported IIGA. Iran took advantage of dissatisfactions with the Saudi-ISI-CIA-Hikmatyar axis to initiate a rapprochement with both its fellow Persian-speakers in Jamiat and with the moderate nationalist mujahidin groups. By 1991 Iran had signed a treaty on cultural cooperation with Tajikistan, Hizb-i

Wahdat, and Jamiat. Mujaddidi and Gailani, the nationalist leaders who had received the least Saudi aid, and Rabbani, who headed the largely Persian-speaking Jamiat, all traveled to Iran and opened offices there.

Mujahidin Parties and Commanders

The withdrawal of Soviet troops from May 15, 1988, to February 15, 1989, greatly reduced the military pressure on the mujahidin. Resistance fighters captured or occupied all of the frontier with Pakistan. They overran the eastern Afghan provincial center of Kunar, where competing shuras vied for power. A largely Hazara shura took control of central Afghanistan. Massoud captured Taliqan, the center of Takhar Province on the border of Soviet Tajikistan. He established a capital there for his Supervisory Council of the North (SCN), which grouped mainly Jamiat commanders in the northeast. Several other provincial garrisons fell and were retaken or negotiated truces with local mujahidin.

The fragmented political and military structures of the mujahidin prevented them from turning these local victories into a national one. The Soviet presence had galvanized Afghanistan's society into a certain unity of action, but for many fighters the withdrawal of Soviet troops meant the end of the jihad, of the religious obligation to unite with Muslims against non-Muslim aggressors. Mujahidin who still believed in jihad after the Soviet withdrawal confronted with disbelief the alliance of Hikmatyar and Tanai. If Khalq and Hizb could ally, there was no more jihad, just a multilateral struggle for power.[10]

Gaining access to the lucrative flows of cash and guns from Moscow and Washington required persistent postures of intransigence or pretenses of ideological unity, but many commanders began to make practical deals with their opponents. As early as 1987, whether because counterinsurgency strategy had softened or because of the deterrent effects of Stinger missiles, agriculture and trade began to revive, increasing the resources available to local commanders.[11] Many commanders seized the opportunity to produce a cash crop for which there was seemingly unlimited demand — opium poppies. In some areas the poppy profits allowed commanders to become powerful warlords, increasingly independent of both the external donors and local society.

The Soviet withdrawal had another important effect. Soviet troops and especially helicopters had made it nearly impossible for commanders to seize booty or charge tolls, as tribal warlords had done for centuries before the strengthening of the Afghan state in the 1950s, and as they had started to do again when that state broke down in 1978–79.[12] The Soviet withdrawal enabled resistance leaders to levy tributes on road transport — traders, smugglers, and government suppliers alike. They also engaged in trade, for many of them had developed business relationships with the transport companies that brought their supplies from Pakistan. In spite of pressure from the ISI, commanders generally preferred to trade with Kabul, Qandahar, Herat, or other major regional centers they surrounded rather than strangle them.

Local commanders also received increasing amounts of foreign aid directly rather than through parties. Supply lines from Peshawar became much more secure, and more aid could travel over roads by truck rather than by pack animals on mountain trails. European and U.N. aid programs generally dealt directly with commanders who could implement programs in areas under their control.

Thus the various foreign plans for a resistance victory were frustrated not just by Kabul and Moscow but by the mujahidin commanders themselves. By mid-1989, commanders had new resources and were so resentful of ISI pressure that some observers said that they were "on strike."

Some commanders used these resources to elaborate independent political strategies, but most returned to traditional modes of behavior, becoming less politicized and emerging as a new stratum of "Islamic khans." The tendency toward politicization of local insurgencies that had grown during the Soviet occupation reversed itself among many groups as a result of decreased military pressure and increased access to local resources. The new local elites, including Islamist intellectuals, were partly reabsorbed into the traditional patterns with which they had grown up.[13]

Most Islamist activists were village youths who had sojourned in Kabul or regional towns for secondary or higher education. These experiences had given them links to national and international networks that provided the resources through which they had consolidated power as a new generation of local strongmen. The khans of the old regime, many of whom had fled, continued to lose power, for the new Islamic khans still opposed them. Just as the old khans had supported the royal regime but resisted government interference in local society, the Islamic khans affiliated themselves with Islamic parties but resisted any impositions by the exiled leaders — to say nothing of the ISI. Najibullah recognized this principle in his counterinsurgency strategy. Before the Soviet withdrawal the regime's pacification program had mainly tried to recruit traditional khans, members of the "big families" who had served in the parliaments of New Democracy, but Najibullah and his militia intermediaries concentrated later efforts on local commanders of all parties, especially on Islamists engaged in local conflicts with rivals.

Hikmatyar was the only leader to exploit opium profits systematically to maintain a hierarchically organized party and conventional army. In the summer of 1988, expecting that the Soviet withdrawal would lead to a decrease in foreign support, he seems to have instructed his men to search for precious stones and to cultivate poppy. Unlike the warlord commanders, who were content to sell the raw opium at bazaars in Afghanistan and Baluchistan (where paper currency was weighed rather than counted), Hikmatyar, in partnership with Pakistani heroin syndicates, seems also to have invested in some processing plants.[14]

In the SCN-dominated areas of the northeast a more differentiated and extensive organization raised funds with taxlike levies on the revitalized agricultural production and the mining of precious gems. In this area only certain parts of Badakhshan seem to have been conducive to opium growing, which played a correspondingly lesser role. Foreign aid to the SCN served to strengthen existing quasi-state institutions with a strong local political base, which made the council an increasingly attractive target for foreign economic and humanitarian aid. Less information is available on Herat, but it seems that a similar process developed there, except that the regime- and resistance-controlled areas were better integrated into a common economy. North-central Afghanistan emerged as a region dominated by Uzbek and Ismaili government militia leaders who developed patron-client relations with local commanders.

As communications and travel within the country became easier, broader regional coalitions arose in those areas where social control was coherent enough to support them, providing a counterpoint to the general tendency toward de-politicization. Some commanders tried to build national organizations independent of the ISI, but they were generally limited by the social structure and geography of Afghanistan to organizing one region of the country. Such regional organizations formed the basis of ethnic politics.

This process started in 1987 in response to second-track proposals for the formation of an interim government. In June and July of 1987, Jamiat Commander Ismail Khan of Herat, a former army officer, convened a meeting of commanders in Ghor Province. Reports stated that over twelve hundred commanders attended, from twenty of the twenty-nine provinces. The meeting "categorically reject[ed] the policy of national reconciliation and coalition government with the Soviet-backed communist regime." The first point of the resolution passed by the commanders, however, seemed to be directed equally at the leaders in Peshawar: "The resistance forces actually present in the battle fronts have the right to determine the future of Afghanistan. No one else is allowed to decide the future destiny of the nation."[15]

The commanders called for a second conference within six months to elect a "Supreme Revolutionary Council of the Jehad," which would "have the task to explore means and ways for the organisation and coordination of warring groups inside Afghanistan and help the oppressed nation of Afghanistan exercise its right of self-determination. . . . Meetings should be held in all provinces and districts in order to elect authorised representatives for the second meeting."[16] Ismail Khan never managed to establish an ongoing organization or to convene a second meeting. The ISI and Jamiat headquarters in Peshawar, alarmed at his excessive independence, set about undermining him by increasing aid to his rivals in Herat. His meeting, however, established the framework that was adopted in 1990 by a new organization.

Soon after the Tanai-Hikmatyar coup, a group of mujahidin field commanders began to organize a National Commanders Shura. Its conveners claimed that the NCS intended only to coordinate military strategy, but most Afghans perceived it as an attempt by internal commanders to seize the initiative from the discredited and foreign-influenced exiled leaders. The NCS held meetings in May and June 1990, with mostly Pashtun participation from eastern Afghanistan, and decided to call a nationwide meeting of commanders the following October. The October meeting was held in Kunar, near the undefined boundary between the Pashtun south and the non-Pashtun north, so that more northern commanders could attend. At Hikmatyar's orders, his commanders boycotted the NCS. Sayyaf also forbade his commanders to attend, but several defied him. ISI officers tried to dissuade some commanders from attending what they called an American shura. The ISI's new director-general, Asad Durrani, insisted on traveling to the meeting, but he was forbidden to participate in the sessions.

The October NCS meeting included a broader representation of regions and ethnic groups than any previous gathering of the mujahidin. It passed resolutions against the ISI-sponsored strategy of a direct attack on Kabul by Hikmatyar's militia units based in Pakistan. Instead, it outlined a plan to capture provincial outposts of the regime and to set up regional administrations (base areas) in nine zones.

The NCS, however, did not choose a national leadership to compete openly with the parties on whom they still depended for aid. Instead of independently pursuing a national political strategy based on local and regional mobilization, the NCS sent Massoud to Islamabad to lobby for their position. Massoud complained that the ISI discriminated against him and other powerful commanders in favor of Hikmatyar. He asked that the most powerful commanders in NCS be given aid directly to carry out plans that they formulated themselves — that is, without ISI interference. In March 1990 he had sent emissaries with the same message to Washington, where they had received backing from congressional mujahidin supporters.[17]

U.S. diplomats in Pakistan promised finally to resolve the problem by supplying Massoud and other major commanders directly. U.S. officials took measures to assure supplies to the major commanders in the NCS, including sophisticated radio communications equipment that would enable them to communicate inside Afghanistan in code, without going through Pakistan. Radio communication, which bypassed the difficulty of transport in this mountainous country, was key to the attempt to form a national coalition. After several months of wrangling within the NCS over who would receive them, the sets were delivered.

A significant amount of arms and supplies finally began to flow to Massoud and other prominent commanders in the NCS.[18] The State Department supported this policy as a means of increasing military pressure on the hard-liners who had taken over Soviet Afghanistan policy after Shevardnadze's resignation. State Department officials also hoped that by strengthening militarily effective commanders inside the country they could offset the strength of Hikmatyar in the event of a change in power. In the event, the failure of the NCS to develop clear national political leadership led to a breakdown of cooperation, which in turn triggered ethnic conflict within Afghanistan.

In fact, the expansion of the political arena promoted ethnic conflict.[19] Soviet control of the axes of communication and the capital had kept resistance units confined to small localities, where the principal social friction was between local qawms. As some resistance units expanded and the battle for Kabul unfolded, these organizations cohered as ethnic cores of larger coalitions, regardless of the ideology of those who led them. National integration is a cooperation problem, which is solved by some combination of a hegemonic power imposing a state and a negotiated agreement among regional powers to delegate powers to a central authority. The buffer state had been consolidated when outside powers gave the ruling dynasty enough resources to conquer competing powers. The breakdown of cooperation over the role of Afghanistan in the international system led to a concatenation of security dilemmas, as the weakening of global powers encouraged competition among regional powers, who in turn encouraged conflict among ethnic and regional coalitions within Afghanistan itself.

As the United States and the USSR disengaged, states in the region aligned themselves with these ethnic coalitions in Afghanistan. Rough affiliations grouped Pakistan and Saudi Arabia with eastern and Ghilzai Pashtun Islamists, and Iran with the Shia and with Persian-speaking and Turkic groups. The latter groups also enjoyed some sympathy in Central Asia, especially Uzbekistan. Pashtun traditionalists and Durranis negotiated with both of these coalitions, while hoping for more involvement by the United Nations and the United States. All groupings found allies within the Kabul regime, largely on an ethnic basis, the Pashtun Islamists with Khalqis and the non-Pashtuns with anti-Najibullah Parchamis.

The Kabul Regime and Armed Forces

The Soviet troops in Afghanistan not only kept the resistance from cutting roads and overrunning government bases, they also prevented the open outbreak of factional feuding in the PDPA. The Red Army enabled the Soviet leadership to impose Karmal on the Khalqis and Najibullah on both the Khalqis and Karmalites. When the troops withdrew, Moscow lost this instrument of direct coercive control of the Kabul regime and ruling party. Instead it tried to influence its clients through advisers and aid, as the United States and Pakistan tried to influence the mujahidin.

The regime, meanwhile, abandoned its ideology in favor of survival. Najibullah presided over the reversal of virtually every element of the PDPA's program. He changed the name of the country back to the Republic of Afghanistan, changed the name of the party to the Watan (Homeland) Party, renounced Marxism, single-party rule, and socialism, and embraced Islam, pluralism, and market economics. Rather than pursue a revolutionary strategy, Najibullah redistributed the massive Soviet aid to the various apparatuses linked to the regime, notably the militias that guarded his lifeline to the USSR. The high level of aid may have constituted the political price that Gorbachev had to pay to obtain his hard-liners' agreement to withdraw Soviet troops and Najibullah's assent to the Geneva Accords with positive symmetry.

Even with the aid, increased Afghan state expenditures that were needed to compensate for the Soviet troop withdrawal provoked a severe fiscal crisis after 1986. As an alternative to dependence on Moscow, Najibullah printed money. The resulting hyperinflation in turn reinforced dependence on Soviet supplies of food and fuel. The Soviets supplied an average of 250,000 tons of wheat per year, more than 100 percent of the total estimated consumption of the population of Kabul.[20]

With these resources Najibullah managed to retain control over the major cities and access to the paved roads that linked them. As the source of Najibullah's power shifted from direct Soviet military presence to the redistribution of resources, he was forced to delegate more power to local commanders, thereby multiplying the bases for factionalism within the regime. Unable to create an effective, modern military, the government moved away from a bureaucratic chain of command toward a system based on brokerage, in which the state pays powerful leaders to supply troops from among their followers.[21] Najibullah relied increasingly on heavily armed qawm-based militias rather than the regular armed forces. The most important militias were those created to guard the regime's lifeline, the road link to the USSR. This road passed through the largely non-Pashtun areas of northern Afghanistan on its way to Uzbekistan. Just before the signing of the Geneva Accords, this whole area received a special status, with its own deputy prime minister. The regime spent large sums to recruit militias that guarded the road and other economic assets. The largest militia was the mainly Uzbek Jauzjanis, led by Gen. Abdul Rashid Dostum. The Jauzjanis (later known as Ghilam Jam, or carpet snatchers) guarded the natural gas fields in the north and the northern part of the road, up to the Soviet border. A militia of Ismaili Hazaras led by their traditional religious leader, Sayyid Mansur Nadiri, guarded the next segment of road, south to the Salang Tunnel.

Najibullah created a military command structure for the northern zone that placed Pashtun generals in charge of coordinating the activities of non-Pashtun militias. Nonetheless, the government's political and economic efforts in the north strengthened the capacity for collective action of that area's inhabitants, once the overlay of foreign-assisted, Pashtun-dominated administration was stripped away.

The regime failed to find any formula for internal coherence that could substitute for its abandoned ideology. Instead, regime figures tried to assure their survival by pursuing links to various social groups within the country, including both mujahidin and militias. Through this process Najibullah and his Soviet backers forfeited influence and invited an ethnic realignment of political forces. One manifestation of this process was the reemergence of open conflict between Khalq and Parcham, whose members found different allies in the resistance and the government armed forces. The March 1990 coup in which Khalqi Defense Minister Shahnawaz Tanai united with Hizb-i Islami leader Gulbuddin Hikmatyar and the Pakistani ISI against Najibullah was only the most dramatic example of an alliance across an ideological gulf. Another manifestation of the process was the increasingly open tug-of-war between Najibullah and the non-Pashtun government militias based in northern Afghanistan.

The struggle over the future of reform in the USSR intensified in 1990 and early 1991, and the various factions in Kabul looked again to their patrons in Moscow. As the Moscow hard-liners prepared for their coup in the summer of 1991, Babrak Karmal returned to Kabul on June 20. His arrival may have been part of a contingency plan to restore a more hard-line Afghanistan policy after the anti-Gorbachev coup. At any rate, the failure of the August coup in Moscow disheartened both the Khalqis and the Karmalites.[22] At this point they may have decided finally that the revolution was over and that they could assure their personal survival only by making ethnic alliances against Najibullah.

Many of the Pashtuns in the Khalqi leadership had already joined Hikmatyar. Sultan Ali Kishtmand, the only Hazara in the party leadership, resigned in the summer of 1991. He complained of Pashtun domination and supported the political demands of the Iranian-based Shia parties for regional autonomy and broad representation in the central government. The emerging independence of the Soviet Central Asian republics, as well as the increased discussion of power sharing in a transitional government, also increased tensions, especially between Tajiks and Pashtuns.[23]

The regime's control over rural areas continued to erode. The mujahidin consolidated their hold over outlying areas, especially the northeast, and the regime had scant control even in many areas dominated by groups that owed nominal allegiance to Kabul. Both the Jauzjanis and Ismailis seemed to exercise nearly as much independence as Massoud's Council of the North, and both the

Qandahar and Herat garrisons had struck deals with local mujahidin groups that left them poised in a tenuous equilibrium between Kabul and the local population. Najibullah fell not because of any onslaught by mujahidin but because the loss of Soviet aid eroded his ability to control factionalism and ethnic conflict in his own ranks.

9 *From Conflict Resolution to State Disintegration*

Just when the United Nations plan was supposed to go into effect, the dissolution of the Soviet Union transformed the regional and global significance of Afghanistan. The two superpowers had devised this plan as an exercise in hegemonic cooperation under the aegis of the United Nations. The United States and the Soviet Union would ask the Secretary General's Office, in accord with General Assembly resolutions, to sponsor an interim government; the superpowers would use their influence with the regional states and with their Afghan clients to assure implementation of the plan and promote stability. With the dissolution of the USSR, however, one superpower disappeared, the other disengaged, and cooperation between them became moot. In the absence of hegemonic power, security dilemmas emerged both for regional states and for the ethnic coalitions within Afghanistan.

The domestic politics of Afghanistan soon offered a close approximation to the anarchy of international relations theory. Some actors were aggressive, with preference orderings as in the Deadlock game, where *DD* is preferred to *CC*, rendering cooperation impossible. But even those who preferred *CC* (a political settlement) to *DD* (civil war) felt constrained to take military action by the threat that their adversaries might do so. The same logic applied to both the ethnic coalitions in Afghanistan and to their regional supporters. The resulting series of military maneuvers that preempted the implementation of the U.N. plan plunged the country into the new round of war that persisted until mid-1995.

Attempt to Implement the U.N. Plan

After the Baker-Pankin agreement of September 13, U.N. Secretary General Pérez de Cuéllar tried to secure cooperation among all states involved. To assure compliance with the superpowers' plan by the regional states, he traveled to Saudi Arabia and then to Tehran, where he met President Ghulam Ishaq Khan of

Pakistan, as well as Hashemi Rafsanjani of Iran.[1] All leaders claimed to support a political settlement. The civilian government in Islamabad felt that a stable Afghanistan was in the national interest of Pakistan. The emerging independence of the Central Asian states could give Pakistan an alternative to its eternally unequal contest with India in South Asia. A peaceful Afghanistan through which the newly independent republics could have access to Pakistan and the sea was essential to that vision.

After Pérez de Cuéllar completed these consultations, he received further encouragement. The Soviet foreign ministry met one of the last demands of the United States and its partners when its U.N. delegation explicitly told Pérez de Cuéllar that Najibullah need not be part of the transition, a policy shift that Najibullah soon confirmed. In October the secretary general said, "I have been given assurances that some of the controversial personalities concerned would not insist on their personal participation, either in the intra-Afghan dialogue or in the transition mechanism."[2]

In November the foreign ministers of the USSR, Russia, and Tajikistan met in Moscow with four of the seven Pakistan-based mujahidin parties (Jamiat and the three traditionalist parties) and the Iran-based Hizb-i Wahdat. These parties had met twice since the spring with the foreign ministries of Pakistan and Iran to discuss implementation of the five points proposed by the U.N. secretary general in May 1991. The three Pashtun-led Islamist parties that were closest to the ISI and Arab Islamists had refused to participate in previous meetings and were not invited to Moscow. The composition of this meeting signaled the seeming success of U.S. policy aimed at marginalizing both Najibullah and Hikmatyar.

A joint statement issued after the Moscow meeting called for the replacement of the current government in Kabul by an "Islamic interim government." The interim government would hold elections with the aid of the Organization of the Islamic Conference and the United Nations (mentioned in that order). The Soviet and Russian side also promised not only to terminate weapons supplies but to withdraw any remaining military advisers and end supply of fuel for military operations. The mujahidin promised to expedite the release of Soviet prisoners of war.

Following the meetings in Moscow, Pérez de Cuéllar invited the permanent representatives of the United States, the USSR, Pakistan, Saudi Arabia, and Iran to a "tea party" in his office to affirm their multilateral cooperation. Iran declined to attend a meeting with the United States, but all five states affirmed support for the U.N. initiative. Nonetheless, to paraphrase Chairman Mao, a tea party is not a Security Council resolution. This informal show of cooperation was not backed up by the level of force employed in Cambodia, where the international community deployed billions of dollars worth of military resources, civilian personnel, and humanitarian aid to assure a transition. The regional powers in this case, aware of the lack of any enforcement mechanism, continued to strengthen their links to groups in Afghanistan that could promote their interests and block their rivals.

This meeting authorized the Secretary General's Office to accelerate its work on the transitional mechanism. The first proposal, from Moscow, was to establish a joint government between mujahidin and non-Communists in Kabul. Moscow suggested that Zahir Shah or Mujaddidi be designated as president while Najibullah's appointee, Fazl Haq Khaliqyar, a nonparty dignitary from Herat, continued as prime minister. Objections by the Pashtun radicals, Hikmatyar, Khalis, and Sayyaf, and by Jamiat leader Burhanuddin Rabbani undercut this simple and direct solution.[3]

Benon Sevan then set off to carry out long-debated plans to use the good offices of the U.N. secretary general to promote negotiations among the various Afghan parties. In January 1992 the new secretary general, Boutros Boutros-Ghali, announced a plan under which all Afghan parties would submit to his office lists of candidates for an "Afghan gathering" (*ijlas*). The United Nations would negotiate agreement among the parties to select about 150 representatives, and the gathering would elect a committee of about 35. This committee would canvass the entire nation and, on the basis of these consultations, would summon a nationwide meeting to decide on an interim government and the holding of elections.

This cumbersome procedure was designed to overcome several obstacles. Power-sharing negotiations remained impossible because, unlike the insurgents in other regional conflicts, the resistance parties still refused even to meet openly with representatives of the existing government. (All of them, however, had their own back channels to individuals in Kabul.) Organizing a multiparty council as in Cambodia, where all four parties signed an agreement, was impossible. Najibullah had offered to hand over power to Zahir Shah or to a neutral force, but not to a fragmented resistance that had not defeated him and that offered no united alternative. Furthermore, any Afghan who tried to convene a gathering would be suspected of promoting his own power, and any non-Afghan — even the U.N. secretary general — would lack legitimacy. The U.N. plan operated on the premise that the Afghan groups assembled could build legitimacy and authority incrementally. The procedure drew on certain Afghan traditions (in particular the emergency Loya Jirga) propounded to the United Nations by exiled officials of the old regime, including the former king and his advisers.[4] The proposal resembled others, going back at least to the Cordovez plan of 1988, that attempted to resolve the conflict by an appeal to prewar Afghan "national" traditions.

The three traditionalist-nationalist parties of the mujahidin submitted a joint list of proposed participants in the gathering, as did the Shia Hizb-i Wahdat. Zahir Shah and his advisers ultimately refused to submit a list to a gathering that gave such weight to the resistance parties. The Sunni Islamist parties (including Jamiat) also refused, suspecting that the U.N. effort was an effort to exclude them from power or to deny their impending victory. Najibullah also postponed giving his list, which would have constituted a more decisive signal that he was prepared to depart than had his previous confidential assurance.

By March, Pakistan and the United States were putting intense pressure on Sevan to force Najibullah to leave. They claimed that an explicit, public commitment by Najibullah to depart would allow them to pressure the "rejectionists" in the resistance. After several long sessions with Sevan in Kabul, Najibullah presented his list and agreed to announce his intention to resign. On March 18, 1992, Najibullah addressed the nation on television and radio. Reading a speech written for him by Sevan, he announced his resignation, which, he said, would take effect once the United Nations had established an "interim government," to which he would transfer all "powers and executive authority."[5] The international community prepared for the implementation of the regime for conflict resolution in Afghanistan.

From Conflict Resolution to State Disintegration

The cutoff of aid, the dissolution of the Soviet Union, and his own announcement, however, soon deprived Najibullah of any "powers and executive authority" to transfer. The broadcast of a clear signal that Najibullah would leave, before the establishment of an alternative to replace him, created a vacuum of power in Kabul into which the regional and ethnic coalitions rushed.

In the past, great powers had tried to consolidate the buffer state by providing a ruler with enough military and financial resources to neutralize other contenders for power. But now the great powers merely promised to cease aid to the armed groups that they had funded and to "support" (verbally) the assumption of authority by a group of men whose names had not even been announced and who controlled no armed forces. The international community acted as if Afghanistan had a law-bound state apparatus that would govern the country once a more legitimate authority took control. The Soviets had made a similar error in 1979, when Brezhnev and his advisers thought that sending their army to seize control of the central state in Kabul would enable their clients to control the country. In 1979, at least, the opposition was still disorganized and poorly armed; by 1992 the principal groups left out of the political settlement also controlled well-armed and organized forces.

After the fall of Najibullah, four principal armed groups fought for power in Kabul. These groups had different ethnic compositions and different sources of foreign support, according to the regions in which they were based. Each group to some extent also enjoyed income from local taxes or customs, as well as from the drug trade and other enterprises.

Abdul Rashid Dostum, a former commander of the Afghan Army's Jauzjani division, led a largely Uzbek group of former government militias that also included members of other ethnic groups from northern Afghanistan. Former leaders of Parcham, including Babrak Karmal, joined him in Mazar-i Sharif. He received support from the Karimov government in Uzbekistan and, perhaps, from Russia.

Massoud and Rabbani led mainly Tajiks, with members of some other northeastern ethnic groups; they were allied to one small but well-organized Shia party that had lost favor with Iran.[6] They drew on the resources of their regional base in the northeastern provinces. After Rabbani became acting president in June 1992, they received some financial support and fuel from the Saudi government and enjoyed the use of Afghanistan's newly printed bank notes.

Hikmatyar led a mainly Pashtun group that consisted of Hizb recruits from the refugee camps and eastern Afghanistan, former Khalqis, and former government militias. He never succeeded in galvanizing the Pashtun tribal shuras behind him, however, and thus lacked a consolidated regional base. The tribes were hardly involved in the struggle for Kabul. Hikmatyar continued to receive help from Arab and Pakistani Islamic radicals — and Massoud continued to capture such foreign volunteers from Hikmatyar's ranks. Hikmatyar also had income from the drug trade and trumped Rabbani's control of the currency by counterfeiting money in Pakistan.

Finally, Hizb-i Wahdat, which had a base in the Hazarajat, organized the Shia of Kabul city, who were armed by the Iranians and Parchamis during Najibullah's fall.[7]

The ethnic structure of the conflict changed over time as the domestic and international balance of power shifted, suggesting that the conflict was fundamentally a struggle for power rather than an ethnic war fueled by "ancient hatreds." At first, Massoud, Dostum, and Hizb-i Wahdat took joint control of Kabul and repulsed an attack by the Hizb-Khalq coalition. This conflict seemed to pit resurgent non-Pashtuns against Pashtuns, who had long dominated the Afghan state. It was also a clash between coalitions backed by Iran, on the one hand, and Pakistan and Saudi Arabia on the other. But by the end of 1992 the ethnic alignment had shifted. By the start of 1994, Hikmatyar's Hizb, Mujaddidi's ANLF, the Shia Hizb-i Wahdat, and Dostum's Junbish allied in a Coordination Council (*Shura-yi Hamahangi*).

The predominance of Massoud and Rabbani in Kabul alienated first Hizb-i Wahdat and then Dostum. Furthermore, the political situation in the newly independent states of Central Asia set formerly allied Uzbeks and Tajiks of north Afghanistan against each other. Dostum's backer, President Islam Karimov of Uzbekistan, worked with Russia to restore to power in Tajikistan a coalition of former Communists and others, including Uzbeks. Massoud, meanwhile, gave refuge to the supporters of the opposition, which included Islamists, Tajik nationalists, and democrats. Karimov apparently wanted Dostum to block Massoud's access to the Tajikistan-Afghanistan border.[8]

Iran, too, differed with Massoud over several issues. As early as the summer of 1992 Iran's establishment of a consulate in Dostum's capital of Mazar-i Sharif created tensions with Rabbani and Massoud. In December 1992 Massoud launched an offensive to take control of Shia neighborhoods of Kabul, leading Hizb-i Wahdat to sign an agreement with Hikmatyar in January. Dostum broke ranks with Massoud; he attacked Jamiat positions in the north in fall 1993 and openly allied with Hikmatyar by New Year of 1994, when the two former enemies launched a joint attack on Massoud's forces in Kabul. This alliance was soon formalized through the establishment of the Coordination Council.

While shifting power relations were tearing the country apart, both outside powers and Afghan groups continued their efforts to reinstate legitimate government. But the fragmentation of social power, the multiplicity of armed groups, and the abdication of the major states doomed those efforts. While foreign ministries negotiated peace plans, intelligence agencies pursued preparations for other contingencies. Iran, Pakistan, Saudi Arabia, and Uzbekistan all worked to ensure, at the least, that forces supported by their rivals would not become too powerful. A more detailed account of these developments will illustrate how they conformed to the model of the security dilemma under anarchy.

Since 1989, Hikmatyar had been using ethnic politics, among other tactics, to counter the State Department's endeavor to marginalize him. He allied with the Khalqis in 1989–90 with the support of Pakistan's ISI in pursuit of a military victory. After the Moscow meeting in November 1991, where neither he nor Kabul was represented, Hikmatyar, using Qaddhafy as an intermediary, wrote to Najibullah with an offer of collaboration. Najibullah later sent a trusted military officer to Peshawar to explore the offer. In Kabul there was talk of a "Pashtun solution."[9]

Meanwhile the non-Pashtun northern alliance was solidifying. Both the largest government militias and the largest mujahidin force — the Islamic Army of the Supervisory Council — were based in this area. Massoud had received large quantities of American materiel since the spring of 1991, enabling him to equip and expand his Islamic Army to about twelve thousand men. Confronted with Massoud's new strength, Dostum began secret negotiations with him. Massoud also continued to gain credibility with the anti-Najibullah Tajik Parchamis in the party and the army, many of whom had long hedged their bets by cooperating with him. Iran nurtured the non-Pashtun alliance through its links to non-Pashtun Parchamis and northern militias.[10] Thus it balanced the opposing Hizb-Khalq alliance that was supported by ISI, the Saudis, and other Arabs.

In January 1992, almost as soon as the aid from the USSR stopped, Dostum went into open revolt. Dostum, like all commanders, received containers of freshly printed banknotes, at least some of which he then redistributed to his men.[11] Deprived of Soviet aid, however, Najibullah halted salaries for the inflated number of soldiers that Dostum claimed to have under his command. The Soviet military had sent one last shipment of weapons and vehicles to Afghanistan. No longer restrained by the threat of reprisals, Dostum seized the whole cargo with the aid of Abdul Mumin, a Tajik Parchami officer aligned with Massoud, who commanded the border garrison through which the aid passed.

Dostum's revolt was a textbook case of the end of defection in a cooperation problem. Cooperation over time between an aid giver and an agent who has partly antagonistic interests can be seen as an iterated Prisoners' Dilemma. The cooperative strategies were for Najibullah to continue giving aid and for Dostum to fight against Najibullah's enemies. If Dostum refused to fight or attacked the wrong targets, Najibullah could retaliate by withholding aid. If Dostum did not receive as much aid as he wanted, he could sit on the sidelines or attack Najibullah's other allies. In addition, the Soviets provided external monitoring and enforcement of the cooperation.[12] Now both the iteration and the external enforcement had ended.

Najibullah turned to other means for control of an agent by a principal. He tried to use ethnic ties to create reliable agents who could monitor the unreliable ones and take sanctions against them. He tried to extend the control of Pashtun military officers who were loyal to him over the northern militias by shifting key Pashtun generals into positions of command. Najibullah's warning that he would no longer pay for phantom soldiers indicated that his new agents would monitor Dostum more closely.[13]

The attempt to strengthen monitoring of the northern militias by Pashtun commanders provoked the revolt. Dostum canvassed support for the revolt from other non-Pashtun militias and the mainly non-Pashtun Parchami forces in Kabul, where officials who saw Najibullah sinking desperately sought protectors among the mujahidin and the militias. These factional and ethnic revolts within the armed forces and party epitomized the failure of institutionalization that rendered an organized transition impossible. The chain of patronage and cooperation that had sustained the vestigial institutions of the Afghan state had broken down with the disengagement and dissolution of the United States and USSR.

The rebel militias solidified their Iranian-brokered alliance with commanders of Hizb-i Wahdat, Jamiat, and other northern resistance groups. The day after Najibullah announced that he would resign, this coalition seized control of Mazar-i Sharif, cutting off Kabul's main supply lines. Dostum announced the establishment of an autonomous administration in the north and the formation of his National Islamic Movement (*Junbish-i Milli-yi Islami*). Massoud, an acknowledged hero of the resistance, emerged as the political spokesman for the alliance, but its most powerful military force consisted of Dostum's troops. Dostum had more than forty thousand men, triple Massoud's force. The northern commanders of both militias and mujahidin felt that they had been ignored in the U.N. process, which had concentrated on mediating between the mainly Pashtun leaders in Kabul and Peshawar. Massoud told the mujahidin that he was acting on behalf of resistance commanders and the NCS, not a regional-ethnic alliance; he may have given a rather different impression to Dostum. Dostum expected an important position in the new government, but Massoud's party leader, Rabbani, an Islamic scholar who opposed deals with "communists," consistently refused.

As the revolt threatened to topple the government before the transition could be completed, the United Nations streamlined its plan. A "pretransition council composed of impartial personalities" chosen from the lists submitted to the United Nations would take over "all powers and executive authority" from the current government.[14] This council would then convene a shura in Kabul to choose an interim government. Under severe pressure from the United States and Pakistan, the major leaders in Peshawar and Kabul agreed, but agreements in Afghanistan, like any reached under anarchy, must be self-enforcing. Both Hikmatyar and the commanders of the northern alliance, who led the most powerful military forces in the country, viewed this process as an attempt to marginalize them.

According to the plan, on the night of April 15–16 a U.N. plane would fly the members of the interim government into Kabul, where Najibullah would transfer power to them at the airport and leave for exile in India on the same plane. During the day of April 15, however, in a meeting of more than eight hours at the Islamabad residence of the prime minister of Pakistan, two of the mujahidin parties expressed misgivings about the pretransition council and asked for a mujahidin government.[15] When the mujahidin leaders were unable to agree on the composition of the council, Sevan flew alone to Kabul in the early hours of April 16. There, however, the Parchami rebels allied with Massoud had seized control of the Kabul airport with 750 to 1,000 troops flown from northern military bases.[16] Najibullah, blocked from reaching the airport, fled to the office of the United Nations.

Led by Karmal's second cousin, Foreign Minister Abdul Wakil, the Parchami rebels denounced their former leader Najibullah as a hated dictator and secretly asked Massoud to enter the capital as head of state. The Parchamis intended to use Massoud as a figurehead who would continue to depend on them.[17] Massoud rejected this offer and asked the leaders in Peshawar to accelerate their efforts to form an interim government of mujahidin. Massoud faced a security dilemma, which arose in part from the failure of the NCS to appoint a national leadership or any decision-making mechanism. If Massoud moved the northern forces to secure Kabul with Dostum's aid, he would provoke resentment from Pashtun commanders, risking ethnic war. But the longer he remained outside the city while the leaders dithered, the more opportunities Hikmatyar and his Khalqi allies had to stage a coup. Similar logic applied to the other side's dilemma.

Massoud constantly spoke on his American radios with prominent Pashtuns in the NCS, trying to assure them he had no intention to take power for himself or for the northern alliance. For ideological reasons, and because he felt he had been insufficiently consulted, he rejected the U.N. interim plan. He claimed to hope that despite their shortcomings the Peshawar leaders would create an interim government that would provide legitimate political leadership. Despite intense Pakistani pressure, however, the leaders in Peshawar argued for ten days about arrangements for a transitional government.[18]

Meanwhile, Pashtuns in the Afghan military — mainly Khalqis, but also some Parchamis close to Najibullah — reacted to the threatened takeover of Kabul by the northerners. Hikmatyar and his ISI supporters prepared to reactivate plans for a military victory in Kabul. When Hikmatyar had sought to take Kabul before, in March 1990 and August–September 1991, the United States had been able to use its sponsorship to halt the offensives. But just as the end of Soviet aid deprived Najibullah of leverage over the militias, so the end of U.S. aid deprived Washington of leverage over Hikmatyar and the ISI.

Khalqi officers permitted Hizb-i Islami fighters to infiltrate the city. Hikmatyar's military force also crossed the Pakistan border and camped south of Kabul, where Khalqi units joined it. Although Islamabad was officially neutral, Hikmatyar continued to recruit fighters and to transfer weapons, oil, and supplies from Pakistan, as well as maintain offices and bank accounts there. Jamaat-i Islami supported him, as did a sector of the intelligence apparatus.

On April 25, with the Peshawar leaders still unable to reach agreement, the forces of Massoud and Dostum, already in control of the airport, entered the city to preempt a coup by Hizb. The non-Pashtun Parchamis, assisted by the Iranian embassy, had also armed the Shia of Kabul city.[19] Hikmatyar portrayed his strategy as a defense against a coup by the northern alliance. After several days of hard fighting, the Massoud and Dostum forces and the Shia expelled the Khalqi-Hizbi forces.

The party leaders, Hikmatyar excluded, finally reached agreement on April 26 and announced the Peshawar Accords. For two months Mujaddidi would be acting president; he would be followed by Rabbani for four months. At the end of the six-month interim, the government would hold a shura to choose a government for the next eighteen months, after which elections would be held. The acting president would answer to a council composed of the leaders of mujahidin parties. Massoud became minister of defense. The interim government arrived in Kabul from Peshawar on April 28 and proclaimed the establishment of the Islamic State of Afghanistan.

The government relied on the forces of Massoud and Dostum for military control of Kabul, and Hikmatyar bombarded the city with rockets and denounced the ISA as a disguised Communist regime. At the same time fighting between Iran-backed Shia and Arab-backed Salafi (Wahhabi) Sunni groups took many lives.

Four months after Rabbani assumed authority as acting president, on October 28, the leadership council reluctantly voted to extend his mandate for forty-five days, on the grounds that continued fighting and the destruction of Kabul had made it impossible for him to summon the shura in the time designated. After the extension, however, the government would summon a nationwide *shura-yi ahl-i hall-u-aqd* (council of those who loose and bind, an Islamic legal term unfamiliar to most Afghans). The shura would elect a president for the following eighteen months. Somewhat belatedly, Rabbani managed to convoke a shura of 1,335 men at the end of December 1992. But most of the parties boycotted the shura, charging that it was manipulated by Rabbani, whom, to no one's surprise, it elected as president on December 29.

The assumption of a near monopoly over the central government by Jamiat accelerated the shifts in alliances that changes in the regional international system had begun. Massoud and Rabbani became more isolated as their former allies turned against them.

The United Nations and most of the international community had by this time virtually dropped Afghanistan from the political agenda. Pakistan and Saudi Arabia began a new initiative, which pro-Hikmatyar forces turned to their advantage. After a January appeal by King Fahd of Saudi Arabia and pressure from Jamaat and its allies in Pakistan, the major party leaders, Sunni and Shia, signed a new agreement in Islamabad on March 7, 1993.[20] The leaders then paid a visit to Saudi Arabia, where they made the pilgrimage to Mecca and took an oath to adhere to the agreement. This oath had little effect, however, because the agreement, among other shortcomings, was internally contradictory. The agreement left Rabbani as president but made Hikmatyar the prime minister, reproducing in Afghanistan a political relation that had undone successive Pakistani governments. The prime minister would appoint the government, including the defense minister, in consultation with the president, who remained supreme commander of the armed forces. The prime minister immediately announced that he would dismiss Defense Minister Massoud, while the president and supreme commander of the armed forces announced that Massoud would remain at his post. When the president traveled to the eastern outskirts of Kabul for a secret meeting with the prime minister, gunmen attempted to assassinate him on the way, and no further meetings were planned. Massoud resigned as defense minister in May but continued to command the same forces.

After months of negotiations in Afghanistan, Pakistan, and Uzbekistan, the new alliance of the anti-Jamiat forces coalesced. On New Year's Day 1994, after receiving fresh military equipment from Pakistan and Uzbekistan, respectively, Hikmatyar and Dostum launched a combined assault on the forces of Rabbani and Massoud. Fighting along these lines also broke out in Mazar and elsewhere in the north, especially in those areas to which refugees had fled from Tajikistan. Despite his lack of consistent foreign support, Massoud gradually gained ground over the year, vindicating his reputation as a military commander, but these military accomplishments brought the country no nearer to peace.

Instead, Rabbani lost whatever legitimacy the Islamabad Accords had conferred on him. He was scheduled to remain as interim president until June 28, 1994, by which time elections were to have been held, but he unilaterally lengthened his own term to the end of the year. By that time, according to conservative estimates based on the numbers of victims arriving at Kabul hospitals, more than twenty thousand had died in the war from April 1992 to December 1994. Many were buried quickly by families or abandoned under the rubble.[21]

In the rest of the country, between the fall of Mazar on March 19 and the surrender of Jalalabad on April 23, 1992, mujahidin had negotiated the surrender of all major government garrisons. Regional councils, some of which included commanders who had formerly fought on opposite sides, formed on the basis of local ethnic and tribal ties. Many regions of the country enjoyed stability under autonomous local leaders or shuras. The fighting in Kabul, however, repeatedly threatened these local arrangements, as national leaders sought regional support or secure base areas.[22]

No one had any reason to secede from such an impotent state, and the regional states let the various Afghan commanders know that they would not countenance any formal partition of Afghanistan. In fact, however, the regionally based ethnic coalitions became autonomous, each with its own armed forces and sources of revenue, however inadequate. All major customs posts, the government's principal sources of revenue in the absence of foreign aid or natural gas exports, were under the control of regional shuras, which kept the revenue for themselves. Tens of thousands of tenuously controlled armed men occupied the streets of the capital. The government, with neither tax revenue nor foreign aid, paid its armed forces by distributing the freshly printed bank notes that continued to arrive by plane from Russia. Many groups funded the continued war through the drug trade. The government was forced to default on promised aid to the regional shuras.

The Mestiri Mission and the Taliban

In 1994 the United Nations tried once more to resolve the conflict in Afghanistan by applying a variant of the regime for conflict resolution. This endeavor resulted from the efforts of midlevel diplomats in the U.N. Department of Political Affairs and the U.N. missions of several countries. These officials had several obstacles to overcome: the United States and Russia were reluctant to involve themselves again in Afghanistan, high officials in the U.N. Secretariat were apprehensive about staking their already shaky prestige on success there, and Pakistan and other regional states did not wish to lose the initiative to others.

These diplomats managed to outmaneuver their opponents, in part by presenting a proposal to the second (economic) committee of the General Assembly. Nestled far down in a resolution of December 21, 1993, entitled "Emergency international assistance for peace, normalcy and reconstruction of war-stricken Afghanistan," was a request to the secretary general "to dispatch to Afghanistan, as soon as possible, a United Nations special mission to canvass a broad spectrum of the leaders of Afghanistan, soliciting their views on how the United Nations can best assist Afghanistan in facilitating national rapprochement and reconstruction."[23] Pursuant to this resolution, on February 12, 1994, Secretary General Boutros-Ghali named former Tunisian Foreign Minister Mahmoud Mestiri as his special envoy to Afghanistan.

According to the analysis of the U.N. officials most closely involved, the 1991–92 plan had failed in part because it had focused too much on reaching agreement among unrepresentative party leaders rather than on pressing Cordovez's strategy to mobilize broader political forces, including the substantial sector of the Afghans who still retained some loyalties to the old regime. The previous U.N. plan had also failed to address the question of how to disarm and separate the antagonists and enforce an agreement.

In line with this analysis, the U.N. special mission met with a wider range of Afghan personalities during its first visit to the region than had any previous mission. The mission virtually created a national public space that had long been absent from Afghan politics. Between March 27 and April 29 the mission traveled to eight cities and towns in Afghanistan, the Pakistani refugee centers of Peshawar and Quetta, Tehran, Riyadh, Jeddah (headquarters of the Organization of the Islamic Conference), Moscow, Ankara, and Rome (the exile home of Zahir Shah). In many places visited by the mission, hundreds or even thousands of Afghans turned out to see it and demand that the United Nations return to Afghanistan and remain involved there. The mission received over three hundred peace proposals, letters, and requests.[24]

These proposals revealed that the expectations of the people of Afghanistan had converged on something like the international regime for conflict resolution. Common themes included an end to the foreign involvement that Afghans claimed was fueling the war; a U.N.-monitored cease-fire; a neutral security or peacekeeping force; a transitional period leading to elections; and the disarming of the population and the principal belligerents. Elections might be preceded by a meeting of a Loya Jirga. Neither Afghans nor potential troop-contributing states favored an international peacekeeping force in Afghanistan. Instead, a neutral Afghan force was envisioned, perhaps recruited from regional shuras, to control security in Kabul.

Mestiri returned to the region from July 30 to September 7. The conclusions of the previous mission encouraged Afghans to step forward to put further pressure on the leaders to make peace. On August 11, for instance, nine hundred tribal elders claiming to represent one million refugees in Pakistan released a petition for peace through the offices of the U.N. High Commissioner for Refugees in Islamabad.[25]

The main protagonists of the civil war tried to use the U.N. mission to reinforce their position. By this time ten parties were involved in the maneuverings, including the seven Sunni parties, the two Shia parties, and Dostum's National Islamic Movement. On the side of "President" Rabbani and Jamiat was Sayyaf. Hikmatyar had organized a Coordination Council that grouped his party with Dostum, the remnants of Mujaddidi's followers, and the Iranian-supported Shia party, Hizb-i Wahdat. The three remaining Sunni parties (Harakat-i Inqilab of Muhammadi, Hizb-i Islami of Khalis, and Gailani's NIFA) and Muhsini's Harakat-i Islami, the Shia party independent of Iran, were considered neutral.

Ismail Khan, the leader of the Herat shura and a member of Jamiat, convened a council in Herat during July 20–25. Some moderates from the old regime who were working with the United Nations attended, but Rabbani reiterated his refusal to permit "communists" such as Dostum to attend, and Hikmatyar was not willing to attend a meeting in an area under Jamiat control. Mestiri worked with the "neutrals" and others all through August and early September but could not obtain agreement on the form of a transition. On September 7 the U.N. secretary general personally visited Islamabad, where he issued a statement noting "with regret that the efforts to convene a joint meeting of the warring factions and leaders of the neutral parties were not successful."[26]

Three weeks later, Mestiri returned to the area. Because the party leaders had once again failed to reach agreement on the terms demanded by the Afghan people, Mestiri now openly and explicitly allied his mission with a group of independent Afghans from the old regime, including a close adviser and relative of Zahir Shah and several prominent individuals and officials from the period of New Democracy.[27] On September 29, Mestiri opened a meeting of a forty-member Afghan "advisory council" in Quetta. The council, which remained in session until October 17, proposed that Rabbani hand over power to an authoritative council that would oversee disarmament of the belligerents and prepare for a Loya Jirga to decide on the future of the country. A neutral security force would take control of Kabul, though it was unclear how this force would be recruited and who would pay for it. The notion of setting up local rather than international peace-keeping forces was an innovation in U.N. conflict resolution and peacekeeping, but organizing and financing such a force posed a new set of problems. Rabbani, Hikmatyar, and other Afghan leaders accepted the proposal in principle (which still left plenty of room for evasion), and it was endorsed by the United Nations Security Council on November 30.[28]

While Mestiri and his team developed their plan, however, both the interests of regional states and the alienation of Afghan public opinion from all the existing political leadership found a new and unexpected form of expression in the sudden appearance of a new armed movement. The appearance of the Taliban — literally religious students — may have owed as much to changes in Pakistan as in Afghanistan.

In October 1993, Benazir Bhutto was once again elected prime minister of Pakistan. She appointed Gen. Naseerullah Khan Babar as interior minister. Babar, a Pashtun military man and PPP loyalist, had served both Bhutto and her father as principal adviser on Afghanistan. In the new government he enjoyed the confidence of both the prime minister and the army and thus occupied a unique position of power. Upon assuming office, Bhutto and Babar presumably found plans for the January 1994 Kabul coup already well advanced and acquiesced in it in hopes that it would stabilize Afghanistan. When it failed, Babar, it appears, began to move Pakistan away from its reliance on Hikmatyar as an agent of Pakistan's influence, a policy that he had begun in 1974 as Zulfiqar Ali Bhutto's governor of the NWFP.

Since the fall of 1991, when the USSR disintegrated, moderates in the Pakistani foreign policy establishment, led by then Minister of State for Economic Affairs Sardar Asif Ali, argued that the focus of Pakistan's foreign policy on its northwest borders should be opening trade with the new states of Central Asia, not an Islamic campaign.[29] Sardar Asif became Benazir Bhutto's minister of foreign affairs in 1993, and General Babar appears to have adopted his policy.

Babar is reported to have argued that Afghanistan would not be a stable or united country for a long time, and that Pakistan could not afford to wait to expand links to Central Asia. Rather than rely on the dubious claims of Hikmatyar that he would take over Kabul and stabilize Afghanistan, Pakistan should deal directly with whatever powers existed on the ground to facilitate the development of overland trade with Central Asia. If the route from Peshawar through Kabul and the Salang Highway to Tashkent was blocked by the war in Kabul, Pakistan should seek to open the western route, from Quetta through Qandahar and Herat to Turkmenistan (see map, pp. xii–xiii).

In June 1994, Bhutto's cabinet decided to proceed with building rail and road links to Central Asia. On September 14, Babar announced that the following week he would travel to Central Asia via Qandahar and Herat to negotiate the transit of a Pakistani convoy that would leave in mid-October. The convoy would be organized by the National Logistics Cell, the same military transport unit that had been in charge of supplying the mujahidin with weapons. A representative of the railway department would accompany Babar to examine the feasibility of constructing a rail line along the route. The World Bank had promised $1.5 million for such a feasibility study.[30]

The convoy was delayed until Benazir Bhutto personally made the final arrangements. While attending independence day celebrations in Turkmenistan on October 25, Bhutto reached agreements with both Ismail Khan and Abdul Rashid Dostum, heads of the shuras in Herat and Mazar-i Sharif, who controlled Afghanistan's border with Turkmenistan and Uzbekistan. Four days later thirty trucks laden with food, clothes, and medical supplies left Quetta, reportedly escorted by Colonel Imam, one of the ISI officers most prominent in Pakistan's Afghanistan policy. Soon after crossing into Afghanistan, on November 1, the convoy was stopped by Afghan tribesmen who had long exacted tolls from travelers and had served Najibullah as a militia in the area.[31] By November 5 the convoy had been freed and sent on its way by a new group — Taliban apparently comprising both Afghan refugees and Pakistani Pashtuns, who had streamed across the border armed with new weapons. After a quick battle the Taliban dispersed the tribesmen and quickly swept into Qandahar city, where with little resistance they captured the two main strategic targets, the airport and the governor's residence.[32]

The students quickly gained popular support by imposing order on Qandahar. The shura that had assumed control of the city and province after the fall of Najibullah had disintegrated, and different parts of the city were held by different commanders, though there was far less fighting than in Kabul. The state of security in Qandahar may be inferred from the fact that the main Hizb-i Islami commander there had been unable to attend the United Nations' advisory council meeting in Quetta because thirty-one of his relatives had recently been killed by a "crazed heroin addict" at a wedding party.[33]

The core leadership of the Taliban movement consisted partly of traditional, privately educated ulama — Islamic scholars — from the southern Pashtun tribes and partly of students studying in traditional Sunni madrasas in Pakistani Baluchistan. Some of these ulama had been commanders in the jihad but had become alienated from the party leaderships. Most of the madrasas where they recruited student followers were affiliated with the Jamiat-ul-Ulema-i Islam in Pakistan. This party, divided into two factions, was virulently opposed to the Islamist radical Jamaat-i Islami and had intermittently allied itself with the PPP. It seems likely that the Taliban received arms from Pakistan (whether Babar's Interior Ministry or the ISI) in support of their effort to free the convoy. Pakistan's policy now replaced cooperation of the ISI, the Jamaat-i Islami, Hikmatyar, and eastern Pashtuns with an axis based on Babar's Interior Ministry, the JUI, the Taliban, and the southern Pashtuns.

As the Taliban consolidated their hold over Qandahar, however, the leaders of this amorphous movement began to articulate the common feelings of people in

Afghanistan, the same feelings that had led to an outpouring of support for the Mestiri mission. They denounced the failure of the mujahidin leaders to establish security and began collecting weapons from the population. They charged the former commanders with having become thieves and even rapists. They tore down all checkpoints set up to extort money and refused all bribes at their own. They imposed a conservative interpretation of Islamic law, especially regarding women, who were to be confined and veiled even more strictly than before. As they moved out of Qandahar west to the Helmand Valley and northeast to Ghazni, they also denounced the drug trade and burned poppy fields, gaining some credibility in the eyes of the United States.

Student fronts had always been one of the components of the jihad.[34] These fronts, recruited from the private madrasas of tribal-rural Afghanistan, generally belonged to traditionalist parties (especially Muhammadi's) and expressed the common people's identification of Islam with justice, not with a radical political ideology. As one journalist noted, "If a reporter asks a Taleb what kind of rule he wants in the future, he will answer 'Islamic,' because that is the only word he knows for the rule of law Afghanistan so sadly lacks."[35] One might also note that the southern Pashtun tribes represented by the Taliban had little if any representation in the leadership of the parties that were involved in the negotiations. Few Qandaharis had attended the modern state educational system, and they were consequently absent from the principal political elites of the mujahidin, the communists, and even the old regime.[36]

The order imposed by the Taliban was in the interest of Pakistan. By mid-December, Pakistani workers were repairing the airport in Qandahar and the Qandahar-Herat highway, now under the joint control of the Taliban and Ismail Khan. Three Pakistani convoys had made the journey to Central Asia; Pakistan was planning direct flights to Qandahar and Herat; and General Babar proposed that Pakistani state-run banks and retail stores open branches in those cities.[37] The Taliban helped provide security for these activities and doubtless received Pakistani aid, but they also had plans of their own and began to march toward Kabul.[38] With both Pakistani aid and an avalanche of public opinion supporting the movement, the mujahidin parties in the southern Pashtun areas collapsed much as Najibullah's forces had in 1992. The Taliban advanced toward Kabul with little if any fighting, as most armed groups either fled or joined them. By February 1995 the Taliban had advanced into Wardak Province and encountered the forces of Gulbuddin Hikmatyar, who was using the area as a rear base for his bombardment of Kabul.

Meanwhile, negotiations related to the U.N. plan continued. Rabbani announced on December 26 that he would step down in accordance with the U.N. plan, but two days later he once again unilaterally extended his term. For the first time in years the United States weighed in directly; in mid-December Assistant

Secretary of State Robin Raphel visited Jalalabad and paid a call on Zahir Shah in Rome, signaling support for the Afghan moderates who were key to the U.N. plan. In early January the U.S. ambassador to Pakistan met Rabbani, Dostum, and Hikmatyar to push for implementation of the U.N. plan. The ostensible obstacle was the composition of the interim authoritative council, but the underlying problem was the unbridgeable antagonism between Hikmatyar and the Rabbani-Massoud forces. Hikmatyar wanted to use the agreement to force Rabbani to resign and Massoud's forces to vacate Kabul; Rabbani and Massoud would not pull out without guarantees — stronger than any the United Nations was likely to be able to give — that Hikmatyar's forces would be disarmed and demobilized to the point where they could no longer threaten the capital. As the negotiations continued, the two sides continued to pound each other with rockets, and the people of Kabul continued to die.[39]

The Taliban broke the deadlock, while posing new problems of their own. On February 10, after several days of hard fighting, they took Maydan Shahr, capital of Wardak province, from Hikmatyar's rear forces, while Massoud kept Hikmatyar's front lines pinned down. That same day, the U.N. secretary general announced from New York that the authoritative council would meet in Kabul on February 20.[40] On February 14 the Taliban occupied Hikmatyar's main base in Charasyab, Logar Province. Hikmatyar fled without a fight, leaving all of his heavy weapons and documents behind. Some reports claimed that many of his troops, who were recently recruited youth enrolled simply to feed their families, deserted or joined the Taliban. Hikmatyar retreated to the hill district of Sarobi, Kabul Province; the Jalalabad Shura offered him safe passage to Pakistan but refused to allow him to establish a base. Massoud moved his front lines south to posts deserted by Hikmatyar, then moved back slightly under an agreement negotiated with the Taliban. Except for a Shia neighborhood dominated by Hizb-i Wahdat, all of Kabul was now under Massoud's control.

The neutralization of Hikmatyar removed one of the obstacles to the U.N. plan, but the arrival of the Taliban created another. The ulama who constituted the core leadership of the movement insisted that they alone would carry out disarmament and oversee security in Kabul. They also insisted that the authoritative council must consist of "good Muslims," which cast doubt not only on some of the officials of the old regime involved but also on all representatives of the existing parties, which the Taliban denounced as criminal. Instead of party representation, they insisted on two representatives from each province, a demand that reflected the relative absence of representatives from Qandahar in the leadership of any of the existing organizations.

As in 1992, the advance on Kabul of a regional force brought ethnic loyalties into play. A takeover of Kabul by the Taliban would replace the mainly Tajik force that now controlled the capital with an all-Pashtun force. From his base in Mazar, Dostum, who had done nothing to aid his ally, Hikmatyar, threatened that if the Taliban attacked him, he would declare the independence of the Republic of South Turkistan. Indeed, while battles were taking place around Kabul, Dostum had been engaged in a series of skirmishes with pro-Massoud forces in north Afghanistan, battles that had more to do with developments in the civil war in Tajikistan than with the battle for Kabul. The Tajikistan Islamic resistance was based in the areas attacked by Dostum, and both Russia and Uzbekistan were aiding Dostum in the hope that he could help neutralize these forces.

The advance of the Taliban, however, proved short-lived. They took over the Hizb-i Wahdat positions in southern Kabul, but Massoud's forces drove them out, virtually leveling the area. Wahdat leader Abdul Ali Mazari was killed while in custody of the Taliban. This incident, as well as their shelling of Kabul during the fight with Massoud and their military defeat, deprived the Taliban of their air of purity and invincibility. Massoud drove them out of rocketing distance of Kabul, consolidating his hold over the capital. He was reportedly strengthened by aid from Iran, which now assisted whoever was fighting the Taliban. The strength of the government removed the pressure that might have led Rabbani to hand over power to an interim council. If the new military balance proved stable, negotiations among the major power centers might begin, but neighboring states might also step in once again to destabilize the country. No cooperative agreement yet regulated Afghanistan's anarchy.

From Buffer State to Failed State

According to the media-image folklore of the Post–Cold War global village, the end of global strategic conflict has uncovered long-simmering hatreds. On those rare occasions when a Western imagemonger wanders far enough off the information superhighway to point a camera along the pitted roads and dusty paths of Afghanistan, turbaned "fundamentalist tribesmen" with automatic rifles and grenade launchers offer a fitting symbol of ancient hatreds revived with modern destructiveness.

But Afghanistan has not reverted to premodern domestic politics. The failed state of Afghanistan, which has proved "utterly incapable of sustaining itself as a member of the international community," is the product of that very community.[41] International cooperation between imperial powers created the buffer state of Afghanistan. Foreign aid enabled a fractious dynasty to maintain its precarious rule over a territory demarcated by Britain and Russia. The breakdown of cooperation between hegemonic powers during the endgame of the Cold War turned that buffer state into an arena of regional conflict. New elites created by the foreign aid–funded schools and bureaucracy used international alliances to build armed organizations linked to different ethnic groups and regions of the country. These elites displaced those who had both ruled the buffer state and created institutions of Afghan nationhood. The Geneva negotiations tried to reinstate cooperation but foundered on the impossibility of defining reciprocity in a violent, ideological conflict. The dissolution of one superpower led to a precipitous disengagement by the other and left the guerrilla organizations armed and in the field without global sponsors. In 1991–92 the United Nations, with U.S. and Soviet/Russian verbal support, failed to create an interim government from the leaders of those organizations. The regional states that supported the combatants had not evolved a cooperative agreement on the role of Afghanistan. They regulated their interstate dealings through the cooperative rules of diplomacy, but the conflict among the contending groups they backed in Afghanistan obeyed only the rules of anarchy. What failed in Afghanistan was not just the Afghan state, but the international system that had first sustained and then undermined its rulers. The independent action of a few U.N. officials and the Afghans who turned out to support their effort could not reverse these harsh realities.

Was the breakdown of cooperation an inevitable result of vast historic change or might it have been averted? Some argue that the anarchy in Afghanistan resulted from mistakes in or sabotage of the peace plan. Some regret that the United Nations acquiesced to U.S. and Pakistani pressure to force Najibullah from power prematurely, creating a power vacuum before an alternative was prepared to fill it. Others blame the attempt by the United States and the United Nations to sideline Hikmatyar, which inevitably provoked confrontation. But if the United States and Pakistan had not initially aided Hikmatyar and other such party leaders, this problem might not have arisen, and Afghan nationalist forces might have reasserted control as in the past. If the Soviet Union had not supported the PDPA and invaded Afghanistan, the United States might not have devoted such resources to building up an Islamist resistance. If Pakistan had not denied the right of self-determination to Pashtunistan, Afghanistan's rulers might not have turned to the USSR. If Afghan rulers had followed Islam rather than nationalism, they might not have provoked the nationalist conflict with Pakistan that pushed Afghanistan into the hands of the Soviets. If the British, pursuing divide-and-rule colonialist tactics, had not separated the tribal territories from Afghanistan, the Pashtunistan conflict might never have arisen. And so on, back to Genghis Khan and beyond. Such arguments lead everywhere and nowhere. In strategic interactions, causality at any moment ultimately lies in the structure of interests and capabilities left by the history that has resulted from a continuous series of such moments, none of which enjoys a privileged place. And these historical legacies (or opportunity sets) often leave all too little room for escape from conflict.

The main task of the scholar is to elucidate these legacies, but even when the weight of argument seems to crush out hope, we can also try to discern those margins for action that might avert the worst. Two seemingly unreal hopes live on in the discourse of both the Afghans and the international community: the hope of Afghanistan as a unified state with a common past and a common future, and the hope of resolving conflict through negotiations and even, perhaps, elections. The absence of social and material resources to translate these discourses into institutions produces the anarchy that is Afghanistan today. The social ecology of this mountain land still produces two tendencies noted by Elphinstone: a stubborn republicanism at the grassroots and a "principle of repulsion and disunion, too strong to be overcome, except by such a force as, while it united the whole into one solid body, would crush and obliterate the features of every one of the parts."[42]

With automatic weapons distributed among all social networks of the country, no power today can crush the parts of Afghanistan, molding it into a state by conquest. In the past such conquest relied on international support to assure a preponderance of force, but the breakdown of international cooperation in Afghanistan has made the country unconquerable.

Can Afghanistan instead be reconstructed through negotiation among representatives of its various "republican" segments? In some regions of Afghanistan, representative shuras have brought civil peace and collected weapons. In Herat, Panjsher, Ghazni, Qandahar, and Jalalabad most people go about their business in peace under weak but representative administrations that are barely linked to the central state. Left to themselves, these shuras might find a way to summon a national assembly, whether called a Loya Jirga or a shura, to resolve the problems of the country. According to the nationalist myth, this is what Afghans have always done, and there are times to mobilize myths rather than debunk them. As the combatants come to realize what the Soviets acknowledged in the mid-1980s — that there is no military solution to the conflict — such ideas are circulating again. Even when leaders put them forward cynically, they can create political processes that take on a life of their own.

The lessons not only of Afghanistan but of Angola, Cambodia, Nicaragua, and other conflicts show that some preconditions must be met before a national assembly can make enforceable, legitimate decisions. The breakdown of agreements in both Angola and Afghanistan argues that disarming contending militias, or at least depriving them of heavy weapons, must precede national elections or power sharing. Such disarmament has already occurred in some regions, and some of the parties have proposed plans for turning over heavy weapons to a third force as components of a national agreement. Subordinating armed forces to an international peacekeeping force or subjecting them to intrusive monitoring — the Cambodian and Nicaraguan models, respectively — may also be effective, but seem even less likely than disarmament in the Afghan context.

The main lesson is that resolution of conflicts in states that have been failed by the international community requires a sustained cooperative effort by that community. But the region around Afghanistan is itself going through the turmoil of revolution and state building. Iran, Pakistan, Uzbekistan, Tajikistan — all are to different degrees insecure states, warily eyeing each other. Any power shift in Afghanistan disquiets some and pleases others. The resulting security dilemmas render extraordinarily difficult the construction of a demarcated domestic political arena in Afghanistan, let alone a stable one. The continued lack of effective engagement by the major powers that provided aid and weapons makes such agreement even more difficult. Skilled and energetic mediation by an envoy of the U.N. secretary general is necessary but probably inadequate by itself.

If the international community seriously wants to rebuild Afghanistan, it must start with a framework for regional cooperation. Intelligence and political action must combine to shut down the sources of money and fuel for the combatants. On the other hand, a more generous program of aid for reconstructing the country is necessary to give the combatants incentives to cooperate, to offer the fighters an alternative livelihood. Some form of peacekeeping to oversee disarmament might also be required.

Just naming the obstacles provides a reminder that the United States and others have let the bleeding wound become "infected," in Haji Mahmud Zamin's words — in large part because no one wants to pay the cost of the uncertain cure. But if the United States and its allies won the Cold War, no ally paid more for this goal than the people of Afghanistan. The maneuvers of party leaders may inspire cynicism or repulsion, but millions of unknown people sacrificed their homes, their land, their cattle, their health, their families, and their lives, with barely a hope of success or reward, at least in this world. Contemplating the "victory" whose benefits Afghans cannot share, I recall the lines of Mirza Asadullah Khan, whose pen name, Ghalib, means "the victor":

> The peoples became part of the faith but were erased.
> So if the Victor is weeping, O people of the world,
> Only look at these cities, that have turned to desolation.[43]

Appendix A
Financing of Government Expenditure, 1952–88

Expenditure

Sources of Financing

Year	Total (millions of afghanis)	Ordinary (%)	Development (%)	Domestic Revenue, Excluding Gas (%)	Sales of Natural Gas (%)	Foreign Aid (%)	(Rentier Income) (%)	Domestic Borrowing (%)
1952	830	80	21	74	0	18	18	8
1953	838	80	21	93	0	7	7	0
1954	1,030	80	20	94	0	6	6	1
1955	1,260	74	26	102	0	9	9	-11
1956	1,291	71	30	89	0	8	8	3
1957[a]	740	71	29	113	0	30	30	-43
1958[b]	2,627	38	62	51	0	52	52	-4
1959[b]	3,228	39	61	48	0	53	53	0
1960[b]	4,177	33	67	38	0	53	53	9
1961[b]	5,805	27	73	36	0	50	50	14
1962[c]	3,221	27	73	22	0	60	60	18
1962	6,440	29	71	33	0	51	51	17
1963	7,079	34	66	38	0	49	49	14
1964	7,348	35	65	42	0	49	49	10
1965	8,107	36	64	49	0	52	52	-1
1966	8,504	40	60	50	0	50	50	-1
1967	8,109	45	55	51	1	41	42	7
1968	8,333	51	49	49	5	39	45	7
1969	8,642	55	45	54	5	29	34	13
1970	8,130	63	37	61	9	23	32	7

Year							
1971	8,964	61	39	59	7	28	34	8
1972	10,298	55	45	53	7	37	44	4
1973[d]	11,318	58	42	55	8	31	38	7
1975	16,187	60	40	63	12	31	42	4
1976	19,594	57	43	62	10	29	39	−1
1977	24,326	49	51	53	8	34	42	4
1978	26,397	47	53	54	9	34	43	4
1979	30,173	56	44	40	13	36	48	12
1980	31,692	62	38	50	33	28	61	−11
1981	40,751	66	34	40	34	26	59	1
1982	42,112	69	31	37	34	28	62	0
1986	88,700	74	26	31	17	29	46	23
1988	129,900	84	16	24	6	26	32	44

Sources: Data from Maxwell J. Fry, *The Afghan Economy: Money, Finance, and the Critical Constraints to Economic Development* (Leiden: E. J. Brill, 1974), 158–59, 170–71; Democratic Republic of Afghanistan (DRA), *Statistical Information of Afghanistan, 1975–1978* (Kabul: Central Statistics Office, 1979); DRA, *Statistical Year Book (SYB) 1358: (March 1979–March 1980)* (Kabul: Central Statistics Office, 1981); DRA, *SYB 1359: March 1980–March 1981* (Kabul: Central Statistics Office, 1982); DRA, *SYB 1360: March 1981–March 1982* (Kabul: Central Statistics Office, 1983); DRA, *SYB 1361: March 1982–March 1983* (Kabul: Central Statistics Office, 1986); Republic of Afghanistan, "Afghanistan 1990," Country Presentation at the Second United Nations Conference on the Least Developed Countries (Geneva: mimeo, April 1990).

Note: Government expenditure equals ordinary plus development expenditure. Foreign aid includes both commodity assistance and project aid, loans, and grants. Rentier income is the sum of foreign aid and sales of natural gas. Domestic borrowing is a residual which does not correspond to figures in monetary surveys. Except as noted, years are Afghan (Islamic solar) years beginning in the given Common Era year. No data available for some years.

[a]First half of 1336.

[b]Common Era years.

[c]Second half of 1340.

[d]Estimate; final figures not available.

Appendix B
Political Actors in Afghanistan, 1973–95

Contemporary political actors who are mentioned in the text are briefly identified here to enable a reader to associate names with major organizations or events.

Transliterating Pashto, Persian, and Arabic names into English is difficult; alphabetizing them satisfactorily is impossible. Many of the actors listed here do not have personal and family names in the Western (or east Asian) sense. I have alphabetized by family name, where such can be said to exist, including cases where a pen-name or nom de guerre (*takhallus*) has become accepted as a family name (Karmal, Massoud, Majrooh). I do not treat "Muhammad" as a principal name when it is conjoined with another. All compounds with "'Abdul" (or 'Abd al-) are treated as one name ('Abdul Rahman, for example, is not presented as Rahman, 'Abdul). If you cannot find someone under one name, try another. The ayn (') and hamza (') are included here where appropriate, but in keeping with standard practice in English-language texts, those diacritics are omitted in the text of the book.

'Abdul Rahman, Akhtar. Pakistani general, intimate of Zia. Director general of ISI, 1977–85. Chairman of Joint Chiefs of Staff committee, 1985–88. Architect with Zia of Pakistan's Afghanistan policy. Died with Zia in airplane explosion, August 17, 1988.

'Abdul Wakil. Kabuli Persian-speaker, second cousin of Babrak Karmal. Foreign minister, 1986–92. Secretly negotiated with Massoud after Najibullah's resignation.

'Abdul Wali. Cousin, son-in-law, and close adviser of Zahir Shah. General, commander of Central Forces in 1973. Imprisoned by Daoud, 1973–76, then joined Zahir Shah in Rome.

Ahmad, Qazi Hussain. Leader (amir) of Jama'at-i Islami of Pakistan.

Amin, Hafizullah. Kharruti Pashtun from Paghman, Kabul Province. Attended Columbia University. Headmaster of teacher's training school, Kabul. Strongman of Khalq. Deputy prime minister of DRA, April 1978. Prime minister, April 1979. President of DRA and secretary general of PDPA after he had Taraki assassinated in September 1979. Killed by KGB special forces, December 27, 1979.

Andropov, Yuri. General secretary, Communist Party of the USSR, 1982–83. Promoted from head of KGB. Began process of extricating Soviet troops from Afghanistan, but soon became incapacitated and died.

Atsak, Juma. Achakzai Pashtun from Farah. Parchami allied with Najibullah. Reportedly the favorite Afghan general of Gen. Valentin Varennikov, commander of Soviet ground forces. Appointed commander of northern zone, Mazar-i Sharif, 1988. Conflict with Dostum contributed to mutiny of northern militias, 1992.

Babar, Naseerullah Khan. Pakistani Pashtun general. Adviser on Afghanistan to Prime Ministers Zulfiqar Ali Bhutto and Benazir Bhutto. Minister of the interior after October 1993. Reported to be major supporter of Afghan Taliban movement.

Baker, James. Secretary of state, United States, 1989–93.

Baryalai, Mahmud. Half-brother of Babrak Karmal, son-in-law of Anahita Ratibzad. Educated in USSR. Parchami, PDPA Central Committee member after 1980, deputy prime minister, June 1989, fired, June 1991, when Karmal returned from Moscow. Sent troops to Kabul airport to block Najibullah's exit, April 1992.

Beg, Mirza Aslam. Pakistan chief of army staff, 1988–90.

Bessmertnykh, Alexandr. Soviet ambassador to United States in 1990. Negotiated with Kimmitt over transitional arrangement in Afghanistan.

Bhutto, Benazir. Daughter of Zulfikar Ali Bhutto. Leader of Pakistan People's Party, 1985–present. Prime minister of Pakistan, 1988–90, 1993–present.

Boutros-Ghali, Boutros. United Nations secretary general, 1992–present. Formerly minister of state for foreign affairs, Egypt.

Brezhnev, Leonid. General secretary of the CPSU at the time of the Soviet invasion of Afghanistan. Died, 1982.

Brzezinski, Zbigniew. National security adviser to President Carter, 1977–81. Formerly professor of political science, Columbia University.

Bush, George. President of the United States, 1989–93.

Carter, Jimmy. President of the United States, 1977–81.

Casey, William. Director of central intelligence, U.S. government, 1981–86.

Chernenko, Konstantin. General secretary of Communist Party of USSR, 1983–85. Conservative who presided over escalation of war in Afghanistan.

Cordovez, Diego. United Nations under secretary general for special political affairs and personal representative of the secretary general for Afghanistan, 1982–88. Chief mediator in Geneva negotiations. Left United Nations to become foreign minister of Ecuador, August 1988.

Daoud, Muhammad. Cousin of Zahir Shah. Prime minister of Afghanistan, 1953–63. Presided over foreign aid–funded growth of Afghan state. Overthrew Zahir Shah in a coup, July 1973, founded Republic of Afghanistan. President, 1973–78. Killed in coup d'état, April 27, 1978.

Dost, Shah Muhammad. Minister of foreign affairs of DRA, 1980–86.

Dostum, Abdul Rashid. Uzbek from Jauzjan. Organized militia in north Afghanistan that developed into 53rd Division. Najibullah's most important militia commander. Mutinied, January 1992, founded National Islamic Movement of Afghanistan. Principal warlord of north after April 1992, based in Mazar-i Sharif. After mutiny allied with northern mujahidin. Allied with Hikmatyar, January 1994.

Durrani, Asad. Pakistani general, director general of ISI, 1990–91.

Ermacora, Felix. Austrian jurist. Special rapporteur on Afghanistan, United Nations Commission on Human Rights, 1984–1995. Died, 1995, of disease contracted on a mission to Afghanistan and Pakistan.

Es'haq, Mohammad. Tajik from Panjsher. Attended Engineering Faculty, joined Muslim Youth. Participated in Panjsher uprising (1975) under Ahmad Shah Massoud and in Panjsheri resistance. Negotiated with Soviet military on behalf of Massoud, 1983. After 1983 political officer of JIA, Peshawar, editor of *AFGHANews*. Deputy minister of civil aviation, 1993.

Gailani, Sayyid Ahmad. Member of family of Sayyid Abdul Qadir al-Jilani of Baghdad.

Pir (elder) of Qadiriyya Sufi order in Afghanistan, leader of NIFA. Related by marriage to major Muhammadzai lineages.

Gates, Robert. Deputy to DCI Casey, 1981–86. Director of central intelligence, 1986–89. National security adviser to President Bush, 1989–93.

Gavrilov, Stanislav. Andropov's special ambassador to Geneva talks. Promised to bring an eighteen-month withdrawal timetable to June 1983 round, but died beforehand.

Ghulam Rasul. Khalqi Pashtun. General, commander of Pul-i Charkhi prison, 1978–79. Commander of 18th Division, Balkh, 1992. Appointment as commander of Hairatan garrison led to revolt by northern militias.

Gorbachev, Mikhail S. First secretary, Communist Party of the Soviet Union, 1985–91; President of the USSR, 1986–91.

Gromyko, Andrei. Minister of foreign affairs, USSR, 1964–85.

Gul, Hamid. General, director general of ISI, 1985–89. Fired by Benazir Bhutto. Strong supporter of Jama'at-i Islami of Pakistan and of Hikmatyar in Afghanistan.

Gulabzoy, Sayyid Muhammad. Khalqi Pashtun from Paktia. General, Soviet-trained tank officer. Key figure in 1978 coup. Minister of interior, 1980–88. Exiled as ambassador to USSR, November 1988.

Haqqani, Jalaluddin. Pakistan-educated mawlawi of Jadran tribe, Paktia. HIK commander. Member of NCS. Led forces that took Khost, March 1991. Headed Gardez shura after April 1992. Appointed minister of justice in first government of the ISA.

Harrison, Selig S. Senior fellow, Carnegie Endowment for International Peace. Consistent advocate of Geneva negotiations and U.S.-Soviet compromise on Afghanistan.

Hikmatyar, Gulbuddin. Kharruti Pashtun from Imam Sahib, Kunduz. Attended Engineering Faculty, joined Muslim Youth. Responsible for student affairs on shura of Islamic movement, 1973, though then in jail for murder of Maoist student. Released, fled to Pakistan, became leader of HIH. Received largest share of aid distributed by ISI during war. Allied with Tanai and other PDPA Pashtun dissidents in March 1990. Named prime minister of ISA by Islamabad Accords, March 1993.

Hussein, Saddam. President of Iraq, invaded Kuwait in August 1990.

Isma'il Khan. Born in Shindand, Farah. Ethnic origin ambiguous, perhaps intentionally. Captain, staff officer of Herat Garrison, JIA member. Led March 1979 Herat mutiny with Capt. A'la'uddin Khan. Amir of resistance in Herat, commander of Amir Hamza division. Amir of Herat shura after April 1992.

Junejo, Mohammad Khan. Prime minister of Pakistan, 1986–88, chosen by parliament elected in nonparty elections under martial law. Dismissed by Zia for interfering with military prerogatives, including Afghanistan policy. Member of Pakistan Muslim League.

Kallu, Shamsur Rahman. Pakistani general, director general of ISI, 1989–90.

Karmal, Babrak. Kabuli Persian-speaker. Founder of PDPA, leader of Parcham. Deputy prime minister of DRA, April 1978. Exiled, July 1978, returned with Soviet troops. Secretary general of PDPA and president of Revolutionary Council, 1980–86. Exiled to USSR until June 1991. Moved to Hairatan after April 1992.

Khalis, Mawlawi Yunus. Mawlawi from Khugiani tribe (Pashtun), Nangarhar, educated in NWFP, British India. Early leader of Islamic movement. Fled to Pakistan, 1974. Leader of HIK.

Khan, Ghulam Ishaq. Pakistani civil servant, former member of Indian civil service. President of Pakistan, 1988–93.

Khan, Riaz Mohammad. Responsible for Geneva negotiations, Foreign Ministry of

Pakistan, 1982–88. Author of *Untying the Afghan Knot.* Ambassador to Kazakhstan, 1992–present.

Khan, Sahibzada Yaqub. Retired general, minister of foreign affairs of Pakistan, 1982–86, 1988–90.

Khan, Shahnawaz. A Muhammadzai settled in Pakistan. Foreign secretary through 1982. Thereafter permanent representative to the United Nations.

Khomeini, Ruhollah. Ayatollah, founding leader of the Islamic Republic of Iran. Died, 1989.

Kimmitt, Robert. Under secretary of state, 1989–91. Negotiated with Ambassador Bessmertnykh over transitional arrangement in Afghanistan, 1990.

Kishtmand, Sultan Ali. Kabuli Hazara, founding member of PDPA and Parcham. Prime minister of DRA, 1981–88, 1989–90. Resigned from Watan Party in summer 1991, protesting Pashtun domination. Badly wounded in assassination attempt soon after.

Kozyrev, Nikolai. Emissary of Gorbachev to Geneva talks on Afghanistan.

Kryuchkov, Vladimir. Chief of KGB, 1985–91. Member of coup committee, Moscow, August 1991.

Majrooh, Sayd Bahauddin. Sayyid of Kunar, son of Shamsuddin. Educated in France, Germany. Chair, Department of Philosophy, Kabul University. Author, *Izhda-yi Khudi (The Monster of Egoism),* an epic poem in Persian. Fled to Peshawar, 1980, founded *Afghan Information Centre Monthly Bulletin.* Assassinated, February 1988, after publishing results of a survey showing that Afghan refugees in Pakistan overwhelmingly preferred Zahir Shah to any of the mujahidin leaders.

Massoud, Ahmad Shah. Persian-speaker of Panjsher, raised in Kabul. Attended Polytechnic Institute, joined Muslim Youth, fled to Pakistan. Led uprising in Panjsher Valley, 1975, returned to Pakistan, joined JIA. Linked to Rabbani by marriage. After 1979 led resistance in Panjsher Valley. Negotiated truce directly with Soviets, 1983. Founded SCN, 1985. Established Islamic Army of SCN, 1988. Cooperated with Dostum in capture of Kabul, April 1992. First defense minister of ISA. Resigned but stayed in command, May 1993.

Mestiri, Mahmoud. Former minister of foreign affairs of Tunisia. Appointed special envoy to Afghanistan of the United Nations secretary general, February 12, 1994.

Muhammadi, Muhammad Nabi. Ahmadzai Pashtun of Logar. Traditionalist mawlawi, head of madrasa. Member of Parliament, New Democracy. Leader of HAR.

Muhsini, Sheikh Asif. Pashto-speaking Shi'a from Qandahar. Early Islamist leader. Leader of Harakat-i Islami. Took title *Ayatollah.* Poor relations with Iran.

Mujaddidi, Sibghatullah. Father's first cousin was last member of his family to be main pir of Naqshbandi order in Afghanistan. Leader of ANLF. President of IIGA, 1989. Acting president of ISA, April–June 1992.

Mu'min, Abdul. This linguistically improbable name is given by several sources. Parchami Tajik from north Afghanistan. Soviet-trained general. Commander of Hairatan garrison, 1992. Najibullah's attempt to remove him led to northern revolt. Close links to both Dostum and Massoud. Died (or killed), January 1994, when Dostum switched to Hikmatyar's side.

Nadiri, Sayyid Mansur. Also called the Sayyid of Kayan. Pir of Isma'ili Hazaras of north Afghanistan. Led large government militia. Allied with Dostum to bring down Najibullah, 1992. Member of council of Dostum's National Islamic Movement.

Najibullah. Ahmadzai Pashtun born in Kabul. Student leader of PDPA-Parcham at Kabul University. Exiled by Taraki, July 1978. Director general of KhAD, January 1980–

November 1985. General secretary of PDPA and president of Watan Party, May 1986–April 1992. President of RA, November 1987–April 1992. Overthrown while in the process of resigning, April 15, 1992, took refuge in U.N. office in Kabul.

Oakley, Robert. U.S. ambassador to Pakistan, 1988–91.

Pankin, Boris. minister of foreign affairs, USSR, August–December 1991.

Pérez de Cuéllar, Javier. United Nations secretary general, 1982–92.

Picco, Giandomenico. Assistant for special political affairs, U.N. Secretary General's Office, 1982–92.

al-Qaddhafy, Muammar. Leader of Libya.

Rabbani, Burhanuddin. Tajik from Badakhshan. Educated at al-Azhar, lecturer at Shari'a Faculty. Leader of shura of Islamic movement, 1974. Fled to Pakistan, where he became leader of JIA after movement split. Second acting president of ISA under Peshawar Accords, June 1992–March 1993. Acting president of ISA under Islamabad Accords, March 1993–June 1994. Extended his term unilaterally by six months, June 1994.

Rafsanjani, Hashemi. Shi'a jurist with the rank of Hojatolislam, president of Islamic Republic of Iran, 1989–present.

Reagan, Ronald. President of the United States, 1981–89.

Sa'ud, Turki al-Faisal. Saudi prince, director of al-Istakhbara al-'Ama, (General Intelligence), the intelligence agency of the Kingdom of Saudi Arabia.

Sayyaf, 'Abd al-Rabb al-Rasul. Original name Ghulam Rasul. Kharruti Pashtun from Paghman, Kabul province. Educated at al-Azhar, lecturer at Shari'a Faculty. Elected deputy leader of shura of Islamic movement, 1973. Arrested, 1975, while about to board airplane to study law at George Washington University. Survived the 1979 prison massacres because of kinship with Hafizullah Amin. Released, January 1980, came to Peshawar. Established his own organization (ITT), based on his ability to raise funds from Arabs. Known for adherence to Salafi Islam. Prime minister of IIGA, 1989. Allied with Hikmatyar, April 1992. Allied with Rabbani, January 1993.

Sevan, Benon. Armenian Cypriot U.N. official. Political officer, UNGOMAP, 1988–90; OSGAP, 1990–92. Returned to Secretariat as assistant secretary general for political affairs, August 1992.

Shahi, Agha. Foreign minister of Pakistan, 1979–82. Resigned in protest when U.S. direct dealing with Zia and General Akhtar undermined his diplomacy on Afghanistan.

Shevardnadze, Eduard. Minister of foreign affairs, USSR, 1985–90. Presided over development of New Thinking in foreign affairs. President of Republic of Georgia, 1993–present.

Shultz, George. Secretary of state of the United States, 1982–89.

Tanai, Shahnawaz. Khalqi Pashtun from Paktia. Soviet-trained general, chief of army staff, 1986–88. Minister of defense, 1988–90. Central Committee member since 1983, Politburo since 1988. Staged coup against Najibullah in March 1990. Allied with Hikmatyar, fled to Pakistan.

Taraki, Nur Muhammad. Pashtun from Ghazni. Self-educated writer. Founder and general secretary of PDPA, leader of Khalq. President of Revolutionary Council and prime minister of DRA, April 1978. Threatened that "those who plot against us in the dark will disappear in the dark." Smothered to death in his bed on orders of Hafizullah Amin, September 17, 1979.

Tomsen, Peter. U.S. State Department special envoy to the Afghan mujahidin, 1989–92.

Vorontsov, Yuli. Deputy foreign minister, USSR, concurrently appointed as ambassador to

Afghanistan, 1988–89. Charged with negotiating an interim government with mujahidin. Permanent representative of Russia to United Nations, 1992–94, then ambassador to the United States.

Whitehead, John. Deputy secretary of state, United States, December 1985. Wrote letter to United Nations in which United States agreed to guarantee Geneva Accords if outstanding issues were settled satisfactorily.

Wilson, Charles. Member, U.S. House of Representatives (D-Texas). Strong advocate of Afghan mujahidin. Chief legislative advocate of supplying Stingers to resistance.

Ya'aqubi, Ghulam Faruq. Parchami Muhammadzai from Kabul. Trained as policeman in West Germany. Succeeded Najibullah as director general of KhAD and joined PDPA Central Committee, November 1985. Minister of state security (WAD), from January 1986. Joined Politburo, November 1986. Reportedly committed suicide in his office, April 15–16, 1992.

Yeltsin, Boris. President of Russian Federation, 1990–present.

Zahir Shah, Muhammad. Son of Muhammad Nadir Shah. King of Afghanistan, 1933–73. Educated in France. Called for Loya Jirga, 1983, and several times since. Met with diplomats from United Nations, United States, USSR, Pakistan, India, in effort to find political solution. Offered to take any role desired by Afghan nation, but ruled out restoring monarchy. Lives in Rome.

Zia ul-Haq, Mohammad. General, chief of army staff, Pakistan, appointed by Zulfikar Ali Bhutto, 1974. Staged coup, July 1977, became chief martial law administrator. Executed Bhutto, April 1979. Ended martial law, proclaimed himself president, December 1985. Died, August 17, 1988, in an explosion on a military aircraft.

Notes

1. The Failure of International Conflict Resolution

1. *New York Times,* February 9, 1988. U.S. government officials at first debunked the notion of a new Soviet approach (United States Central Intelligence Agency, "USSR and Regional Conflicts").

2. Definition of *regime* from Krasner, "Structural Causes and Regime Consequences," 1.

3. Helman and Ratner, "Saving Failed States," 3.

4. Haji Mahmud Zamin, interviewed by Tim Weiner of the *New York Times,* Asadabad, Kunar Province, Afghanistan, September 1993. Personal communication from Weiner, June 30, 1994.

5. For estimates of casualties based on demographic surveys, see Sliwinski, "Decimation of Afghanistan"; for a conservative revision, see Khalidi, "Demographic Consequences of War." Refugee figures are very loose approximations based on estimates by the United Nations High Commission for Refugees in conjunction with the governments of Pakistan and Iran. An incomplete census begun in 1979 estimated Afghanistan's population at 15.5 million. The 1993 population was estimated at about 16.5 million (Central Intelligence Agency, *World Factbook, 1994,* accessed via Internet courtesy of the Libraries of the University of Missouri-St. Louis).

6. Kolodziej, "Cold War as Cooperation"; Kremenyuk, "Cold War as Cooperation"; Garthoff, *Détente and Confrontation.*

7. *Washington Post,* November 15, 1992, quoting Politburo files released to the public.

8. Shultz, *Turmoil and Triumph,* 1090; Mendelson, "Internal Battles and External Wars," 356.

9. Rubin, "Fragmentation of Afghanistan."

10. *New York Times,* March 19, 1992.

11. United Nations Office for the Co-ordination of Humanitarian and Economic Assistance Programmes relating to Afghanistan (UNOCA), "Immediate Humanitarian Needs in Afghanistan"; United Nations Department of Humanitarian Affairs, "Note on Winter Emergency Needs in Afghanistan," 2; *New York Times,* March 8, 1993.

12. "Introduction," in United States, Department of State, *Country Reports on Human Rights Practices for 1984,* 5–6; Forsythe, *Human Rights and World Politics,* 110–20; Jacoby, "Reagan Turnaround on Human Rights."

13. Brown, *With Friends Like These,* 120–22.

14. Attempts to link social structure to regime type date back to Aristotle, who linked

inequalities of wealth to tyranny. Canonical modern examples of this school of thought include Lipset, *Political Man,* and his critic, Guillermo O'Donnell, *Modernization and Bureaucratic Authoritarianism.* Pye, *Asian Power and Politics,* and Wiarda, *Corporatism and National Development,* made arguments for cultural prerequisites of democracy in Asia and Latin America, respectively.

15. The landmark in the study of the breakdown of democracy was Linz, *Breakdown of Democratic Regimes,* accompanied by a series of case studies on Europe and Latin America edited by Linz and Stepan. A similarly influential role in the study of redemocratization was played by O'Donnell and Schmitter, *Transitions from Authoritarian Rule,* and the accompanying edited volumes with Whitehead. Huntington sought a synthesis of the two schools in *Third Wave,* where he argued that social and economic "development" must reach a certain level before a society reaches the "Zone of Choice," where strategic choices can lead to the establishment and consolidation of democracy. On the role of political learning see Bermeo, "Democracy and the Lessons of Dictatorship." Many articles in this vein were published in the *Journal of Democracy,* published by the National Endowment for Democracy. The NED was established by Congress to promote the new strategy of supporting the spread of democracy, which was endorsed with slightly different emphases by both the Republican and Democratic Parties.

16. Shain and Linz, "Role of Interim Governments," 74; Shain and Linz, *Between States,* 10–14.

17. Helman and Ratner, "Saving Failed States," 17; Shain and Berat, "International Interim Government Model Revisited."

18. Shain and Berat, "International Interim Government Model Revisited," 63.

19. Berat and Shain, "Provisional Governments in Democratization," 34.

20. Helman and Ratner, "Saving Failed States."

21. Posen, "Security Dilemma and Ethnic Conflict," argues that security dilemmas produced by imperial collapse lead to competitive group mobilization, which is likely to turn violent under certain conditions.

22. This is an observation, not a figure of speech. In southern Tajikistan in May 1993, I was told by UNHCR officials that they had taken months to obtain two hundred shovels needed to clear out canals filled with debris from the civil war of the previous year. At the same time, nothing was more common than groups of men armed with Kalashnikovs riding around in cars.

23. Shain and Linz, *Between States,* 8. An earlier version omitted the word "almost" (Shain and Linz, "Role of Interim Governments," 75).

2. The International System, State Formation, and Political Conflict

1. In Putnam's model of two-level games (in "Diplomacy and Domestic Politics"), for instance, a negotiator or chief executive must both reach agreement with another state and assure domestic ratification. This model provides a metaphor for interaction only when the boundaries of states are clear not only geographically but institutionally. On formation of systems of states as prior to formation of states, see Tilly, *Capital, Coercion, and European States.* On effects of boundaries, see Kratochwil, "Systems, Boundaries, and Territoriality."

2. On the effect of state formation on "patterns of politics" see Skocpol, "Bringing the State Back In," 20–27.

3. Tilly, *Formation of National States in Western Europe,* analyzed this process.

4. Kratochwil and Ruggie, "International Organization"; Puchala and Hopkins, "International Regimes," 67–75. Lisa Anderson (personal communication, September 1994) suggested the periodization of colonialism.

5. Kratochwil, "Systems, Boundaries, and Territoriality," 40, discusses buffer states, citing Afghanistan as the classic example.

6. Jackson and Rosberg, "Why Africa's Weak States Persist," and Jackson, "Quasi-States, Dual Regimes, and Neoclassical Theory."

7. Milner, "Assumption of Anarchy."

8. The background information on Afghanistan in this chapter derives from Rubin, *Fragmentation of Afghanistan,* which in turn relied on works by numerous scholars cited there. I restrict citations here to specific facts or quotations or to assertions that did not appear in the previous book.

9. A readable, accurate account is Hopkirk, *Great Game.*

10. Ibid., 304.

11. On the general problem, see Jervis, *Perception and Misperception.* Jervis, "Cooperation under the Security Dilemma," 167, illustrates the security dilemma with one example from the Great Game—British and Russian railroad building in Persia near the Afghan border. See Hopkirk, *Great Game,* 430–46, the chapter entitled "The Railway Race to the East."

12. The first strategy label always applies to the actor from whose perspective the game is being viewed. These games are analyzed widely in the literature, and I explore them more in Chapter 4. Snyder and Diesing, *Conflict Among Nations,* use such models in the analysis of specific international crises.

13. Hopkirk, *Great Game,* 519–22. Kratochwil, "Systems, Boundaries, and Territoriality," 40, discusses the creation of the Afghan buffer state and the Wakhan corridor as an example of the cooperative formation of the state system.

14. Elphinstone, *Kingdom of Caubul* 1: 230–31.

15. Ibid., 1: 235.

16. Kipling, "The Ballad of the King's Mercy," *Complete Verse,* 243, 245. Another chorus describes the use of Uzbek troops against the Ghilzais. "The Ballad of the King's Jest," ibid., 245–48, also deals with the amir's cruelty, in the context of the continual rumors and fears of a Russian invasion of Afghanistan.

17. Arnold, *Afghanistan's Two-Party Communism,* 6, gives the founding dates of Communist Parties in other countries on the Soviet border: Korea (1925), China (1921), Mongolia (1921), Iran (1920), Turkey (1920), Romania (1921), Czechoslovakia (1921), Poland (1918), Finland (1918), and Norway (1923). Afghanistan was no "readier" for a communist movement than was Mongolia in 1921, so foreign policy considerations must have influenced the Comintern's decision.

18. Dupree, *Afghanistan,* 526–30, and Kamrany, *Peaceful Competition in Afghanistan,* are among the observers who remarked on the tacit collaboration that developed between the aid givers.

19. Bradsher, *Afghanistan and the Soviet Union,* 24–25, 29. Kakar ("Fall of the Afghan Monarchy," 212) gives higher figures of 7,000 trained in the USSR and Czechoslovakia and 600 trained in the United States.

20. Luciani, "Allocation vs. Production States," 69. Luciani suggests defining "allocation states as all those states whose revenue derives predominantly (more than 40 percent)

from oil or other foreign sources and whose expenditure is a substantial share of GDP." Afghanistan during much of this period met the first part of the definition but not the second.

21. Callaghy, *State-Society Struggle,* uses the term "cover-over strategy." This appears to be quite similar to the more standard anthropological concept of "encapsulation," as described in Tapper, "Introduction."

22. There has never been a complete census of Afghanistan, let alone a count of ethnic groups. Nor is the concept of ethnicity universally accepted as a basis for identity. Local meanings of the identities applied in the text need to be studied, not assumed. Afghans frequently deny that ethnicity means anything to them and claim that it is an external imposition; some make this argument even — or especially — when they are expounding grudges against other ethnic groups, whom they accuse of exploiting ethnicity.

23. For simplicity's sake, I am using the term *Tajik* for Sunni Persian speakers in Afghanistan. Members of this group have complained to me that they do not consider themselves Tajiks and that this identity was foisted on them by either the Soviets or the BBC. Elphinstone noted that "The name of Taujik is rather loosely used" (*Kingdom of Caubul* 1: 404), and the 180 years since his work was published do not seem to have clarified matters. Elphinstone concludes that the term "is more properly confined to those inhabitants of countries where Toorkee and Pushtoo are spoken, whose vernacular language is Persian." This is close to common usage today, but Hazaras, although they speak a type of Persian, are distinguished from Tajiks by their eastern Turkic racial type and their adherence to Shiism. Here all Sunni Persian speakers will be treated as a group, sometimes denoted as Tajik.

24. On the breakdown of détente, see Garthoff, *Détente and Confrontation;* Kratochwil, "Systems, Boundaries, and Territoriality," 47. For details and references on these events in Afghanistan, see Rubin, *Fragmentation of Afghanistan.*

25. *Khalq* (the masses) and *Parcham* (the flag) were the names of the factions' newspapers.

26. The principal work on this movement is Roy, *Islam and Resistance.*

27. Interviews with officials of the United Nations, Iran, and the USSR. See also Garthoff, *Détente and Confrontation,* 927–31; Herrmann, "Soviet Behavior in Regional Conflicts."

28. Garthoff, *Détente and Confrontation,* 928.

29. Anwar, *Tragedy of Afghanistan,* describes how Amin was killed after a failed Soviet plan (which involved feeding him drugged food and forcing him to resign while hospitalized) degenerated into something like a Keystone Cops film directed by Sergei Eisenstein.

30. On the pattern of repression, see Laber and Rubin, *"A Nation is Dying."* The cost estimate was given by the Soviet Premier Nikolai Ryzhkov in 1989 (*Far Eastern Economic Review,* July 13, 1989, pp. 16–17; see also an identical estimate in the archives of the CPSU Central Committee Politburo, quoted in *Washington Post,* November 15, 1992.

31. *New York Times,* June 24, 1989; *Washington Post,* November 16, 1992, citing Politburo documents. Republic of Afghanistan, "Afghanistan 1990," Country Presentation at the Second United Nations Conference on the Least Developed Countries, Geneva, April 1990, 5, gives the average amount of wheat supplied. The mayor of Kabul estimated in January 1989 that the city consumed 630 tons of flour per day, or about 230,000 tons per year (SWB/FE, January 28, 1989, C1). Soviet Politburo documents from 1990 give a slightly lower figure of 15,000 tons per month, or 180,000 tons per year (*Washington Post,* November 16, 1992).

32. Garthoff, *Détente and Confrontation,* 927–28.

33. Harrison, "Inside the Afghan Talks," 50. For slightly different figures see Khan, *Untying the Afghan Knot,* 351–52. On the 1984 and 1985 increases, see *Washington Post,* January 13, 1985.

3. Structures of War and Negotiation

1. On this effort, see Rubin, *Fragmentation of Afghanistan,* chapter 6.

2. Yousaf and Adkin, *Bear Trap,* 209.

3. I have not found any evidence to support the belief then voiced by critics of the U.S. effort, including Soviet officials, that the U.S. wanted to keep the Red Army tied down to prevent the Soviets from reaping the political benefits of a withdrawal. American policy-makers did not believe that the Soviets would withdraw from Afghanistan if aid to the mujahidin were stopped and hence did not believe that their aid was preventing a with-drawal. I analyze this debate more rigorously below, using a game theory model.

4. I have heard this view expressed by government officials myself. For quotations attributed to DCI William Casey and U.S. Congressman Charles Wilson (D.-Texas) see Yousaf and Adkin, *Bear Trap,* 63, 79.

5. Harrison, "Dateline Afghanistan," 177–80, was one of the few outside observers to call attention to the Jirga. See also Rubin, *Fragmentation of Afghanistan,* chapter 8. On the parties, see ibid., chapter 9.

6. Axelrod, *Evolution of Cooperation.*

7. Yousaf and Adkin, *Bear Trap,* 97–112.

8. Many of these accounts were reputed to be in the Bank of Credit and Commerce International.

9. Yousaf and Adkin, *Bear Trap,* 106.

10. Interview with logistics officer of a traditionalist-nationalist party, Khyber Agency, Pakistan, February 1989. According to a NIFA commander of Pashtuns in Kunduz, quoted in files of the Swedish Committee for Afghanistan, "In NIFA party there is no transportation cost for mujahedin. . . . Usually weapons of NIFA and Professor Mojaddedi are sold because of this transportation cost."

11. On the use of a multistate environment such as conference diplomacy or the U.N. General Assembly to promote autonomy of international organizations, see Ness and Brechin, "Bridging the Gap," 251–52.

12. On the problem of reciprocity see Keohane, "Reciprocity in International Relations," 11–12; Jervis, "Realism, Game Theory, and Cooperation," 336; Milner, "International Theories of Cooperation," 470; Gowa, "Anarchy, Egoism, and Third Images," 184. On regimes and cooperation, see Milner, "International Theories of Cooperation," 475–78

13. As quoted by Cordovez, November 21, 1985. Cordovez was describing the Soviet position, not endorsing it.

14. Khan, *Untying the Afghan Knot,* 28.

15. Garthoff, *Détente and Confrontation,* 947.

16. Khan, *Untying the Afghan Knot,* 121.

17. Ibid., 73.

18. UNGA Resolution 35/37 on the Situation in Afghanistan and Its Implications for International Peace and Security, 20 November 1980, reproduced in Khan, *Untying the Afghan Knot,* 336–37.

19. Harrison, "Inside the Afghan Talks," 39.

20. According to Khan, *Untying the Afghan Knot,* 43, Pérez de Cuellar persuaded Shahi to address the issue of "self-determination" only indirectly by including "consultations with refugees," a group that was understood to include the exiled parties. According to Harrison ("Inside the Afghan Talks," 38), "in April 1982 Cordovez persuaded the new Pakistani foreign minister, Yaqub Khan [Agha Shahi had resigned in January], to drop self-determination as an agenda item."

21. Lipson, "Why Are Some International Agreements Informal?" 498, 528–31.

22. Interview with Farouq Azam, political officer, National Islamic Front of Afghanistan (Gailani), Peshawar, November 1986.

23. Khan, *Untying the Afghan Knot,* 15; interviews with Diego Cordovez, United Nations, November 21, 1985, and April 22, 1986.

24. Interview, November 21, 1985.

25. Interview, April 22, 1986.

4. International Conflict and Cooperation

1. Keohane, *After Hegemony,* 51–52; the definition is based on Lindblom's more general definition of "policy coordination" in *Intelligence of Democracy,* 46. See the discussion of the definition in Milner, "International Theories of Cooperation," 467.

2. In addition to Snyder and Diesing, *Conflict Among Nations,* works that apply game models to the problem of international cooperation include Jervis, "Cooperation under the Security Dilemma"; Axelrod, *Evolution of Cooperation;* many works by Snidal, including "Game Theory of Cooperation," "Coordination Versus Prisoners' Dilemma," and "Relative Gains"; Lipson, "International Cooperation"; Stein, "Coordination and Collaboration"; and Wagner, "Theory of Games." On the realist argument about relative gains see Grieco, *Cooperation Among Nations.*

3. Snyder and Diesing, *Conflict among Nations,* 74–85. Putnam, "Diplomacy and Domestic Politics," 435, notes that in half of Snyder and Diesing's cases, the decision makers were not unified.

4. Allison, *Essence of Decision,* discusses the effect of bureaucratic politics on foreign policy decision making. Haas, *Saving the Mediterranean,* popularized the notion of epistemic communities in international relations; Mendelson, "Internal Battles and External Wars," modified it for application to the case of the Soviet withdrawal from Afghanistan. Jervis, *Perception and Misperception,* shows how cognitive biases systematically affect decision making through, among other things, the elaboration of enemy images. Blum, "Soviet Perceptions," discusses the various images of the United States in Moscow. Jervis summarizes many of these considerations in "Realism, Game Theory, and Cooperation."

5. This structure is similar to that used to manage cooperation among banks in international debt negotiations. See Lipson, "Bankers' Dilemmas."

6. Some in the USSR, Kabul, and Pakistan accused U.S. hard-liners of wanting to keep the Soviet Union tied down in Afghanistan. Such views, I believe, did not hold that the United States preferred continued war to a unilateral and ignominious Soviet withdrawal. They meant instead that the United States preferred war to a Geneva-like compromise, without which the Soviets would not withdraw. In other words, the argument supposed that the order of preference for the United States was SC > War > Geneva > AC (the position called *Rollback* in Table 4.1, corresponding to the game of Deadlock), whereas the Soviets'

ranking was AC > Geneva > War > SC (*Dealer* in Table 4.1, corresponding to a Prisoners' Dilemma). Such an argument in a way accused American Rollback proponents of being realists, illegitimately concerned with relative gains, instead of neorealists, who would more productively focus on absolute gains, including gains from cooperation with the USSR.

7. Snidal, "Game *Theory* of International Politics," 43.

8. Herrmann, "Soviet Behavior in Regional Conflicts," 434. Herrmann discusses only Soviet strategies, but the same analysis can be applied to the United States.

9. Jervis describes the general problem in *Perception and Misperception.* He applies it to the problem of cooperation in "Realism, Game Theory, and Cooperation," 336–39. For an application of attribution theory to Soviet-American interaction during this period, see Blum, "Soviet Perceptions."

10. Jervis analyzes the implications of this game in "Cooperation under the Security Dilemma."

11. The difference between these two strategies would be the amount of resources devoted to building up defensive military capabilities within one's borders or previous security perimeter, an item which did not figure on the Geneva agenda. See Herrmann, "Soviet Behavior in Regional Conflicts," 434.

12. On bandwagoning see Snyder, "Introduction."

13. This table analyzes the games only in terms of ranked outcomes and pure strategies. If we assign cardinal utilities to the outcomes and allow mixed strategies, a larger range of negotiations become theoretically possible. For instance, under some assumptions about cardinal utilities, the upper left-hand game (between the hard-liners of both sides) yields results in which a coordinated mixture of outcomes AC and SC is superior to War for both sides. One might interpret such a mixed strategy set as an agreement to fight while showing some degree of mutual restraint, but such analyses do not add much to our understanding. In some cases where Geneva is feasible, analysis using cardinal utilities reveals a set of possible agreements (a negotiation set) that mixes Geneva with either AC or SC, depending on which side is more belligerent. One might associate such mixtures with negotiations over the length of the timetable for troop withdrawal (the more AC or the less SC mixed with Geneva, the longer the troop withdrawal) or over the degree or timing of linkage to the troop withdrawal with ending aid to the resistance (the more AC or less SC mixed with Geneva, the sooner the end of aid and the looser the Soviet obligation to reciprocate fully). I have not found that adding the considerable degree of complexity that such analysis requires gives a proportionate benefit in additional insight.

14. Axelrod, *Evolution of Cooperation*; Oye, "Explaining Cooperation"; Axelrod and Keohane, "Achieving Cooperation"; Stein, "Coordination and Collaboration."

15. Snyder and Diesing, *Conflict Among Nations,* 245–46.

5. Progress and Stalemate

1. Interview, November 21, 1985.

2. Ibid.

3. Harrison claims that Andropov's offers created a "lost opportunity" ("Inside the Afghan Talks," 40). Riaz Mohammad Khan, a member of the Pakistani delegation at Geneva, instead refers to "the illusion of missed opportunity" (*Untying the Afghan Knot,* 118).

4. Khan, *Untying the Afghan Knot,* mentions no such commitment and claims that the

Soviets agreed later in the process only to an explicit mention of a starting date for the troop withdrawal.

5. Harrison, "Inside the Afghan Talks," 42; Cordovez gave the same account to me at our first meeting, on November 21, 1985.

6. Khan, *Untying the Afghan Knot*, 107.

7. Harrison, "Inside the Afghan Talks," 41.

8. Khan, *Untying the Afghan Knot*, 116; more generally, Lipson, "Why Are Some International Agreements Informal?"

9. Harrison, "Inside the Afghan Talks," 49.

10. Interview with Es'haq, Peshawar, November 1986.

11. Interview, November 22, 1986.

12. Interview, November 21, 1985.

13. The two available accounts of that meeting are contradictory. Harrison, "Inside the Afghan Talks," 45–46, gives an account based on Cordovez's summary of "stenographic notes" of the meeting shown him by the Soviets. Khan, *Untying the Afghan Knot*, 120–21, gives an account based on either the records of the Pakistan foreign ministry or his own notes as a participant.

On Geneva

Harrison: "Yaqub had insisted that the agreement was 'wide open.' Pakistan would not commit itself even hypothetically to an aid cutoff until the terms of the withdrawal had been negotiated."

Khan: "In a meticulously prepared presentation, Yaqub Khan began by stating Pakistan's seriousness in pursuing a political settlement. . . . He spoke of his efforts to seek the support of the other permanent members of the Security Council for the U.N. process and to explain to them the elements of a 'package deal' being forged at Geneva. . . . He then declared the major outstanding issues to be a short time frame [for troop withdrawal], guarantees, and consultations with the refugees. . . . Gromyko proceeded to reiterate the well-known Soviet view emphasizing interference from Pakistan as the basic issue . . . and stated in clear terms that the question of withdrawal of the Soviet contingent would not arise until Afghanistan felt fully secure. . . . [A] dour Gromyko firmly maintained that inclusion of withdrawal in a U.N. document was unacceptable. 'These were Soviet troops, not Afghan or Pakistani,' he said."

On the second track

Harrison: "Yaqub had also failed to acknowledge the A.B.K. understanding — requiring only a fresh face on the existing Kabul regime — but had demanded instead a new, noncommunist government as the precondition for a settlement."

Khan: "The aim of Pakistani interference, Gromyko asserted, was to influence the internal situation of Afghanistan. He dismissed such aspirations as 'unrealistic fantasies.' In response, Yaqub Khan disavowed any policy on the part of Pakistan to determine the nature of the government in Kabul, which he said was the business of the Afghans. Later in the meeting, however, he delicately made the point that a future regime in Kabul required a wide support base in the interests of peace in Afghanistan."

14. On these points see Mendelson, "Internal Battles and External Wars," 341–48.

15. On these programs see Laber and Rubin, *"A Nation is Dying,"* and Rubin, *Fragmentation of Afghanistan*, chapter 6.

16. Allan and Stahel, "Tribal Guerrilla Warfare."

17. Krakowski, "Defining Success"; interview with Krakowski, Department of Defense, May 16, 1985. Krakowski, a professor of international relations then at Yeshiva University,

worked as a special assistant to Richard Perle, the neoconservative assistant secretary of defense who had been an aide to Sen. Henry Jackson of Washington. As late as October 1988, after the Soviet withdrawal had begun, Krakowski argued that "Soviet objectives in the region include not only control of Afghanistan but the dismemberment of Pakistan as an independent state" (Krakowski, "Post-Soviet Afghanistan," 108).

18. U.N. Commission on Human Rights, "Report on the situation of human rights in Afghanistan." Jeri Laber and I wrote the first Helsinki Watch report on Afghanistan, released in November 1984, *"Tears, Blood, and Cries."* We shared our files and prepublication draft with Ermacora.

19. The latter lobbying tactic was particularly exasperating to the State Department. But the commanders may have been telling the truth. Not only were Pakistani officers skimming and selling supplies, but according to some reports arms intended for the mujahidin were diverted to Iran as the "back door" of the Iran-Contra operation. See Lifschultz, "Iran-Contra's Secret Back Door."

20. Harrison, "Inside the Afghan Talks," 50. For somewhat different figures see Khan, *Untying the Afghan Knot,* 351, 352.

21. Harrison, "Inside the Afghan Talks," 31.

22. Krakowski, "Defining Success."

23. Harrison, "Inside the Afghan Talks," 50.

24. Interview, Washington, May 16, 1985. Wilson later mounted the first Stinger fired in Afghanistan on the wall of his congressional office, next to pictures of himself with resistance commander Abdul Haq.

25. *New York Times,* April 18, 1988; interview with the late Dr. Shah Bazgar, Peshawar, November 1986.

26. Yousaf and Adkin, *Bear Trap*; *Washington Post,* July 15, 16, 1992; interview with Robert Oakley, Washington, October 1992.

27. Interview with Department of State source, May 14, 1985.

28. Interview with Department of State source, May 17, 1985.

29. The State Department official cited above said that only Sayyaf, Hikmatyar, Rabbani, and Khalis mattered politically. His office also contained the first copy I ever saw of Roy, *L'Afghanistan,* which argued that the Islamists represented the political future of Afghanistan.

30. Khan, *Untying the Afghan Knot,* 80.

31. Ibid., 159. After Rabbani met Reagan, the Arab volunteers in Chitral and Parachinar refused for several weeks to pay for Jamiat's transport.

On several occasions I was involved in trying to organize parts of the delegation's program, which led to my first brief meeting with Hikmatyar, among others. The State Department was trying to lure the alliance away from several right-wing organizations that had adopted it. In November 1986 the delegation was assaulted by members of the DRA's U.N. mission en route to a press conference in the Secretariat.

32. "US AID Humanitarian Assistance to Afghanistan." I owe thanks to Amb. Robert Oakley for supplying me with this document.

6. New Thinking and the Geneva Accords

1. Mendelson, "Internal Battles and External Wars."

2. The first interpretation has been the dominant American one, as expressed, for instance, in Shultz, *Turmoil and Triumph,* 570, 987, and Khalilzad, "Soviet-American

Cooperation in Afghanistan," 77. Harrison, "Inside the Afghan Talks," emphasizes the importance of U.N. mediation. Herrmann, "Soviet Decision to Withdraw," and Mendelson, "Internal Battles and External Wars," argue that the withdrawal was mainly the result of internal changes in the USSR.

3. *Washington Post,* April 14, 1988.

4. Interview with Cordovez, April 22, 1986.

5. Lipson, "Why Are Some International Agreements Informal?" 508–9.

6. Harrison, "Inside the Afghan Talks," 50.

7. Interview, November 21, 1985.

8. According to Mendelson, "Internal Battles and External Wars," 356, "After the summit at Reykjavik, Gorbachev and his advisers came to the conclusion that the United States would not entertain seriously the idea of new political thinking until a Soviet withdrawal from Afghanistan was complete."

9. Interview with former State Department official, November 1988.

10. Harrison, "Inside the Afghan Talks," 52.

11. Whitehead, "Afghanistan's Struggle for Freedom," 3.

12. Harrison, "Inside the Afghan Talks," 52. He quotes a CIA official as saying, "The general belief is that the settlement isn't going anywhere, so it was felt there was nothing to be lost in agreeing to guarantee." Khalilzad, who worked on Afghanistan in the Reagan administration, confirmed that the United States did not take the negotiations seriously at first ("Soviet-American Cooperation in Afghanistan," 71–72). Shultz, *Turmoil and Triumph,* 1087, quotes Shevardnadze as leveling a similar charge, which the author does not deny.

13. Quoted in interview with Najibullah in *Pravda,* translated in *Current Digest of the Soviet Press* 41, no. 50 (1989), 16–17, cited in Khan, *Untying the Afghan Knot,* 361. A Soviet expert on Afghanistan (interview, Washington, November 1989) recounted the same speech, although he placed it at a different time than did the *Pravda* article.

14. Interview with Cordovez, January 1986 (date unavailable); the same incident is described in Khan, *Untying the Afghan Knot,* 144.

15. *New York Times,* June 17, 1988. In June 1988 I discussed the contents of this letter in Moscow with a variety of Party members who were concerned with Afghanistan. According to the *Times* the letter strongly implied but did not explicitly say that the decision to send troops was a mistake, but all of my official interlocutors interpreted it in that light. Dissidents, in contrast, described the invasion as a "crime."

16. For more details see Rubin, "Next Round."

17. FBIS/SU, February 26, 1986, O-31.

18. Interview with Cordovez, April 22, 1986.

19. Interview with Cordovez, June 5, 1986.

20. U.N. General Assembly Document A/41/505, 13–14.

21. See Gorbachev, *Perestroika.*

22. Mendelson, "Internal Battles and External Wars," 356.

23. Interview with Cordovez, Islamabad, November 26, 1986.

24. UNDPI, "Press Briefing by Under-Secretary-General for Special Political Affairs," December 9, 1986.

25. *Washington Post,* November 15, 1992.

26. *Washington Post,* April 14, 1988.

27. Interview with Cordovez, November 17, 1986,

28. Interview with Cordovez, October 17, 1986.

29. I played a small personal role in the second track at this point. In discussions with Cordovez on October 17 and November 13, 1986, I said that the resistance objections to political negotiations with the PDPA in general and Najibullah in particular seemed sincere and unshakable. I nonetheless agreed to sound out various party leaders informally during my visit to Peshawar in November–December. I reported to him on these consultations in Islamabad on November 26.

30. Interview with Cordovez, May 6, 1987.

31. Khan, *Untying the Afghan Knot,* 181–82.

32. Interview with former PDPA Central Committee member, Almaty, October 8, 1992; interview with Yuri Gankovsky, Washington, April 1988. Gankovsky stated that Najibullah's goal throughout was to be an "absolute dictator with no opposition."

33. Khan, *Untying the Afghan Knot,* 190.

34. Ibid.

35. Yousaf and Adkin, *Bear Trap;* also see the accounts from various sources in National Security Archive, *Afghanistan* 1: 167–69.

36. "Statement by Robert A. Peck, Deputy Assistant Secretary of State, Bureau of Near East and South Asian Affairs before the subcommittee on Asia and Pacific Affairs, House Foreign Affairs Committee," March 5, 1987, cited in National Security Archive, *Afghanistan* 1: 167; Cordovez said in an interview on May 6, 1987, that the Pakistanis would not move until after the aid package was passed.

37. Interview with Cordovez, May 6, 1987.

38. Harrison, "Inside the Afghan Talks," 53–54; Cordovez described this proposal to me in a meeting on July 22, 1987.

39. Interview with Cordovez, July 22, 1987.

40. Harrison, "Inside the Afghan Talks," 53–54.

41. Khan, *Untying the Afghan Knot,* 231–32.

42. Cordovez used me to try to set up a back channel of communication with the mujahidin leaders at this time. He had met them only once, at the OIC summit in Kuwait the previous January. Pakistan had given what he considered to be evasive answers to his subsequent requests to meet them. At a meeting on July 22, 1987, he suggested that a request by the leaders in Peshawar to meet him would put pressure on the Pakistanis. He asked me to suggest a credible intermediary who could introduce the idea to the mujahidin leaders. I suggested Anders Fänge, head of the Swedish Committee for Afghanistan in Peshawar. Cordovez, who had a friend in the Swedish Foreign Ministry, liked the idea. Cordovez met his friend in Geneva and persuaded him to ask Fänge to raise the idea. In an article published on the opinion page of the *New York Times* on August 14 and also (without my knowledge) in the *Muslim* (Islamabad), I outlined the status of the war and the negotiations and argued that the mujahidin leaders should ask to meet Cordovez to discuss a change of government in Afghanistan in conjunction with the Geneva Accords. (A member of the Soviet U.N. mission invited me to lunch shortly thereafter to try to find out what Cordovez was doing.) Fänge showed my article to the leaders and discussed the proposition. Most of them agreed, more or less, that it was a good idea, and they agreed to present it at the next meeting of the alliance shura. But they never did: all meetings of the shura took place under the watchful eyes of the ISI.

Cordovez then proposed that I go to Pakistan to sound out the leaders. At about this time, the Geneva talks hurriedly reconvened on September 7. I already had my ticket to Pakistan when I received a call from Cordovez's office in New York saying that Fänge had leaked information about the initiative to the *Christian Science Monitor.* An article on September

9, 1987, in that newspaper reported that "U.N. special envoy Diego Cordovez has indirectly approached the [mujahidin] parties for their views, but the leaders have yet to respond." Cordovez feared Pakistan's reaction and called off my mission.

43. Harrison, "Inside the Afghan Talks," 54.

44. Shultz, *Turmoil and Triumph,* 987.

45. Ibid., 1087.

46. *Washington Post,* April 14, 1988.

47. Interview with Yuri Gankovsky, Villanova, Pa., October 31, 1992.

48. Shultz, *Turmoil and Triumph,* 1087–88. Some mujahidin supporters did not accept the possibility of a Soviet troop withdrawal even after it happened, claiming that various pro-regime militias were actually Soviet troops in disguise. See Klass, "Next Steps," 274.

49. National Security Archive, *Afghanistan* 1: 182; Khan, *Untying the Afghan Knot,* 234, 245–48.

50. Shultz, *Turmoil and Triumph,* 1087.

51. *Wall Street Journal,* December 1, 1987; *Washington Post,* December 14, 1987; *Washington Post,* April 14, 1988. For a more detailed explanation of Zia's thinking, as well as of the complex factional fighting within the government of Pakistan at the time, see Khan, *Untying the Afghan Knot,* 235–38.

52. "Press Briefing by Under-Secretary-General Cordovez," January 18, 1988.

53. Khan, *Untying the Afghan Knot,* 251–52 . The meeting did not deal with any matters of substance (interview with Cordovez, May 4, 1988).

54. *New York Times,* February 9, 1988.

55. "What Do the Afghan Refugees Think?" In my view the survey methodology was somewhat flawed, as Majrooh's field workers did not have the resources to carry out a genuine random survey of the entire refugee population. The survey did, I believe, accurately reflect the views of elders living in refugee camps. The younger generation, who would not have contradicted the elders in front of outside visitors, probably was less favorable to the old regime.

56. Khan, *Untying the Afghan Knot,* 258; *The Independent,* September 13, 1988; "Gouvernement introuvable."

57. Senate Resolution 386.

58. Interview with State Department official, Washington, May 11, 1988; Shultz, *Turmoil and Triumph,* 1087.

59. Shultz, *Turmoil and Triumph,* 1093.

60. Ibid., 1091.

61. Keohane, "Reciprocity in International Relations," 8.

62. Interview with Robert Kimmitt, Washington, D.C., June 15, 1994.

63. *Washington Post,* April 8, 14, 1988; cited in National Security Archive, *Afghanistan* 1: 186.

64. For the full texts see United Nations Press Release SG/1860, April 14, 1988. Most of the text of the four instruments was printed in the *New York Times* on April 15, 1988.

65. Instrument 1, Article 2, paragraphs 10, 12.

7. Cooperation Between the Superpowers

1. This is the central theme of Migdal, *Strong Societies and Weak States.*

2. Miller, "Explaining Great Power Cooperation."

3. Katz, "Future of Superpower Conflict Resolution," 174–75.

4. In an interview on May 4, 1988, Cordovez described the agreement as "negative implied symmetry." The Soviets would refrain from aiding Kabul but would not explicitly commit themselves to such forbearance, and the United States would reciprocate in accordance with Secretary Shultz's call for "balanced restraint." See also *New York Times,* April 15, 1988.

5. Shultz, *Turmoil and Triumph,* 1090.

6. Borovik, "Preliminary Results."

7. Milner, "International Theories of Cooperation," 482; Keohane, "Reciprocity in International Relations," 11; Gowa, "Anarchy, Egoism, and Third Images," 184; Jervis, "Realism, Game Theory, and Cooperation," 336.

8. This analysis is based on interviews with American, former Soviet, and U.N. diplomats who were involved in these negotiations.

9. In November 1988 the CIA estimated that if Soviet troops withdrew, leaving the PDPA "still in control of Kabul and the main cities, . . . the Kabul regime will collapse within six to twelve months . . . if not sooner" (United States Central Intelligence Agency, "Soviet and Resistance Objectives," 6). In February 1989 the CIA predicted: "The communist regime in Afghanistan is likely to collapse politically within three to six months, although technically regime members have enough military resources to hold the capital for up to a year" (United States Central Intelligence Agency, "Outlook for Afghanistan," 1).

10. Shultz, *Turmoil and Triumph,* 1088.

11. *New York Times,* February 26, 1989.

12. *Independent,* June 20, 1989; *Far Eastern Economic Review,* July 13, 1989. U.S. aid was also reportedly held up by a devastating fire in a Chinese factory where many of the weapons were manufactured (interview with U.S. diplomat).

13. On the struggle over institutional prerogatives in military and postmilitary regimes, see Stepan, *Rethinking Military Politics.*

14. When Brig. Mohammad Yousaf first visited Ojhri after being appointed head of the ISI's Afghanistan operations, he was shocked to observe that "just about every safety rule I had ever been taught about arms storage was being broken, and this within a densely populated area" (Yousaf and Adkins, *Bear Trap,* 28).

15. London *Telegraph,* June 6, 1988; Yousaf and Adkins, *Bear Trap,* 221.

16. Hamid Gul recounted these negotiations in an interview in *Far Eastern Economic Review,* October 15, 1992.

17. For a fuller account of this effort, see Rubin, "Next Round."

18. Khalilzad, "Soviet-American Cooperation in Afghanistan," 74.

19. UNGOMAP's mandate lapsed as of February 14, 1990, one year after the end of the Soviet withdrawal. The U.N then established a successor, the Office of the Secretary General in Afghanistan and Pakistan (OSGAP). Sevan headed OSGAP's main office in Islamabad.

20. Touval, "Why the U.N. Fails."

21. Kabul Domestic Service, October 19, 1988, in Federal Broadcast Information Service (FBIS)/Near East and South Asia (NES), October 20, 1988, 50; *New York Times,* October 19, 26, 29, 31, 1988; *Guardian,* October 20, 1988; interview with Soviet adviser to the Afghanistan Ministry of Defense, Washington, D.C., November 1989. According to the Soviet adviser, Gulabzoy had told Shevardnadze that he would never accept Najibullah's leadership. Karmal himself had already been exiled to Moscow.

22. Interviews with Pakistani, Afghan, and Soviet sources.

23. Interview in Riyadh, March 1989; Cronin, "Afghanistan After the Soviet Withdrawal."

24. *The Independent,* February 2, 1989.

25. Rubin, "Political Exiles."

26. Interview with USAID official, Peshawar, January 1989.

27. For analyses of the defeat of the mujahidin at Jalalabad see Rubin, "Fragmentation of Afghanistan"; Yousaf and Adkins, *Bear Trap.*

28. Katz, "Future of Superpower Conflict Resolution." 171; interview with Robert Kimmitt, Washington, June 15, 1994.

29. I made this case in detail in "Prepared Statement."

30. *Washington Post,* September 2, 9, 1989; *New York Times,* November 19, 1989. Other sources have confirmed these reports and added some details.

31. *Los Angeles Times,* November 19, 1989; *Far Eastern Economic Review,* December 7, 1989; *Independent,* May 28, 1990; *Independent,* August 1, 1990; interviews with U.S. and Congressional officials.

32. Regimes are one of several factors that facilitate cooperation (Milner, "International Theories of Cooperation," 475–78). Robert Kimmitt, who was under secretary of state for political affairs during most of this period, said of these negotiations, "We [U.S. and Soviet bargainers] all agreed on where we wanted to end up but disagreed on how to get there. This made the job both easier and more difficult. There was no ideological disagreement — we were arguing about fine points" (interview, Washington, D.C., June 15, 1994).

33. Lipson, "Bankers' Dilemmas."

34. On the first anniversary of the end of the Soviet withdrawal, U.N. Secretary General Pérez de Cuéllar stated, "I welcome the progress of constructive dialogue that has begun between the two guarantors. . . . It is essential to develop an international consensus in order to enable the Afghan people to develop their own national consensus. Only then shall the Afghans be able to exercise their right of self-determination" (U.N. Department of Public Information, press release, February 15, 1990).

35. Interview with Robert Kimmitt, Washington, June 15, 1994. Kimmitt's statements were only one source of the analysis in the text, for which I alone bear responsibility. On game theory and integrative bargaining, see Sebenius, "Challenging Conventional Explanations."

36. "Communique of Baker and Shevardnadze."

37. This demand came to be known as "negative symmetry plus."

38. Speech by Under-Secretary of State Robert Kimmitt, Asia Society, Washington, D.C., April 18, 1990: "A stable political settlement is not achievable so long as the Najib regime remains in power. This is not a U.S. demand; it is a statement of Afghan reality." Unpublished text of speech, 8.

39. See the rather circumspect discussion of this issue by Baker and Shevardnadze at their press conference in Irkutsk, August 2, 1990.

40. *Wall Street Journal,* September 27, 1990; *Washington Post,* October 23, 1990; Robert Kimmitt, interview, Washington, June 15, 1994.

41. Unpublished text of press conference furnished by the Department of State.

42. Babrak Karmal hinted strongly that it was Kryuchkov who came to Kabul in 1986 to inform him that he would have to leave for exile in the USSR (*The Guardian,* November 19, 1991).

43. *New York Times,* February 17, 1991; Reuters, March 5, 1991.

44. *Time,* June 24, 1991; *Washington Post,* October 1, 1991; *Far Eastern Economic*

Review, October 3, 1991; *New York Times,* May 11, 1991; *Telegraph,* October 30, 1991.

45. United Nations Department of Public Information, "Statement of the Secretary General on Afghanistan."

46. Interviews with U.N. and Iranian diplomats.

47. Communique of meeting between Foreign Minister Boris Pankin and Secretary of State James Baker, Moscow, September 13, 1991; *Washington Post,* September 14, 1991.

8. Decline of Hegemonic Control

1. *New York Times,* April 24, 1989; see also *Financial Times,* February 1, 1989, and *Le Monde,* March 19, 1989.

2. Reuters, May 25, 1989; *Independent,* May 26, 1989; *New York Times,* May 26, 1989; *Far Eastern Economic Review,* June 8, 1989.

3. Yousaf and Adkin, *Bear Trap,* 8.

4. Asia Watch, *Forgotten War,* 50.

5. On the beginnings of the Hizb-Khalq alliance, see *Financial Times,* August 7, 1989; *Independent,* August 12, 1989. On the coup, see *Washington Post,* March 17, 1990, and *Insight,* April 9, 1990, 8–18. U.S. State Department sources stated that the ISI was involved in this coup attempt "up to their necks." Pakistani diplomats have denied this to me, but I am not convinced.

6. While in Pakistan in October 1990 to observe the elections, I heard reports of CIA involvement with this effort. See *Independent,* October 2, 1990; *New York Times,* January 3, 1991. In September 1990 I also received briefings on these events from State Department officials and Afghan exiles linked to moderate mujahidin parties.

7. *New York Times,* February 17, 1991; interviews with State Department officials, March 1992.

8. Interview with officials of Ministry of Foreign Affairs of Iran, Tehran, April 1994.

9. *The Times,* June 21, 1989; *Washington Post,* July 9, 1989; *The Independent,* July, 31. 1989; Olivier Roy, personal communication.

10. I heard this often from mujahidin interlocutors — party officials excepted — in 1990.

11. Swedish Committee, *Agricultural Survey,* 38, written before the Geneva Accords went into effect, attributes the revival to the missiles.

12. Based on data in files of the Swedish Committee for Afghanistan Cash for Food Program, Peshawar. On this source see Rubin, *Fragmentation of Afghanistan,* Appendix A.

13. Roy, "La guerre comme facteur."

14. *Washington Post,* May 13, 1990. I have also conducted interviews on these subjects with a number of informants who are in a position to know the truth of what they claim.

15. "Meeting of Resistance Commanders," 9.

16. Ibid., 10.

17. I met with them during their visit. See also *Washington Times,* May 8, 1990.

18. *Washington Post,* April 1, 1991.

19. This is a prediction of the *competition* model of ethnic conflict; see Nagel and Olzak, "Ethnic Mobilization."

20. For details and sources, see Rubin, *Fragmentation of Afghanistan,* chapter 7.

21. Tilly, *Coercion, Capital, and European States,* 29, 53.

22. Interview with former member of Indian Embassy in Kabul, New York.

23. *AFGHANews* 7, no. 15 (August 1, 1991): 3; *Washington Post,* October 20, 1991.

9. From Conflict Resolution to State Disintegration

1. *Le Monde,* September 17, 1991.
2. "Situation in Afghanistan," 12.
3. Interviews with mujahidin leaders and Pakistani diplomats, New York, October 1991; Reuters (Islamabad), October 11, 1991.
4. Interview with Zahir Shah, Rome, July 31, 1991.
5. *New York Times,* March 19, 1992.
6. This was the Harakat-i Islami of Ayatullah Asif Muhsini, a largely non-Hazara (Qizilbash) party.
7. Other groups shifted alliances around the poles of Hizb and Jamiat. Sayyaf was at first in league with Hikmatyar but shifted to Jamiat after January 1993, when Hikmatyar allied with the Iranian-supported Hizb-i Wahdat. Mujaddidi, who had denounced Hikmatyar for years, joined with him after Rabbani insisted on supplanting Mujaddidi as acting president in July 1992. Other parties and shuras also vacillated between the two poles, but these alliances had little military effect, which was the only effect that mattered.
8. For a more complete analysis, see Rubin, "Fragmentation of Tajikistan." Supporters of the Tajikistan opposition who had formerly been refugees in Afghanistan stated in interviews in southern Tajikistan (January 1994) that troops of Dostum had destroyed their homes while fighting alongside the Popular Front in the Tajikistan civil war.
9. On the "Pashtun solution" see *Washington Post,* October 20, 1991. Hikmatyar reportedly wrote to Najibullah, "You and I could do something in Afghanistan." Najibullah's emissary was Manokai Mangal, hero of the defense of Jalalabad and political director of the Khalqi-dominated Ministry of the Interior. (Interview with exiled Parchami Central Committee member, Almaty, October 1992.)
10. Massoud described his underground work in Kabul in "Massood Reviews History of Victory," 6. According to several sources, after 1989 Iran worked both to unite Shia mujahidin and to establish close contacts with non-Pashtun members of the ruling party. It brokered an alliance between Dostum and Hizb-i Wahdat. Iran supposedly sought to balance the rise of Saudi and Pakistani influence among the Sunni mujahidin, especially Pashtuns. Tehran sought a special relationship with the northern, non-Pashtun, part of Afghanistan, which constituted a land bridge between Iran and the newly independent states of Uzbekistan and Tajikistan. (Interview with Afghan diplomat, New York, November 1991; "Foreign Interference Fuels War," 7.) U.N. officials interviewed in New York claimed that Najibullah shared this view. Foreign Ministry sources in Tehran (April 1994) denied any such role.
11. On the expansion of the money supply in Afghanistan under Najibullah, see Rubin, *Fragmentation of Afghanistan,* especially chapter 7.
12. This model is a straightforward application of Axelrod, *Evolution of Cooperation.*
13. In January, immediately after the aid cutoff, Najibullah instructed Gen. Juma Atsak, the Pashtun commander of the northern zone, based in Mazar-i Sharif, to replace Gen. Abdul Mumin, the Tajik commander of the border garrison, with General Rasul, a Pashtun Khalqi who was much hated for his service as commander of Pul-i Charkhi Prison under Taraki. Rasul commanded a Khalqi Division of the army in Balkh, the garrison between Hairatan and Mazar-i Sharif.
14. "Statement by the Secretary-General on Afghanistan," April 10, 1992.
15. Rabbani, whose forces seemed on the verge of taking Kabul with the support of the

northern rebels, wavered. The son of Mujaddidi, who harbored ill-concealed ambitions to serve as president of the country, suggested a mujahidin government instead.

16. According to U.N. and Afghan diplomats, the operation was coordinated by Karmal's brother, Mahmud Baryalai. Massoud claims that it was carried out by officers loyal to him ("Massood Reviews History of Victory," 6). If both stories are true, the events would assume a still more interesting character. That same night Najibullah's close associate, secret police chief Ghulam Faruq Yaaqubi, died of an apparently self-inflicted gunshot wound while sitting at his desk in the headquarters of the secret police.

17. Interviews with Parchami former Central Committee members, New York, April 1992, and Almaty, October 1992.

18. For Massoud's account, see "Massood Reviews History of Victory." During the crisis I received frequent indirect updates on Massoud's activities and thinking from his representative in Paris, Daoud Mir. Mir communicated with Peshawar, where Massoud's brother was in radio contact with the commander.

19. Interview with exiled Parchami Central Committee member, Almaty, October 1992, and State Department official, Washington, March 1993.

20. The text of the agreement was printed in English in *Dawn* (Karachi), March 8, 1993. It is identical with a faxed text supplied to me by the Afghan Mission to the United Nations. The Pakistani delegation that convinced the leaders to come to Islamabad included Hamid Gul, former director of ISI, and Qazi Hussein Ahmed, leader of Jamaat-i Islami, both prominent supporters of Hikmatyar. At this time Prime Minister Sharif of Pakistan needed the support of these political groups in his battle with the president, who dismissed him soon after.

21. Associated Press, Kabul, January 31, 1995.

22. For more details of the situations in different regions of the country, see Rubin, *Fragmentation of Afghanistan,* chapter 12.

23. U.N. General Assembly, "Emergency International Assistance," para. 4 (a).

24. U.N. General Assembly, "Progress Report." The cities visited in Afghanistan were Jalalabad, Kabul, Mazar-i Sharif, Shibirghan, Herat, Bamiyan, Qandahar, and Khost.

25. Voice of America, Islamabad, August 11, 1994.

26. U.N. Department of Public Information, "Secretary-General Urges Afghan Leaders."

27. These were Sultan Mahmud Ghazi, cousin of Zahir Shah; Sayyid Shamsuddin Majrooh, principal author of the constitution of New Democracy; Dr. Mohammad Yousof, prime minister 1963–65; Abdul Samad Hamed, deputy prime minister 1967–69; Ghulam Ali Ayeen, former Governor of Kabul; and Abdul Sattar Sirat, former member of the Supreme Court.

28. U.N. Security Council, "Security Council Welcomes"; U.N. General Assembly, "Strengthening the Coordination."

29. Rashid, *Resurgence of Central Asia,* 215–16.

30. Reuters, Islamabad, September 14, 1994.

31. The group that held up the convoy was the Achakzai clan formerly led by the late Ismatullah Muslim (Rubin, *Fragmentation of Afghanistan,* 158–59, 199, 244, 245). Some of the information on this incident is derived from a posting to usenet newsgroup soc.culture.afghanistan on November 7, 1994.

32. Reuters, Quetta, November 5, 1994.

33. Reuters, Qandahar, November 3, 1994.

34. Roy, *Islam and Resistance,* 112–18.

35. Smith, "Rebels Aren't So Scary."

36. The old regime is commonly said to have been dominated by Durranis, but these were nearly all either Muhammadzais or other aristocratic clans mainly settled in Kabul. These groups became both Persianized and Westernized and were perceived in Qandahar as insufficiently Islamic.

37. Agence France Presse, Islamabad, December 7, 1994; Reuters, Islamabad, December 11, 1994.

38. Reports relayed from Qandahar claimed that the Taliban had all new weapons and even metal detectors to aid in the disarmament of the population (post to soc.culture.afghanistan, December 13, 1994). Smith, "Rebels Aren't So Scary," says that when she met some Taliban in Qandahar in September 1994, they were already planning their march on Kabul.

39. In September and October, in addition to the usual Hizb-Jamiat clashes, a civil war broke out in the previously relatively calm Shia areas of Kabul, as the pro-Jamiat and pro-Hizb Shia parties bombarded each other.

40. U.N. Department of Public Information, "Head of Special Mission."

41. Quotation from Helman and Ratner, "Saving Failed States," 3.

42. Elphinstone, *Kingdom of Caubul* 1: 235.

43. Translation by author.

Bibliography

Adler, Emanuel, and Peter M. Haas. "Conclusion: Epistemic Communities, World Order, and the Creation of a Reflective Research Program." *International Organization* 46 (1992): 367–90.

Allan, Pierre, and Albert A. Stahel. "Tribal Guerrilla Warfare Against a Colonial Power." *Journal of Conflict Resolution* 27 (1983): 590–617.

Allison, Graham T. *Essence of Decision: Explaining the Cuban Missile Crisis.* Glenview, Ill.: Scott, Foresman, 1971.

Anwar, Raja. *The Tragedy of Afghanistan: A First-Hand Account.* Trans. Khalid Hasan. London: Verso, 1988.

Arnold, Anthony. *Afghanistan's Two-Party Communism: Parcham and Khalq.* Stanford, Calif.: Hoover Institution, 1983.

Asia Watch. *The Forgotten War: Human Rights Abuses and Violations of the Laws of War in Afghanistan Since the Soviet Withdrawal.* Washington, D.C.: Human Rights Watch, 1991.

Axelrod, Robert. *The Evolution of Cooperation.* New York: Basic, 1984.

Axelrod, Robert, and Robert O. Keohane. "Achieving Cooperation under Anarchy: Strategies and Institutions." In *Cooperation under Anarchy,* ed. Oye, 226–54.

Barry, Michael. "La deuxième mort de l'Afghanistan." *Politique Internationale* (1993): 279–312.

Berat, Lynn, and Yossi Shain. "Provisional Governments in Democratization: The 'International Interim Government' Model and the Case of Namibia." *Coexistence* 29 (1992): 31–46.

Bermeo, Nancy. "Democracy and the Lessons of Dictatorship." *Comparative Politics* 24 (1992): 273–91.

Blum, Douglas. "Soviet Perceptions of American Foreign Policy after Afghanistan." In *Dominoes and Bandwagons,* ed. Jervis and Snyder, 190–219.

Borovik, Artem. "Afghanistan: Preliminary Results — Ogonyok Correspondent Artem Borovik Interviews Maj. Gen. Kim Tsagolov, Doctor of Philosophy and Chairman of the Department of Marxism-Leninism at the M. V. Frunze Military Academy." *Ogonyok* (July 23–30, 1988): 25–27.

Bradsher, Henry S. *Afghanistan and the Soviet Union.* Durham: Duke University Press, 1983.

Brown, Cynthia, ed. *With Friends Like These: The Americas Watch Report on Human Rights and U.S. Policy in Latin America.* New York: Pantheon, 1985.

Callaghy, Thomas M. *The State-Society Struggle: Zaire in Comparative Perspective.* New York: Columbia University Press, 1984.

"Communique of U.S. Secretary of State James Baker and Soviet Foreign Minister Eduard Shevardnadze," Jackson Hole, Wyo., September 1989.

Cronin, Richard. "Afghanistan after the Soviet Withdrawal: Contenders for Power." Washington, D.C.: Congressional Research Service, May 1989.

Dupree, Louis. *Afghanistan.* Princeton: Princeton University Press, 1980. [First ed. 1973.]

Elphinstone, Montstuart. *An Account of the Kingdom of Caubul and its Dependencies in Persia, Tartary, and India . . .* Karachi: Oxford University Press, 1972. [First ed. 1815.]

"Foreign Interference Fuels War in Afghanistan," *AFGHANews* 10 (May 1994): 6–7.

Forsythe, David P. *Human Rights and World Politics.* Lincoln: University of Nebraska Press, 1989. [First ed. 1983.]

Fukuyama, Francis. *The End of History and the Last Man.* New York: Basic, 1990.

Garthoff, Raymond L. *Détente and Confrontation: U.S.-Soviet Relations from Nixon to Reagan.* Washington, D.C.: Brookings Institution, 1985.

Gorbachev, Mikhail. *Perestroika: New Thinking for Our Country and the World.* New York: Harper and Row, 1987.

"Un gouvernement introuvable." *Défis Afghans* (February–June 1988): 14–15.

Gowa, Joanne. "Anarchy, Egoism, and Third Images: *The Evolution of Cooperation* and International Relations." *International Organization* 40 (1986): 167–86.

Grieco, Joseph. *Cooperation Among Nations: Europe, America, and Non-Tariff Barriers to Trade.* Ithaca: Cornell University Press, 1990.

Haas, Peter M. *Saving the Mediterranean: The Politics of International Environmental Cooperation.* New York: Columbia University Press, 1990.

———. "Introduction: Epistemic Communities and International Policy Coordination." *International Organization* 46 (1992): 1–35.

Harrison, Selig S. "Dateline Afghanistan: Exit through Finland." *Foreign Policy* 64 (1980–81): 163–87.

———. In Afghanistan's Shadow: Baluch Nationalism and Soviet Temptations. New York: Carnegie Endowment for International Peace, 1981.

———. "Inside the Afghan Talks." *Foreign Policy* 72 (1988): 31–60.

Herrmann, Richard. "The Soviet Decision to Withdraw from Afghanistan: Changing Strategic and Regional Images." In *Dominoes and Bandwagons,* ed. Jervis and Snyder, 220–49.

———. "Soviet Behavior in Regional Conflicts: Old Questions, New Strategies, and Important Lessons." *World Politics* 44 (1992): 432–65.

Helman, Gerald B, and Steven R. Ratner. "Saving Failed States." *Foreign Policy* 89 (1992–93): 3–20.

Hopkirk, Peter. *The Great Game: The Struggle for Empire in Central Asia.* New York: Kodansha International, 1992. [First published as *The Great Game: On Secret Service in High Asia* (London: John Murray, 1990).]

Huntington, Samuel P. *The Third Wave: Democratization in the Late Twentieth Century.* Norman: University of Oklahoma Press, 1986.

Jackson, Robert H. "Quasi-States, Dual Regimes, and Neoclassical Theory: International Jurisprudence and the Third World." *International Organization* 41 (1987): 519–49.

Jackson, Robert H., and Carl G. Rosberg. "Why Africa's Weak States Persist: The Empirical and Juridical in Statehood." *World Politics* 35 (1982): 1–24.

Jacoby, Tamar. "The Reagan Turnaround on Human Rights." *Foreign Affairs* 64 (1986): 1066–86.

Jervis, Robert. *Perception and Misperception in International Politics.* Princeton: Princeton University Press, 1976.

———. "Cooperation under the Security Dilemma." *World Politics* 30 (1978): 167–214.

———. "Realism, Game Theory, and Cooperation." *World Politics* 40 (1988): 317–49.

———. "Rational Deterrence: Theory and Evidence." *World Politics* 41 (1989): 183–207.

———. "Domino Beliefs and Strategic Behavior." In *Dominoes and Bandwagons,* ed. Jervis and Snyder, 20–50.

Jervis, Robert, and Jack Snyder, eds. *Dominoes and Bandwagons: Strategic Beliefs and Great Power Competition in the Eurasian Rimland.* New York: Oxford University Press, 1991.

Kakar, Hasan Kawun. "The Fall of the Afghan Monarchy in 1973." *International Journal of Middle East Studies* 9 (1978): 195–214.

Kamrany, Nake M. *Peaceful Competition in Afghanistan.* Washington, D.C.: Communication Service Corporation, 1969.

Kanet, Roger E., and Edward A. Kolodziej. *The Cold War as Cooperation.* Baltimore: Johns Hopkins University Press, 1991.

Katz, Mark, ed. *Soviet-American Conflict Resolution in the Third World.* Washington, D.C.: United States Institute of Peace, 1991.

———. "Introduction." In *Soviet-American Conflict Resolution,* ed. Katz, 3–12.

———. "The Future of Superpower Conflict Resolution in the Third World." In *Soviet-American Conflict Resolution,* ed. Katz, 169–88.

Keohane, Robert O. *After Hegemony: Cooperation and Discord in the World Political Economy.* Princeton: Princeton University Press, 1984.

———. "Reciprocity in International Relations." *International Organization* 40 (1986): 1–27.

Khalidi, Noor Ahmad. "Afghanistan: Demographic Consequences of War, 1978–1987." *Central Asian Survey* 10 (1991): 101–26.

Khalilzad, Zalmay. "Soviet-American Cooperation in Afghanistan." In *Soviet-American Conflict Resolution,* ed. Katz, 67–94.

Khan, Riaz Mohammad. *Untying the Afghan Knot: Negotiating Soviet Withdrawal.* Durham: Duke University Press, 1991.

Kipling, Rudyard. *Complete Verse: Definitive Edition.* New York: Doubleday, 1989.

Klass, Rosanne. "Afghanistan: The Next Steps." *Orbis* 33 (1989): 273–76.

Kolodziej, Edward A. "The Cold War as Cooperation." In *The Cold War as Cooperation,* ed. Kanet and Kolodziej, 3–30.

Krakowski, Elie D. "Defining Success in Afghanistan." *Washington Quarterly* (Spring 1985): 37–46.

———. "Toward a Post-Soviet Afghanistan." *The World and I* (1988): 106–9.

Krasner, Stephen D., ed. *International Regimes.* Ithaca, N.Y.: Cornell University Press, 1983.

———. "Structural Causes and Regime Consequences: Regimes as Intervening Variables." In *International Regimes,* ed. Krasner, 1–22.

Kratochwil, Friedrich. "Of Systems, Boundaries, and Territoriality: An Inquiry into the Formation of the State System." *World Politics* 39 (1986): 27–52.

Kratochwil, Friedrich, and John Gerard Ruggie. "International Organization: A State of the Art on an Art of the State." *International Organization* 40 (1986): 753–75.

Kremenyuk, Victor A. "The Cold War as Cooperation: A Soviet Perspective." In *The Cold War as Cooperation,* ed. Kanet and Kolodziej, 31–64.

Laber, Jeri, and Barnett R. Rubin. *"Tears, Blood, and Cries": Human Rights in Afghanistan Since the Invasion, 1979–1984.* Helsinki Watch: New York, 1984.

———. *"A Nation is Dying": Afghanistan under the Soviets, 1979–1987.* Evanston, Ill.: Northwestern University Press, 1988.

Lifschultz, Lawrence. "Pakistan was Iran-Contra's Secret Back Door." *Sunday Times of India,* November 24, 1991.

Lindblom, Charles Edward. *The Intelligence of Democracy.* New York: Free Press, 1965.

Linz, Juan J. *The Breakdown of Democratic Regimes: Crisis, Breakdown, and Reequilibration.* Baltimore: Johns Hopkins University Press, 1978.

Linz, Juan J., and Alfred Stepan, eds. *The Breakdown of Democratic Regimes: Europe.* Baltimore: Johns Hopkins University Press, 1978.

———. *The Breakdown of Democratic Regimes: Latin America.* Baltimore: Johns Hopkins University Press, 1978.

Lipset, Seymour Martin. *Political Man: The Social Bases of Politics.* New York: Harper and Row, 1960.

Lipson, Charles. "International Cooperation on Economic and Security Affairs." *World Politics* 37 (1984): 1–23.

———. "Bankers' Dilemmas: Private Cooperation in Rescheduling Sovereign Debts." In *Cooperation under Anarchy,* ed. Oye, 200–225.

———. "Why Are Some International Agreements Informal?" *International Organization* 45 (1991): 495–538.

Luciani, Giacomo. "Allocation vs. Production States: A Theoretical Framework." In *Nation, State and Integration in the Arab World.* Vol. 2: *The Rentier State,* ed. Hazem Beblawi and Giacomo Luciani, 49–82. London: Croom Helm, 1987.

"Massood Reviews History of Victory: Transcript of Sandy Gall's Interview with Ahmad Shah Massood, in Jabulseraj, on Monday, June 28th, 1993," *AFGHANews* 9 (November 1993): 6–8.

"A Meeting of Resistance Commanders Inside Afghanistan." *Afghan Information Centre Monthly Bulletin* no. 77 (August 1987): 9–10.

Mendelson, Sarah E. "Internal Battles and External Wars: Politics, Learning, and the Soviet Withdrawal from Afghanistan." *World Politics* 45 (1993): 327–60.

Migdal, Joel S. *Strong Societies and Weak States: State-Society Relations and State Capabilities in the Third World.* Princeton: Princeton University Press, 1988.

Miller, Benjamin. "Explaining Great Power Cooperation in Conflict Management." *World Politics* 45 (1992): 1–46.

Milner, Helen. "The Assumption of Anarchy in International Relations Theory: A Critique." *Review of International Studies* 17 (1991): 67–85.

———. "International Theories of Cooperation Among Nations: Strengths and Weaknesses." *World Politics* 44 (1992): 466–96.

Nagel, J., and S. Olzak. "Ethnic Mobilization in New and Old States: An Extension of the Competition Model." *Social Problems* 30 (1982): 127–43.

National Security Archive, ed. *Afghanistan: The Making of U.S. Policy, 1973–1990.* Alexandria, Va.: Chadwyck-Healy, 1991.

Ness, Gayl D., and Steven R. Brechin. "Bridging the Gap: International Organizations as Organizations." *International Organization* 42 (1988): 245–73.

Neuman, Stephanie G. "Arms, Aid and the Superpowers." *Foreign Affairs* 66 (1988): 1044–67.

O'Donnell, Guillermo. *Modernization and Bureaucratic Authoritarianism: Studies in South American Politics.* Berkeley: University of California Institute of International Studies, 1973.

O'Donnell, Guillermo, and Philippe Schmitter. *Transitions from Authoritarian Rule: Tentative Conclusions about Uncertain Transitions.* Baltimore: Johns Hopkins University Press, 1986.

O'Donnell, Guillermo, Philippe Schmitter, and Laurence Whitehead, eds. *Transitions from Authoritarian Rule: Comparative Perspectives.* Baltimore: Johns Hopkins University Press, 1986.

———. *Transitions from Authoritarian Rule: Prospects for Democracy.* Baltimore: Johns Hopkins University Press, 1986.

———. *Transitions from Authoritarian Rule: Latin America.* Baltimore: Johns Hopkins University Press, 1986.

Oye, Kenneth A., ed. *Cooperation under Anarchy.* Princeton: Princeton University Press: 1986.

———. "Explaining Cooperation under Anarchy: Hypotheses and Strategies." In *Cooperation under Anarchy,* ed. Oye, 1–24.

Posen, Barry. "The Security Dilemma and Ethnic Conflict." *Survival* 35 (1993): 27–47.

Przeworski, Adam. "Democracy as a Contingent Outcome of Conflict." In *Constitutionalism and Democracy,* ed. Jon Elster and Rune Slagstad, 61. New York: Cambridge University Press, 1988.

Puchala, Donald J., and Raymond F. Hopkins. "International Regimes: Lessons from Inductive Analysis." In *International Regimes,* ed. Krasner, 61–92.

Putnam, Robert D. "Diplomacy and Domestic Politics: The Logic of Two-Level Games." *International Organization* 42 (1988): 427–60.

Pye, Lucian, W. *Asian Power and Politics: The Cultural Dimensions of Authority.* Cambridge, Mass.: Belknap Press, 1985.

Rashid, Ahmed. *The Resurgence of Central Asia: Islam or Nationalism?* Karachi: Oxford University Press; London: Zed, 1994.

Roy, Olivier. *L'Afghanistan: Islam et modernité politique.* Paris: Seuil, 1985.

———. *Islam and Resistance in Afghanistan.* Cambridge: Cambridge University Press, 1986.

———. "La guerre comme facteur du passage au politique." Paper presented at the Congrès National de l'Association Française de Science Politique. Bordeaux: October 5–8, 1988.

Rubin, Barnett R. "Prepared Statement." In *The Situation in Afghanistan,* Hearing before the Subcommittee on Asian and Pacific Affairs of the Committee on Foreign Affairs, House of Representatives, May 1, 1986 (Washington: U.S. Goverment Printing Office, 1986), 79–98.

———. "Afghanistan: The Next Round." *Orbis* 33 (1989): 57–72.

———. "The Fragmentation of Afghanistan." *Foreign Affairs* 68 (1989–90): 150–68.

———. "Afghanistan: Political Exiles in Search of a State." *Journal of Political Science* 18 (1990): 63–93.

———. "The Fragmentation of Tajikistan." *Survival* 35 (Winter 1993–94): 71–91.

———. *The Fragmentation of Afghanistan: State Formation and Collapse in the International System.* New Haven: Yale University Press, 1995.

Saikal, Amin, and William Maley, eds. *The Soviet Withdrawal from Afghanistan.* Cambridge: Cambridge University Press, 1989.

Sebenius, James K. "Challenging Conventional Explanations of International Cooperation: Negotiations Analysis and the Case of Epistemic Communities." *International Organization* 46 (1992): 323–65.

Senate Resolution 386. *Congressional Record – Senate.* One hundredth Congress, Second Session, February 29, 1988, S1588–S1608.

Shain, Yossi, and Lynn Berat. "The International Interim Government Model Revisited." In *Between States,* vol. 1, ed. Shain and Linz: 63–75.

Shain, Yossi, and Juan J. Linz. "The Role of Interim Governments." *Journal of Democracy* 3 (January 1992): 73–89.

———, eds. *Between States: Interim Governments and Democratic Transitions.* Cambridge: Cambridge University Press, 1995.

Shultz, George P. *Turmoil and Triumph: My Years as Secretary of State.* New York: Scribner, 1993.

"The Situation in Afghanistan and its Implications for International Peace and Security: Report of the Secretary-General, U.N. General Assembly and Security Council." U.N. Doc. A/46/577, S/23146. New York: United Nations, October 12, 1992.

Skocpol, Theda. "Bringing the State Back In: Strategies of Analysis in Current Research." In *Bringing the State Back In,* ed. Peter B. Evans, Dietrich Rueschmeyer, and Theda Skocpol, 3–43. Cambridge: Cambridge University Press, 1985.

Sliwinski, Marek. "The Decimation of Afghanistan." *Orbis* 33 (1988–89): 39–56.

Smith, Nancy DeWolf. "These Rebels Aren't So Scary." *Wall Street Journal,* February 22, 1995.

Snidal, Duncan. "Coordination Versus Prisoners' Dilemma: Implications for International Cooperation and Regimes." *American Political Science Review* 79 (1985): 923–42.

———. "The Game *Theory* of International Politics." In *Cooperation under Anarchy,* ed. Oye, 25–57.

———. "Relative Gains and the Pattern of International Cooperation." *American Political Science Review* 85 (1991): 701–26.

Snyder, Glenn H., and Paul Diesing. *Conflict Among Nations: Bargaining, Decision Making, and System Structure in International Crises.* Princeton: Princeton University Press, 1977.

Snyder, Jack. "Introduction." In *Dominoes and Bandwagons,* ed. Jervis and Snyder, 3–20.

Stein, Arthur A. "Coordination and Collaboration: Regimes in an Anarchic World." In *International Regimes,* ed. Krasner, 115–40.

Stepan, Alfred. *Rethinking Military Politics: Brazil and the Southern Cone.* Princeton: Princeton University Press, 1988.

Swedish Committee for Afghanistan Agricultural Committee. *The Agricultural Survey of Afghanistan: First Report.* Peshawar: The Swedish Committee for Afghanistan, May 1988.

Tapper, Richard. "Introduction." In *Conflict of Tribe and State in Iran and Afghanistan,* ed. Richard Tapper, 1–82. New York: St. Martin's, 1983.

Tilly, Charles, ed. *The Formation of National States in Western Europe.* Princeton: Princeton University Press, 1975.

———. *Coercion, Capital, and European States, A.D. 990–1990.* Oxford: Basil Blackwell, 1990.

Touval, Saadia. "Why the U.N. Fails." *Foreign Affairs* 73 (1994): 44–57.

United Nations Department of Humanitarian Affairs. "Note on Winter Emergency Needs in Afghanistan." New York: November 1, 1992.

United Nations Department of Public Information. "Press Briefing by Under-Secretary-General for Special Political Affairs." New York: December 9, 1986.

——. "Press Briefing by Under-Secretary-General Cordovez." New York: January 18, 1988.

——. Press Release SG/1860. New York: April 14, 1988.

——. "Statement of the Secretary-General on Afghanistan." New York: May 21, 1991.

——. "Statement by the Secretary-General on Afghanistan." Geneva: April 10, 1992.

——. "Secretary-General Urges Afghan Leaders to Cooperate with United Nations in Search for Lasting Cease-Fire." U.N. Document SG/SM/5405: September 7, 1994.

——. "Head of Special Mission to Afghanistan Says Mechanism for Transitional Transfer of Power Will Be Assembled by 20 February." U.N. Document SG/SM/555, AFG/67: February 10, 1995.

United Nations Economic and Social Council. Commission on Human Rights. "Report on the situation of human rights in Afghanistan prepared by the Special Rapporteur, Mr. Felix Ermacora, in accordance with commission on Human Rights resolution 1984/55." U.N. Document E/CN.4/1985/21. Geneva: February 19, 1985.

United Nations General Assembly. Gorbachev's Vladivostok speech. U.N. Document A/41/505: July 28, 1986.

——. "Emergency International Assistance for Peace, Normalcy and Reconstruction of War-Stricken Afghanistan." U.N. Document A/RES/48/208: December 21, 1993.

——. "Progress Report of the Special Mission to Afghanistan, March 27–April 29, 1994. Report of the Secretary-General." U.N. Document A/49/208; S/1994/766: July 1, 1994.

——. "Strengthening the Coordination of Humanitarian and Disaster Relief Assistance of the United Nations, Including Special Economic Assistance: Emergency International Assistance for Peace, Normalcy and Reconstruction of War-Stricken Afghanistan: Report of the Secretary-General." U.N. Document A/49/688: November 22, 1994.

United Nations Office for the Co-ordination of Humanitarian and Economic Assistance Programmes relating to Afghanistan (UNOCA). Press Release, "Immediate Humanitarian Needs in Afghanistan Resulting from the Current Hostilities," August 23, 1992.

United Nations Security Council. "Security Council Welcomes Acceptance by Afghan Parties of Phased National Reconciliation Process." U.N. Document S/PRST/77: November 30, 1994.

United States Central Intelligence Agency. "The USSR and Regional Conflicts after Afghanistan: No Rush to Retreat." June 3, 1988. Some text excised.

——. "Soviet and Resistance Objectives in Afghanistan: Is There Any Common Ground?" November 29, 1988. Some text excised.

——. "Outlook for Afghanistan after the Soviet Withdrawal." February 7, 1989. Some text excised.

United States Department of State. *Country Report on Human Rights Practices for 1984.* Washington: U.S. Government Printing Office, 1985.

"US AID Humanitarian Assistance to Afghanistan." Unpublished document, July 1990.

Wagner, R. Harrison. "The Theory of Games and the Problem of International Cooperation." *American Political Science Review* 77 (1983): 330–46.

"What Do the Afghan Refugees Think? An Opinion Survey in the Camps." *Afghan Information Centre Monthly Bulletin* 7 (July 1987): 2–8.

Whitehead, John C. "Afghanistan's Struggle for Freedom: Address before the World Affairs Council in Washington, D.C., on December 13, 1985." *Department of State Bulletin* 86 (February 1986): 1–12.

Wiarda, Howard J. *Corporatism and National Development in Latin America.* Boulder, Colo.: Westview Press, 1981.

Yousaf, Mohammad, and Mark Adkin. *The Bear Trap: Afghanistan's Untold Story.* London: Mark Cooper, 1992.

Index

Abdul Haq, 165
Abdul Mumin, 131, 172
Abdul Rahman, Akhtar, 34, 65, 66, 100
Abdul Rahman Khan, Amir, 19, 21, 23, 28
Abdul Sattar, 79
Abdul Wakil, 132
Abdul Wali, 80
Afghan National Liberation Front (Mujaddidi), 36, 129
Afghanistan, 144; abandonment of, 6–7; anarchy in, 132; border of, 117; breakdown of state in, 95, 117; as buffer state, 16, 17, 18, 19, 71, 76; and Cold War, 21–30; domestic politics of, 57, 58–59, 60, 71, 85–86, 88, 91, 125, 142–43, 145, 164, 167; eastern, 129; formed through cooperation, 18–21; geography of, 119; internal consolidation of, 19–21; invasion of, 29; neutrality of, 83; northeast, 123; northeastern, 129; northern, 122–23, 130; as party to Geneva Accords, 70; population of, 157; as rentier state, 22, 159; Republic of, 84; secession from, 135, 142; signs Geneva Accords, 7; state structure of, 21; and state system, 15; type of government in, 20–21, 33, 34, 78–79; and U.N., 99
Agriculture, 4, 117, 119
Ahmad, Qazi Hussein, 110, 173
Alexander II, Czar, 18
Amanullah Khan, 21
Amin, Hafizullah, 26, 29, 59, 160
Anarchy, 6, 16, 17, 85, 125, 130, 132, 142, 143, 144
Andropov, Yuri, 59–61
Anglo-Afghan wars, 23, 25; first, 20; second, 18, 19
Anglo-Russian Convention (1907), 19, 21
Angola, 97, 144
Arabs, 111, 165; aid Hikmatyar, 115–16, 129;

aid Hizb-Khalq alliance, 130; aid to mujahidin, 38, 39, 105, 126; in Afghanistan, 4
Armacost, Michael, 83, 84
Atsak, Juma, 172
Attribution theory, 18, 50, 83, 90
Axelrod, Robert, 38
Ayeen, Ghulam Ali, 173
al-Azhar University, 27, 37

Babar, Naseerullah Khan, 138, 139, 140
Badakhshan, 37
Baker, James, 107, 109, 111, 125
Baluch, 41
Baluchistan, 119, 139
Bargaining, 43, 46, 54–55, 55–56, 72, 78, 98, 107
Baryalai, Mahmud, 173
Beg, Mirza Aslam, 100, 113, 115, 116
Bessmertnykh, Alexander, 109
Bhutto, Benazir, 89, 101, 103, 113, 115, 138, 139
Bhutto, Zulfiqar Ali, 27, 138
Borders, 16, 18, 19
Boutros-Ghali, Boutros, 127, 136
Brezhnev, Leonid, 26, 28–29, 40–41, 59, 128
Brezhnev doctrine, 104
Britain, 3, 4, 18, 19, 21, 29, 142, 143
Brzezinski, Zbigniew, 41
Buffer state, 3, 17, 25, 29, 42, 121, 128, 142
Bureaucratic politics, 46
Bush, George, 99, 108
Bush administration, 10–11, 99, 104, 105, 107, 109, 110–11, 112

Cambodia, 13, 97, 126, 127, 144, 145
Carter, Jimmy, 30, 40, 41, 51
Casey, William, 65, 81, 99, 161
Central Asia, 113, 121, 172; attacks on, 55, 65,